HUM BOWS,
NOT
HOT DOGS!
Hope you enjoy
our little adventure

HUM BOWS, NOT HOT DOGS!

Memoirs of a savvy Asian American Activist

By Bob Santos

International Examiner Press
Seattle, Washington

Cover photos: Activist Sherrie Chinn marching in support of elderly low-income housing, 1973; (background design) Community activists at the ground breaking ceremony for the Kingdome, 1973 — Eugene Tagawa photos, courtesy of *Asian Family Affair*

Printed in the United States of America

ISBN 0-9717829-0-3

The paper used in this publication meets the minimum requirements of American National Information Sciences — Permanence of Paper for Printed Library Materials, ANSI Z39.48-1984.

Table of Contents

Introduction 10

Chapter One: Childhood Memories 14

In the Beginning.... 14

Growing Up 15

Sockin' Sammy Santos 16

Growing Up in Chinatown — "No Money, No Honey" 19

Uncle Joe 25

The Japanese Kids Leave — "I Am Filipino" 26

Jazzing It Up 28

Cannery Work — Two Separate Worlds 29

It Takes a Filipino Village to Raise a Filipino Child 31

Liking the Laigos 36

Keeping in Touch with the Old Gang 38

Chapter Two: Growing as a Young Adult 40

Pursuing the American Dream — Family Life in the 50s 40

Chapter Three: Civil Rights Activism 46

Civil Rights and Civil Wrongs 46

St. Peter Claver — At the Heart of the Struggle 48

Tyree Scott — The Live Wire 51
Bernie Whitebear — Storming the Fort 56
Roberto Maestas — Compadre and Caballero 60
Larry Gossett — CAMP Director 63
The Gang of Four 64
From Filipino to Asian 67
Asian American Activism — Yellow Power/Brown Power 69

CHAPTER FOUR: PRESERVING AND DEVELOPING THE INTERNATIONAL DISTRICT 74
The Jackson Street Community Council 74
Inter*Im — Leading the Way 76
The Kingdome — Casting a Giant Shadow 78
The Party Is Crashed 80
Gearing Up — The March to HUD 81
Getting Busy — The Effort to Get More Housing 83
Laying the Foundation — Making the Case for More Housing 85
Concerned Asians for the International District — Listing the Demands 87
Selecting the Director of the Kingdome — Aloha Means Goodbye 88
Diana Bower — The Compassionate Consultant 88
The Health Clinic — Patients and Patience 90
Food and Nutrition Programs — I Can Vouch for It 92
The Legal Clinic — Storefront Lawyers 94
Working the Foundation Madness 94
ACRS — Solving Our Own Problems 95
The International Examiner — Read All About It 97
Inter*Im's Parking Lot — Housing for Cars 98
The I.D. Emergency Center — The First Line of Defense 100
Community Garden — From Bushes to Bok Choy 101
Turning the Pig — The Annual Pig Roast 106
Someone to Watch over Me — Denise Louie Day Care Center 108

Back to Basics — A Community Cultural Center 110
Being Our Own Developer — The Public Development Authority 110
First Things First — The Bush Hotel 113
The New Central — The Short End of the Stick 115
Keeping the Culture — The Bush-Asia Annex 117
Acting Up — Northwest Asian American Theatre 118
The Best Causes Are the Lost Causes — The Milwaukee Hotel 120
Two Plans for a Jail in the I.D. — Do Not Pass Go 124
Union Station — Derailing a Transportation Center 126
A Garbage Burning Facility — Trash Talk 130

Chapter Five: It's Just Politics **131**
Three Campaigns Equal Zero 131
Be Like Mike — Working for Congressman Lowry 135

Chapter Six: Justice for Cannery Workers **141**
Canneries, Corruption, and Conspiracy to Commit 141
Gus the Gecko 146
Revenge Is Sweet — The Civil Trial 147
Wards Cove — Justice Denied 150

Chapter Seven: From the Wah Mee to Village Square **152**
Lunar Madness — The Wah Mee Shootings 152
But Life Goes On.... 153
Redeveloping Chinatowns — The National Perspective 154
To Park or Not to Park 156
International District Village Square — The Real Deal 156
The Dreamers and Schemers — Key Board Members, Staff, and Community Supporters 163
Greasing the Wheel — The Political Process 168

Chapter Eight: Life Outside the I.D. 171
The Move to HUD — Bob the Bureaucrat 171

Chapter Nine: Hanging Out with Uncle Bob 179
Uncle Bob's Hangouts 179
Marriage on the Rocks 182
Santos, A Name You Can Trust — Sharon Tomiko Santos 183
We Are Family — My Family 185

Epilogue: The End of an Era, The Beginning of a New Era 187
The Battle Rages On — What the I.D. Is Now 187
The Doomed Stadium 188

Bibliography 191

Acknowledgments 195

Index 197

In memory of Sammy, Virginia, brother Sam, Auntie Toni,
Uncle Joe, Grandma Gilbert, Grampa Nicol, and Joyce,
who helped create these stories

For Danny, Simone, Robin, Tom, John, Nancy,
the grandchildren, and Sharon Tomiko,
who are here to share them

Introduction

EVERY NEIGHBORHOOD HAS ITS roster of local heroes. The mention of a hero's name prompts a cocked ear and summons a round of stories, some true, some half-true and some wholly legend. More often than not, it's nice to hear from the heroes themselves – for what they remember and what they choose to reveal. Heroes – especially those tested in the fires of social activism – can inspire us to believe in the possibility of changing things for the better.

Bob Santos is a hero in an urban hamlet called the International District, an Asian neighborhood along the southern edge of downtown Seattle. For reasons unknown, the District is the only location in the continental United States where the various Asian settlers – Chinese, Japanese, Filipino, and Vietnamese – settled together and built one community. Perhaps it's because the Asian Pacific population in Washington state is relatively small – less than six percent of the total population – that we've found ways to cohabit peacefully for generations. Whatever the reason, Seattle is a model for "pan-Asian cooperation" in the United States.

In the 1970s and 80s, as executive director of the International District Improvement Association (Inter*Im), Bob Santos provided the vision and inspiration to move this neighborhood – the "I.D." – from the brink of physical decay and neglect to rebirth, galvanizing a multi-ethnic coalition of elderly residents, small shopkeepers and idealistic students to restore vacant buildings, construct new housing, develop social service agencies, and create a dynamic new sense of community. Later, in the early 1990s, he helped conceive the International District Village Square project – a remarkable public-private partnership combining apartment units, offices, social services, and retail businesses.

In this book, *Hum Bows, Not Hot Dogs*, he describes what happened, from his choice vantage point, as leader of a powerful grassroots movement, folding wonderful little stories around a vibrant cast of local characters and events. For those who lived through this eventful era, this book replays fond memories: moments of humor, merry-making, trouble-making, confrontation, negotiation, anger, surprise, elation, sadness, fear and pride. This book illuminates pieces of the unexplained past for outsiders who may look with curiosity or puzzlement at how the community came to acquire its distinctive complexion and personality.

Santos also tells about his childhood days in the modest Chinatown hotel room with his father, a famous local boxer; his participation in the drive for racial equality in Seattle in the 1960s; and his rise to political worlds beyond Seattle as a congressional aide and, later, as an official for the U.S. Department of Housing and Urban Development.

For those who don't know "Uncle Bob" Santos – and it's rare to find anyone in Seattle who hasn't made his acquaintance – a brief description is in order. Uncle Bob is insatiably social – as likely to be spotted in a local karaoke bar as at a political rally or a Seattle City Council hearing. He's an irrepressible ham – clowning and joking if you give him even a sliver of an opening. He'll put forth an incredibly corny word pun – "Get it?" – followed with an impish grin, a chuckle, then "Just kidding." Over the years, Bob's ability to poke fun has allowed him to build legions of allies, melt down barriers and develop the credibility to bargain with those in seats of power.

I first met Bob in 1973, shortly after he became director of Inter*Im. I was a reporter for the University of Washington *Daily*, gathering information for a story about the potential impact of a stadium on the International District. I remember entering a nondescript building on South Jackson Street – one of the main thoroughfares running through the heart of the I.D. – and climbing a flight of stairs to meet him. As I came up, he was seated in an office chair at a desk, dressed in a pullover sweater and khaki work slacks. I caught him in mid-sentence, cussing loudly into a phone receiver, "What kind of bullshit is that?" He punctuated the rest of his conversation with other even more pungent phrases and hung up. Then, in one easy motion, he swiveled in my direction, stood up – changing his demeanor almost instantly from ornery to sweet and inviting. "Hey guy!" he said to me, extending his hand. "What's up? Are you from the U-Dub? Have a seat, guy." I was, needless to say, somewhat startled. That was my introduction to Bob Santos.

I never did learn the source of his anger – whether it was, perhaps, an insensitive public official or a former ally with whom he had just had a testy spat – but over the years I've had other opportunities to see the fiery side of his personality. Uncle Bob has never been one to hold his tongue or kiss up to someone he didn't like, despite his congeniality and patience at building political coalitions.

Through the late 1980s, working as editor and reporter for the *International Examiner*, I saw Uncle Bob in action, usually in front of a gathering of elderly residents at the cramped International Drop-In Center on Weller Street or at the scruffy cannery union hall on South Main Street. He would exhort the residents to sign petitions and stand up for their rights: "No one can force you out of your homes," he would say in a firm voice. "But we need all of you and your friends to pack the City Council hearing and let the officials know that they've got to act on behalf of *your* interests." Uncle Bob's words, delivered with fire and a down-home touch, would rouse the irrepressible seniors – like Al Masigat, Leo Lorenzo, Sam Figueros or Mrs. Chin – to come to the microphone to share a personal story about their struggle to retain an affordable apartment and stay in the place they cherished as home.

In times of great stress, heroes are steadying influences, too. After the shocking murders of young cannery union leaders Silme Domingo and Gene Viernes in 1981, Uncle Bob calmed the grieving community and hastened the justice efforts by the simple – yet courageous – act of stepping up to the media microphones and onto the witness stand in court. His visibility, in a time of great paralyzing fear, made others more confident about coming forward and testifying about what they knew. Over the past four decades, in situation after situation, he's stepped forward to speak out, helping bring credibility to credible causes and giving voice to the disenfranchised.

For the record, *Hum Bows, Not Hot Dogs* had its sputtering beginnings about 15 years ago, during a time when both Uncle Bob and I were International District neighbors, living in separate "market-rate" hotels restored with City support. Gary Iwamoto – a long-time I.D. activist and writer – and I met several times at Uncle Bob's modest apartment, trying to steer Uncle Bob to create his autobiography. This first effort didn't get beyond a couple of chapters, quick victim of our inability to make time.

The project – "*The* Book" we sheepishly called it – sat on the shelf and was resuscitated in the past year, as Uncle Bob – in between jobs – carved out blocks of time at the computer to write, aided by Gary Iwamoto, serving as researcher, fact-checker, editor and general co-collaborator. Iwamoto and Uncle Bob are kindred spirits, sharing their great passion for I.D. and social justice causes, not to mention a shameless penchant for corny humor.

A word of explanation about the title of this book. *Hum bow* is a Chinese term for a barbecue pork bun. It's a term used by Chinese Americans in Seattle who speak Toisanese, the dialect of the early settlers, and by others who know and appreciate down-home Chinese lunch cuisine. "Hum Bows, Not Hot Dogs" was a slogan coined in the early 1970s – appearing often on protest signs – expressing opposition to the development of a large sports stadium on the western fringe of the International District. It was adopted as a rallying cry by Uncle Bob and others who feared that large-scale projects would threaten the beloved mom-and-pop restaurants in the area.

"Things are a lot easier now," Uncle Bob said to me recently, commenting on the difference between today and the 1970s, when Inter*Im was first making its mark as an advocate of neighborhood improvement. By a twist of fate, as we were talking, Uncle Bob had been coaxed to return as director of Inter*Im, working out of the same storefront space in the N.P. Hotel where he got started, his desk in the exact same spot it occupied 30 years ago, downstairs from his dad's old apartment, now remodeled. "A lot of people didn't really care for the activists back in the old days. But we learned how to work the system. Some of us moved into positions where we could make a difference. And we got a lot of things done and built. That's a legacy that we can look back on with pride, something for the next generation to build on."

Here, within these pages, is Uncle Bob's legacy – a story that belongs to all of us, given back to us in his own words. As we read from *Hum Bows, Not Hot Dogs*, we laugh, marvel and revisit a triumphant era – not so long ago – when our community was reborn under a shared vision made possible by great leadership.

Ron Chew
Executive Director
Wing Luke Asian Museum

CHAPTER ONE

Childhood Memories

In the Beginning....

LOCATED IN THE HEART of the city, the International District has been the historical, cultural, and political center for Seattle's Asian American communities. The International District was one of the few places in Seattle where Chinese, Japanese, and Filipino immigrants could live. For first generation immigrants, it was their first home in America. For their children, the second generation, it was the neighborhood they grew up in. For their grandchildren, the third generation, it was the neighborhood which gave them their identity as Asian Americans and the opportunity to repay their elders. For me, the International District became a central part of my life, beginning with the times I spent as a child in my father's hotel room, and in the restaurants, barbershops, gambling parlors, and pool halls of the area. For all of us, the International District meant a sense of community.

The International District is a distinct neighborhood just south of downtown Seattle. Its boundaries are Fifth Avenue South (west), South Dearborn Street (south), 12th Avenue South (east), and Yesler Way (north). Going from west to east, the avenues are numbered progressively from Fifth to 12th with the exception of Maynard Avenue South between Sixth Avenue South and Seventh Avenue South. Going from north to south, the streets are named Yesler, Washington, Main, Jackson, King, Weller, Lane, and Dearborn.

While the Chinese, Japanese, and Filipino immigrants settled together in the International District, the three major Asian ethnic groups rarely interacted with each other for many years. There were language and cultural differences between the groups which prevented opportunities for social recreation and political action. As a result, each group formed their own community — the Chinese had "Chinatown," the Japanese had "Nihonmachi" (Japantown), and the Filipinos had "Manilatown." The International District was a racially segregated community restricted to Asian immigrants, but for me, as a kid growing up, it was a place in which I felt very comfortable. Growing up, we called it Chinatown.

Growing Up

I still have vivid memories of impressions, images, and odors from the Chinatown of my early childhood days. I remember old wooden fish barrels that collected rainwater which dripped from leaky roof gutters. The water was used to irrigate family vegetable gardens behind the buildings. I remember the sight of decaying boardwalks, crushed and replaced by cement sidewalks.

From the old Filipino cafes, I remember the smell of vinegar and garlic and the sound of pork sizzling. Chinese kitchens like the Tai Tung, Don Ting, and Linyen were always busy: metal utensils clanged against woks while waiters shouted orders at cooks who, in turn, yelled at whoever listened. In the N.P. Hotel, on the hill on Sixth Avenue South between Jackson and Main streets, where my father lived, the strong aroma of mackerel permeated the room, its blue smoke entering through the transom.

There was always the smell of Lysol in the bathroom and shower and, of course, roach spray in each room. In the lobby of all the hotels, spittoons were strategically placed for use by cigar smokers and tobacco chewers. I remember the smell of stale beer and cigar and cigarette smoke that poured out of Dukes II Tavern (on Maynard and King Street) and Tiger Al Lewis' Tavern (up the block on Jackson Street). The best aromas came out of the barbershops: flowery scented brilliantine hair sheen with brand names like Dixie Peach and Three Flowers, talcum powder, and aftershave lotion that pinched the cheeks when it was slapped on.

One of my earliest memories was seeing Judy Garland in the "Wizard of Oz" in 1940 at the Atlas Theater. During intermission, the Atlas featured local talent on its stage. Two kids I grew up with, Helen and Bill Mamon, did a tap dance routine. We sat in the balcony, yelling and hooting in appreciation.

I also remember visiting the Nippon Kan Theater up on the hill on Washington Street when I was six years old. The Nippon Kan (Japanese Hall) was built in 1909 and served as both a meeting place and a performance theater for the Japanese community. The night I went to the Nippon Kan, there was a performance of Kabuki dancers. I had never seen Kabuki before. The scary makeup on their faces, the ominous drumming — it scared the "shit" out of me for days.

Sockin' Sammy Santos

It was my dad, Sammy Santos, who introduced me to Chinatown. Macario "Sammy" Santos was born in the Philippines in 1902. Times were tough then in the Philippines. As a young man, my dad couldn't find work. With few options available to him, he joined the United States Navy in the Philippines in 1919. While in the Navy, my dad got in a fistfight with a junior grade officer and went AWOL (absent without leave). With no employable skills, he turned to boxing, the only love of his life at that time. He became a prizefighter.

Macario became "Sammy," in part to avoid the military police, but also because "Sammy Santos" was a catchier name for boxing than "Macario Santos." The military police eventually found my dad in California and arrested him in the middle of a boxing match. But they did allow him to finish the fight before they hauled him off to the brig. At least he won, or so he told me. Sammy did his time. When he got out, he went back into the ring.

Dad fought as a lightweight in California, Oregon, and Ohio, then ended up in Seattle, a popular fight town in the old days. In Seattle, each ethnic neighborhood had its boxing heroes. The black neighborhood had Wildcat Carter and Bearcat Baker. The Jewish community had Abe Israel. The Germans had Doc Snell. The Japanese had Jimmy Sakamoto. The Chinese brought up a fighter from Portland named Aw Wing Lee. The Filipinos had several: Pat Yanko, Joe Calder, Mariano Guiang, Mission Bolo, who took up the name of Little Dempsey, after the popular and successful California-based boxer, and of course, my dad Sammy Santos. There was also Tommy Santos, my dad's distant cousin. Uncle Tommy wasn't very successful. He lost more times than he won, but he did have a cauliflower ear, a boxer's badge of honor that attracted all the ladies.

My dad began his life in Seattle as a local sports hero: a prizefighter who fought world class boxers. The press called him "Sockin' Sammy Santos." Having a popular father was a plus for me because everyone in Chinatown and the Filipino community looked up to him.

I used to read his old boxing scrapbook from cover to cover. I knew every boxer Dad knocked out and the round he did it in. He never made it to the title fight, but he was close. In 1931, he lost a close, six-round decision to a boxer named Tod Morgan. Press reports said my dad had been the more aggressive fighter and his loss to Morgan was unpopular and controversial. If he had beaten Morgan, he would have been up for a shot at the title. Still, it was great being able to say to another kid, "My dad can beat your dad."

Sammy met, fell in love with, and married Virginia Nicol, a beautiful local Filipina who worked part-time at the Rizal Cafe while a student at the University of Washington. Virginia's father, Cornelias Nicol, my grandfather (Grampa), immigrated from the Philippines in 1905 and settled in Vancouver, Canada, where he found work in a local sawmill. Grampa married Adaline Gilbert, who was part Canadian Indian and French Canadian. Together they had three children: Lawrence, Antonia (Toni), and Virginia. After Adaline died when the kids were still young, Grampa packed up the family and moved across the border, settling in Port Blakely on Bainbridge Island, where he plied his trade in the local sawmill.

When the Nicol kids were old enough for high school, the family moved to Seattle, where the kids attended Broadway High on Capitol Hill. The Nicol family attended all the Filipino picnics, dances, and dinners. One year, around 1928, Virginia entered the Filipino community queen contest where she was voted first runner-up and earned the title of princess.

Auntie Toni and Mom both worked in Chinatown restaurants while still students. They were very popular with the hundreds of young Filipino bachelors who lived in Chinatown. But the Filipino prizefighters, a fun-loving, free-spirited bunch who earned some pretty good paydays, got all the attention from the young ladies in the community. And so it was with Virginia and Sammy. They were a natural match.

In 1932, soon after Sammy retired from the ring, Sammy Jr. (he was called Sammy Boy) was born. Eighteen months later, a second son, Robert Nicholas, yours truly, was born. Our family lived in the James Apartments located near Sixth Avenue South and James Street. Years later, the building was demolished and a ramp to Interstate 5 was built.

When I was a still a baby, Mom became stricken with tuberculosis. She didn't want to leave her young babies for treatment at the Firlands Sanitarium. Mom deteriorated quickly and died at the young age of 23 in 1935. I never got to know her, but I cherished every picture that my dad kept of my mom. In those pictures, she looked young and healthy. That's how I remember her.

Sammy, the young widower, found it very difficult, if not impossible, to raise two young energetic boys, so he reached out to the in-laws for help. Caroline Gilbert, my great grandmother on my mom's side, whom we called "Grandma," brought Sammy Boy to live with her in Tacoma, Washington while I went to live with Auntie Toni and Uncle Joe Adriatico in Seattle's Central Area.

After Dad retired, he stayed with the sport of boxing as a trainer at the Druxman boxing gym at Seventh Avenue and Pike Street. Dad trained the best fighters in the Druxman stable. One of the toughest fighters to show up at the gym was a kid named Al Hostak from Georgetown, a neighborhood in the industrial area of Seattle. Dad liked Al immediately because the young Hostak, said Dad, "hit like a ton of bricks," just like Dad did.

Hostak won all his fights as a local middleweight. He fought contenders down to California and throughout the Midwest, earning a reputation as a national middleweight contender. A championship bout was held in Seattle between Hostak and the middleweight champ at the time, Freddie Steele, from Tacoma. More than 30,000 people watched the fight. The great Jack Dempsey served as referee. Hostak won the championship and became a local sports hero. When *Sports Illustrated* listed Washington state's top 50 athletes of the century, Al Hostak was on that list. My dad had trained him!

Another young prizefighter Dad trained was Harry "Kid" Matthews, who was managed by "Deacon" Jack Hurley. Hurley was more famous as a fight promoter. In 1956, he promoted the world's heavyweight title fight in Seattle between Floyd Patterson and Pete Rademacher at Sick's Stadium. Hurley managed many fighters in his long career, such as local heavyweight Boone Kirkman (who once fought and lost to George Foreman), but Matthews was probably his best boxer. The Kid was a light heavyweight, a sharp hitter who piled up a long winning streak. Dad was fired as the Kid's trainer after he was suspected of having an affair with the Kid's wife. He didn't complain. The Kid's road to the top ended when he was knocked out by Rocky Marciano. Maybe the Kid would have done better with Sammy Santos in his corner.

When Sammy Boy was around nine years old and I was seven, he came to Seattle with

Grandma Gilbert for regular visits with Dad. Sammy Boy and I would spend all of our Saturdays at Druxman's gym to be with him. After the boxers finished their training, Dad often put the gloves on Sammy Boy and me, and we entertained the boxers and onlookers with a few rounds of wild swinging. Whenever Sammy Boy connected, which I thought was often, I cried, which was also often. The spectators laughed and always threw money into the ring after bouts between the battlin' Santos brothers. We had made it as young prizefighters.

The years of taking too many punches had taken its toll on my dad. He retired early in his career because of blurred vision in his left eye. But he couldn't stay away from the ring. He resumed his career despite the blurred vision. He even won a couple of times. But soon, the vision in his right eye began to deteriorate. In 1945, after an unsuccessful operation on his battered eyes, Dad was blind.

Growing Up in Chinatown — "No Money, No Honey"

When I was eight years old, I worked with Jim Beltran at his dad's Union 76 gas station at the corner of 10th Avenue South and South Jackson. I filled tires with air and radiators with water. In those early days, there were always things to do in Chinatown.

For 10 cents, people checked out the latest movie at the Atlas Theater on Maynard Avenue South. Built in 1922, the Atlas Theater arrived just as the movie industry was beginning to boom. The 475-seat theater became a popular place for families and children. As the country moved into the Great Depression, movies were a cheap form of entertainment. While kids of later generations had television and video games, we had Saturday matinee movie serials featuring the adventures of Flash Gordon and Buck Rogers.

By the 1950s, television became popular and the movie business at the Atlas Theater fell off. In 1960, the theater was renamed the Kokusai Theater, specializing not only in Japanese movies, but movies from Hong Kong and Manila as well. Later, when videotapes made Asian movies more accessible, business at the Kokusai Theater fell off. Then one day, they stopped showing movies. Local businessman Danny Woo took an option on the building with plans to renovate the theater, but he died before the project could get off the ground.

Higo's was a popular novelty store where a dime bought a couple of comic books with a couple of pennies to spare for candy. Founded in the early 1900s by Sanzo Murakami, Higo's was the place to go for toys, clothing, and kitchen goods, among hundreds of other items. In 1957, Higo's Ten Cent Store became Higo's Variety Store when the building was remodeled. Aya and Masako Murakami ran the store for more than fifty years after their father died. Higo's was one of the last remaining Japanese American family-run businesses from the pre-World War II era.

Shigeko Uno and her husband, Chick, had an ice cream parlor, Chick's Ice Creamery, in a storefront at the Bush Hotel. Before World War II, Shigeko's family ran the White River Dairy at Eighth and Weller, the first Japanese American-owned dairy in the United States. At Chihara Jewelers, Dad was able to purchase his radio on credit — nothing to sign, no credit check, just your word. Life was very simple then. Russell's Meat Market was another store that gave credit, one of the oldest stores in Chinatown which later closed after 80 years at the same location.

The best of the restaurants, as I remembered growing up, were the Golden Pheasant, across the street from the N.P. Hotel on Sixth Avenue South, and the Gyokko-Ken at Fifth Avenue South and South Main, which served Chinese food, but was owned by a Japanese family. Two doors east from the Gyokko-Ken was the Chiba Drug Store where we purchased all of my dad's prescriptions; next to them was Sagamiya's, where *mochi* (pounded rice cake) was made.

Over at the Don Ting restaurant, owned by the Chan family, the kids — John, Mary, and Vera — helped out. When Vera grew up, she married Joey Ing and became active in community efforts to preserve the District. The Hong Kong restaurant on Maynard was very popular with the Filipino Alaskeros (Alaskan cannery workers) because it was located in the center of what was considered Manilatown, with the popular Filipino Improvement Club a few doors south and four Filipino barbershops near the corner of Maynard and King Street.

During the weekdays, I lived with Aunt Toni and Uncle Joe. But I spent every weekend with my father, who lived in the N.P. Hotel on Sixth Avenue South. The N.P. Hotel was named after the Northern Pacific Railway. Like many of the hotels in the area — such as the Fujii, Eastern, Panama, Puget Sound, Bush, and Washington — the N.P. Hotel was Japanese-owned. At one time, the N.P. Hotel was considered the "number one" hotel among the Japanese-owned hotels on the Pacific Coast, a place where visiting Japanese dignitaries stayed.

It also served as a Japanese American community center of sorts. Many meetings were held in the hotel's Maneki restaurant.

My father was assigned room 306 because it was right across from the elevator, which made it easier for him to maneuver. The room was nine feet by 13 feet. All of his possessions were crammed into a tiny closet. The double bed took up half the room's space even though it was jammed against the corner. Across from the bed was a low bureau with three drawers on each side and a mirror encased in an oval frame on top. All of Dad's important stuff was arranged in order of importance: dark glasses, wallet, change, hotel key, and cigars.

We often sat on the edge of the bed, facing the radio, where we listened to Dad's favorite shows like Jack Benny, Fibber McGee and Molly, the Shadow, and Seattle Rainiers baseball games. On the face of the radio was a half circle with station numbers printed on tinted glass. I tapped on the glass any time a resident cockroach circled it. Dad often said, "Don't play with that glass, Bobby," and I answered, "But there's static on the radio, Dad."

Mission Bolo was my dad's best friend and another Filipino prizefighter who never quite made it as a professional. He fought mainly in California and according to my Uncle Joe, lost more fights than he won. After Mission Bolo moved to Seattle in the early 1930s, many of Seattle's fight fans mistook Mission for world class contender Little Dempsey, a Filipino who fought in the big boxing cities along the Pacific Coast. Bolo had suffered severe brain damage during his boxing years and began to think he was actually Little Dempsey.

The old *manongs* (a term of respect for elderly Filipino men) used to tease Mission or Little Dempsey, as he preferred to be called, by telling him he owned the Boeing Company and was very wealthy. More than once, Mission took a taxi from downtown Seattle to the N.P. Hotel where he lived and told the taxi driver to collect the cab fare from the Boeing Company. After Mission took a few trips to the King County Jail for non-payment of cab fare, my dad lectured him not to take cabs any longer. Mission had a very difficult time walking in a straight line, but my dad liked his company. They were a familiar sight, as they walked through Chinatown, arm in arm, crazy Mission Bolo navigating through the streets while my blind dad held him up.

On a typical Saturday, I took my dad on a walk around Chinatown, beginning with breakfast at either the Jackson Cafe or the Paramount Cafe. His favorite place was the Jackson Cafe, next to Higo's Ten Cent Store. The Egashira family operated the cafe. I often ordered a hamburger from Rose Yamaguchi, the waitress who hollered to the cook, "hambogu," just like the customers in John Belushi's famous "Saturday Night Live" fast food routine. The hamburger always came on plain white bread. I remember one day, while we were sitting at the cafe, I announced to Dad that there was a new invention...hamburger buns. Dad looked a little bewildered when I said that.

After breakfast, I led Dad around, arm in arm, to his other hangouts in the area. Our routine was to pass by Delfin's Barbershop (six chairs, no waiting, the largest barbershop in Chinatown) or Vince's Barbershop (four chairs, they were the second largest), stop in for a beer at Duke's II, and walk down Maynard Avenue to the Filipino Improvement Club, where lunch was served. At these hangouts, people often gave Sammy a cigar or two and gave me, if I was lucky, a quarter or two. A couple of quarters was a lot of money in those days.

The Filipino Improvement Club, located in the basement of the Freedman Building, was one of the most popular gambling houses in the area. While gambling was illegal, it was no secret. Everybody knew about it. The cops and prosecutors were paid off to look the other way. Rudy Santos, a leader in the Filipino community, was the owner of the club. Everyone went to him for help. He brought a family atmosphere to the club by providing free daily meals to anyone who was hungry. I didn't know if this was done in the spirit of community service or to attract people to gamble. My dad, even though he was blind, frequently gave money to Mission Bolo to gamble. Mission Bolo was punch drunk and couldn't keep up with the fast play. I don't think he ever won, but Dad didn't seem to mind. Years later, when I was asked by Uncle Rudy, a shirt-tail relative, to pay off my dad's gambling debt, I knew that blood was not thicker than greed.

After lunch, I regularly took Dad down King Street to the bathhouse by the alley next to the American Hotel. The hotels in the International District provided single room occupancy units with shared baths and toilets that were usually located at the end of hallways. In the N.P. Hotel where we lived, there were two bathtubs per floor. There was always a long line of bathers waiting for the bathtub. The bathhouse next to the American Hotel had six individual private bathtubs available for 25 cents. After you were clean, you had the choice of also getting cleaned out at the four gambling tables in the back room of the bathhouse.

After we left the bathhouse, we usually walked up Fifth Avenue to Washington Street and dropped in at the Bataan Recreation Club where he visited with all of his pals. Dad was always the center of attention. He and his pals swapped stories about the Philippines or boxing for hours. If it was the first of the month, when my dad got paid, we stopped at the Rice Bowl Cafe or the Manila Cafe.

I remember one day when Dad wanted to have a beer at Mike's Tavern on the corner of Sixth and South King. Inside, a really rowdy guy was picking on a few of the old timers. After the guy had gone on a nonstop tirade for 15 minutes, my dad asked me to bring him up to the bar. When we were in front of this boisterous guy, my dad whispered in my ear, asking me to place his hand on the stranger's shoulder. I was looking the other way when I heard a pop, then a boom. The guy had landed on his back with a little help from a well-placed thump by Dad. Then Dad said, "Bobby, we better go now."

So there we were, my dad pulling me down King Street, tap, tap, tap from his cane, until halfway down the block, I heard two cops yell, "Hey, Sammy, hold up." Dad tugged on my hand and asked, "Who's that?"

"The cops," I replied.

"I'll do the talking."

The two uniforms approached. The older officer wore a sergeant's badge and said, "There's a report out about trouble at the tavern."

My dad, with blood trickling down his knuckle, answered, "I don't see na-ting, officer." The cops had a great laugh and stuck a cigar in my dad's coat pocket.

Even though Dad was blind, he could really cook up some mean *adobo*, neck bones and bitter melon, and pork *inihao. Inihao* is a Filipino dish, which translated means "barbecue." But it's actually cooked with garlic, pork or beef, sautéed in soy sauce, and poured over fresh chopped tomatoes and green onions. Dad's cooking was legendary. There was always a well-fed crowd in that room. I remember all the company who gathered in Dad's hotel room to eat, including the down and outers, Mission Bolo, and the house call girls.

Most of the kids who lived in the I.D. were ashamed to bring their school chums home to their small single room units, but not me. I loved bringing my school friends to room 306 of the N.P. Hotel to show off my dad's two cauliflower ears. These visits also provided the opportunity for my friends to go with me and my dad to the gambling halls. But the ultimate "high" was to actually talk with real call girls. Now don't forget, we were only 11- and 12-year-old boys, so it was only talk. We couldn't afford them, anyway.

Every once in a while, these young ladies, the house pros, came to room 306. Dad regularly poured them a shot of Seagram's with a Seven-Up chaser and the party was on. There were two very young ladies who were friendly and interested in the goings-on in my 11-year-old life. Dixie, a blonde who coined that name after Bing Crosby's wife, and Margie, who had dark red hair, were regular visitors to room 306. When my brother and I thought we were old enough, we tried to make the play, but Dixie and Margie just patted each of us on the head and said, "No money, no honey."

There were a few times on Saturday afternoons, after Margie and Dad had a few drinks, when Margie would say, "Oh! Sammy, I really had a rough night yesterday. Could you give me one of your famous massages?" Dad would then turn to me and say, "Bobby, you go to the Atlas and watch the movie 'Over Da Rainbow.'" He gave me a quarter, which paid for admission, popcorn, and a Coke. I had seen the movie so often I could recite many of the lines and sing all the songs. When I went back to our room after the movie, Dad would yell through the door, "You go get ice cream and come back one more hour."

Margie became my dad's girlfriend before the last operation on his damaged right eye. He had already lost the sight of his left eye while still boxing. Margie was a former call girl who worked exclusively in the hotels of the International District. She often took me shopping to buy me shoes and dress clothes. I was the only guy in school who wore dress slacks with two-toned, brown and white leather shoes.

Soon after Dad lost the sight in his right eye, Margie took off. I saw her one last time as I was walking my dad along King Street. I saw her with her new boyfriend. She motioned me over without acknowledging my dad, kissed me, and said goodbye. She was leaving for California. Years later, I wondered what happened to the beautiful, tall redhead who bought me those really neat shoes.

It became a little ritual for me to light Dad's cigarettes. When he got ready for a light, my brother and I took two of his cigarettes out of the pack, lit them up on his match, and the three of us just puffed away. When I was 12, my brother Sam and I found Dad's hiding place for his whisky stock. We experimented with a tiny drop of whiskey and a whole lot of Seven-Up. Sometimes, when Dad wasn't looking, we poured the booze, lit some smokes, and sat back, smoking and drinking like some real cool dudes.

Uncle Joe

After my mother died in 1935, I went to live with Aunt Toni and Uncle Joe Adriatico during the weekdays while attending parochial school (Maryknoll School for kindergarten and first grade, Immaculate Conception School, and O'Dea High School) in the Central Area of Seattle. On weekends and holidays, I stayed with my dad in Chinatown. Meanwhile, my brother Sam, a year older than I, went to Tacoma to stay with our great grandmother, Caroline Gilbert, a Native Canadian originally from Nanaimo Island, west of Vancouver, Canada. Sam attended St. Patrick's Grade School and Bellarmine Prep High School, both in Tacoma. At Bellarmine, Sam lettered in baseball during his junior and senior years.

Uncle Joe fled the Philippines at an early age because he didn't want to follow the Adriatico family tradition into politics. His father, Macario Adriatico, was a political foe of Manuel Quezon, the first president of the Republic of the Philippines. Uncle Joe became a merchant seaman. It was he, more than anyone else, who first shaped my political awareness. He was a tough, wiry sailor who was well-read and took advantage of his ports of call to learn, first-hand, the politics of the country he was in. Uncle Joe worked on deck as an able-bodied seaman because he refused to serve as a steward or cook as most of the Filipinos did on every ship which sailed out of American ports.

Aunt Toni was somewhat of a saint. She attended mass daily and joined the Marion Club, a Catholic women's group that served the poor. Aunt Toni provided chore services before there were social service programs which did so. I walked with her nightly to the home of Ann Castillio, who was recovering from serious surgery. Aunt Toni bathed her and cooked her meals. If Aunt Toni got paid, it wasn't very much. She also took in and provided for foster children. I grew up with Aunt Toni and Uncle Joe's daughter, Adela, their son Joe Paul, and an adopted cousin, Patrick. The Adriatico home was always filled with lots of kids.

One of the memorable characters who lived in the N.P. Hotel was Fidel Jamilosa, a Filipino from the same province as my dad. Fidel was an old family friend who also visited my aunt and uncle at our home in the Central Area. Fidel worked as a handyman in a downtown beauty shop, was well-read, and spent several years as a student at the University of Washington. He was hired by Boeing during World War II and became a machinist. On weekends about town, Fidel always dressed with class, in not too flashy three-piece suits topped off with a black or gray derby. Fidel could talk about any subject that came up in conversation around my Aunt Toni and Uncle Joe's dinner table, from classical music to Seattle Rainier baseball. He, Uncle Joe, Aunt Toni, and my dad would sit for hours, sipping from a bottle of Old Forrester whiskey and dissecting the War that was raging over Europe and the South Pacific. After World War II ended, the discussions were about politics and the influence of the labor movement on the Filipino community.

The Japanese Kids Leave — "I Am Filipino"

While at Auntie Toni and Uncle Joe's home, I attended the parochial school at Maryknoll, on 16th Avenue and Jefferson, across the street from Providence Hospital. Maryknoll was a missionary church and school. Japanese American kids made up the majority of the students at the school, with the rest from Filipino families who lived in the neighborhood. I don't remember much of kindergarten. But I do remember that in the first grade, I was placed close to the back of the classroom. I really wanted to be up front close to Pauline Matsudaira, the prettiest girl in the whole school. We sat two kids at a square desk facing each other. It took me several months to move up to the front. Finally, I made it to the same desk where Pauline sat. I was in heaven.

However, my world came to an abrupt standstill when one day in the early spring of 1942, Maryknoll School was closed. Japan's attack on Pearl Harbor incited widespread anti-Japanese feeling in the United States, especially on the West Coast where large communities of Japanese Americans lived and worked. President Franklin D. Roosevelt signed Executive Order 9066 on February 19, 1942, which authorized the evacuation and internment of all West Coast Japanese — both American- and foreign-born — "in the interest of national security." Everyone with at least one-sixteenth Japanese ancestry was ordered to leave.

The only possessions they were allowed to take with them were those they could carry. Some families were forced to sell their possessions, homes, and businesses for a fraction of their worth. Local newspapers were filled with "evacuation sale" ads. Others stored their possessions in churches or entrusted them to non-Japanese friends. Businesses not sold to non-Japanese were boarded up. Some businesses, like Shigeko Uno's family-owned White River Dairy, never reopened.

A few weeks later, on a Sunday morning, a convoy of buses showed up across the street from Maryknoll Church. The buses came to drive our Japanese American schoolmates and their families to the Puyallup fairgrounds. There, they were forced to live in horse stalls under armed guard for a short time until the construction of a more permanent internment camp was completed in Minidoka, Idaho, where they spent the duration of the War.

The government believed our Japanese American schoolmates and their families were the "enemy." But even as little kids, we knew we were in a war not only with Japan, but Germany as well. So why weren't the Dodenhoeft or Schmidt families, who also lived in the neighborhood, but were of German descent, sent off to a concentration camp? We knew there was something very wrong with this difference in treatment.

Shortly after the Maryknoll School closed, my schoolmates and I moved three blocks north to the Immaculate Conception School. One lunch period, shortly after I had become a second grader at Immaculate, a blonde sixth grade boy with lots of freckles grabbed me and yelled, "Are you a Jap, huh? Are you a Jap?" Crying, I answered, "No, honest. I'm a Filipino." These kinds of incidents were common and not too long after, kids in our neighborhood had to wear badges printed "I AM FILIPINO" or "I AM CHINESE." At the age of eight, I had my first real personal experience with racism.

Immaculate, which had virtually been an all-White school, had a few African American students enrolled, such as Patty Bown. She graduated from Immaculate Girls High School in 1950 and became a very popular jazz pianist, playing at local clubs when she was barely out of high school. Seattle was a hot jazz town in the early 1950s, but even this cool scene couldn't keep Patty home. She moved to New York in the mid-1950s and became a jazz artist who played with the best jazz stars of the era. Quincy Jones was an early contemporary in Seattle and followed Patty to New York, where she introduced Quincy to major jazz players. When Patty made her infrequent visits home, some of her old friends usually found her playing with a local jazz trio at the New Orleans Jazz Club in Pioneer Square.

After the end of World War II, I can still remember the day when Pauline and the Matsudaira family came home from camp. Mr. and Mrs. Matsudaira left with a large family and came back with even more members (a couple of kids were born in camp). Mrs. Mary Beltran, a prominent member of the Filipino community who lived with her family on 16th Avenue, marched up the stairs of the Matsudaira home with a large chocolate cake to welcome them back to the neighborhood. Other Japanese American families such as the Chiharas, the Nakagawas, and the Horiuchis were also welcomed back to the neighborhood. I was also glad to see the return of the Caasi family. Mrs. Caasi was a Japanese American, but Mr. Caasi was a Filipino American who chose to be interned with his wife.

Jazzing It Up

After the end of World War II, many Japanese American families chose not to return to Seattle or settled elsewhere outside the Chinatown area. Shortly before the War, Yesler Terrace — a major public housing project which eventually covered 12 city blocks — was built on the northern edge of the Chinatown-International District boundary, where the Japanese community had been. As the Japanese left, African Americans began to reside in the area, especially during World War II when war industry jobs were plentiful. They established diners, groceries, taverns, tailor shops, and night clubs.

For many years, Seattle's after hours jazz scene thrived on Jackson Street — clubs like the Ubangi at 710 South King Street; the 416, next to the Atlas Theater; the Congo Club, on the north side of Jackson, on the top floor of a building between Maynard Avenue South and Sixth Avenue South; the Chinese Gardens (which later became the Gim Ling restaurant, then the China Gate restaurant); the Basin Street Club, in the basement of the Bush Hotel extending outward beneath what later became Hing Hay Park; the Elks Club at 662 South Jackson; and the Ebony Cafe at Fifth Avenue South and Jackson.

The walk from Dad's home to my weekday home with my aunt and uncle was always an experience. As a 12-year-old, I became interested in jazz. The walk up Jackson Street to the apartment where we lived on 14th Avenue and Spruce Street was filled with music and a party atmosphere. Walking east, I regularly strolled by the Club Maynard; the Elks Club (the building which later housed the Japanese American Citizens League), where Ray Charles got his start; the Main Event; Bowman's Joint; and the Ebony Clu.

Up on the corner of 12th Avenue South and South Jackson, I was surrounded by street activity, with people going in and out of the taverns, bars, and joints. The Hill Top Tavern held down the northeast corner. Two doors east on Jackson from the Hill Top was the World of Music record shop owned by Bob Summerise; next door was the Monarch Pool Hall, where, even as a kid, I was hustled by pool sharks. The building on the southeast corner of 12th Avenue South and Jackson housed the Tazuma 10 Cents Store on the street level and the Black and Tan Club in the basement, where every major Black band played.

Yesler Way between 12th Avenue South and 14th Avenue South was the rowdy section of town. I knew it was safer to walk on the north side of Yesler. Next to the Chinese meat market on 14th Avenue South and Yesler was the Rocking Chair Club where I watched the swingers, the "hep cats," stroll in and out. The big Black bouncer at the Rocking Chair allowed me, on occasion, to peek in and listen to a couple of numbers played by the band, then shooed me off when the owner approached the front door.

A Chinese man we called "One-Armed Jack" owned a local pool hall. Why he got his nickname was obvious, but none of us had the guts to ask him how he lost his arm. Even with one arm, he was not one to mess with. I brushed up on my pool shooting, hoping to compete with the Monarch hustlers and got hustled by the local Chinese kids. I guess word of my pool skills got around. I became an easy mark.

Cannery Work — Two Separate Worlds

During the summers of my junior and senior years in high school, 1951 and 1952, I went the way of most Filipino males and traveled north to Alaska, where I worked in the fish canneries. My father had been out of boxing for 20 years, but still held the respect of many Filipino community leaders, including the officers of the Cannery Workers Union, Local 7. I didn't have to buy the favor of Gene Navarro, the union dispatcher at that time, who sent me up as his protégé.

Ugashik, Alaska was a very small fishing village on the Ugashik River, which flowed into Bristol Bay. As we approached the village from the river in a pontooned aircraft, I saw a red, weather-beaten fish house on pilings next to the big warehouse. Up on a knoll boardwalk stood a large, two-story white house where the White superintendent, his wife, and their daughter lived during the canning season. The superintendent was a tall, white-haired man, probably in his early 60s. His wife was a short, dark-haired woman, considerably younger than her husband, probably in her 40s. Their daughter was a teenager, the only female close to my age at the cannery. I'm sure her father told her to stay away from "those boys."

Down the boardwalk were a series of single-story duplexes that housed the fishermen and the mechanics who kept up the maintenance of the cannery machinery. They were all White. Next to these stood six low shacks that housed the husky sled dogs. At the very end of the boardwalk, 50 yards further down, was the small bunkhouse where we — the Filipino cannery workers — stayed eight to a room. Four double-bunk beds were crammed into the house with two feet of aisle space down the center to spare.

There were about 150 in the crew. During the first year, I worked in the warehouse and never even touched a fish. As a 17-year-old first-timer, I had no seniority. Instead, I was assigned to place tops on the cans of fish, then load the cans into boxes for shipment, eight hours a day, during the six-week season from the beginning of June to mid-August. It was hard work.

Since we were all members of Local 7 of the Cannery Workers Union, we were guaranteed $1,200 per month, plus overtime for working over 40 hours per week. I netted $2,500 for a season which was a lot of money in the early 50s. I bought my first car, a used 1939 black four-door Chevy, with my earnings.

In my second year at Ugashik, with one year of seniority under my belt, I was assigned to the fish house as a "slimer." When the fishing boat unloaded its catch, fish came off the boat down the chutes into the fish house and plopped onto conveyor belts. As the fish went down the conveyor belts, butchers lopped off the heads and split the fish lengthwise. Slimers like me stood at work stations with faucets, cleaned out the guts, and placed the cut fish into cans. Sliming was a job no one wanted. It was the lowest of the low in the fish house, but even so, a slimer had more status than a warehouse worker. The hours were irregular. Sometimes, we worked around the clock, especially when four or five fishing boats were lined up with full loads. We worked until all the boats were empty.

There were two mess halls, one for Whites where they served steak, pork chops, BLTs, waffles, eggs, bacon, and turkey daily, and one for the Filipinos that featured fish and rice with chicken on Sundays. Don't get me wrong, the fish was prepared 10 different ways and it was always fresh, but we never had the variety of meals available to the White workers.

Although we all lived in this tiny village, it might well have been two worlds. The other world had all the amenities, and we got what was left. We felt a little vindicated when we watched the back of the mess house and saw our chief cook, Benny, sneak into the warehouse with the superintendent's wife for a quickie, and saw our roommate, Buster, have this fling with the superintendent's daughter in the late evening down by the river. We nicknamed them our "two Filipino boys with plenty love to give."

It Takes a Filipino Village to Raise a Filipino Child

The Filipino community had a life and spirit all of its own. Much of the leadership was prominent in "finance," some owned the biggest gambling establishments in Chinatown. Among the most powerful and influential in the community was the leadership of Local 7, the Cannery Workers Union (which later became Local 37 of the International Longshoremen and Warehousemen's Union). They were a mini Mafia. There were instances of power struggles, payoffs, graft, assaults, and murders.

For example, in December of 1936, Virgil Duyungan, president of Local 18257 of the Cannery Workers' and Farm Laborers' Union, and Aurelio Simon, secretary, were murdered in their union offices. Both left widows with large families. There were indictments of Filipino union leaders accused of being communists during the McCarthy witch hunts of the late 1940s and early 1950s. Back in those days, we never questioned our Filipino community leaders. They were respected elders, even if they were crooked or out for personal gain. Most of them were my dad's friends.

My friends and I were too young to get involved in community politics. We were more interested in being teenagers and doing the fun things that teenagers did. The more memorable times we spent as teenagers were on spring weekends at Seward Park. We spent sunny days on "Pinoy Hill," on the top of a curvy road where open space gave room for softball games and volleyball. "Pinoy Hill," a term coined by us young teenagers, served as the site where the Filipino community held its annual July Fourth picnics. Even today, the term "Pinoy Hill" can be found in official informational brochures of the Seattle Parks and Recreation Department.

On most Saturday nights, we were almost always at the Filipino community dances held in Washington Hall at 14th Avenue South and Fir Street or down Washington Street at the Finnish Hall. The dances brought out all the single Filipino guys who always outnumbered the Filipino women and girls. The guys were charged admission, while the women were allowed in without having to pay. A colored ribbon was pinned on our lapels to show proof that we had paid. A different color was used each week to prevent freeloaders from sneaking in. We tried to outsmart them. We always came as a group to the door where the girls checked in. After we found out the right color of the ribbon for the night, the guys trotted down to the Bon Rob Drug Store to buy the same color ribbon for our admission. It was cheaper. If and when we were challenged, the girls threatened to leave, which would have left the older women as the only dance partners for the packed dance hall, full of bachelors.

The band that played for the dances we attended as teenagers was led by Frank Osias, and the piano player was a young teenager by the name of Lois Bolero. Lois later married Phil Hayasaka, and both became active in the local civil rights movement.

The neighborhood "gang" included the kids from the Maryknoll Church, Immaculate Conception High, Garfield High, Franklin High, and O'Dea High as well as all the kids who lived on 16th Avenue. Our close-knit group included my best friend Jim Beltran, who always seemed to get me in trouble as we cruised in his dad's car all over Seattle, Auburn, and Bremerton, looking for his girlfriends. Jim was the toughest guy in the group, the quickest and the best rebounder on our basketball team. Even though he was older and bigger than me, I always loved to box him because when I hit him just once in his nose, he started sneezing. I attacked and wouldn't stop even when he called, "Ding, ding, ding — the round's over. Time out!"

As young kids, we had a *Shopping News* route, making weekly deliveries to every house in the neighborhood. We started at Jim's folks' grocery store at 14th Avenue and Spruce Street, loaded up a baby buggy with papers, soda, cookies, and Twinkies, and off we went. Jim sat in the buggy, folding the papers while I pushed it. I didn't complain. After all, he provided all the eats. While being pushed along, he threw the papers on the porch as we passed.

One day as we went down the steep hill on James Street from Broadway, I couldn't hold the buggy and it got away. I heard Jim yell, "Hey! I think we're going too fast," as the papers were thrown out at a rapidly faster pace. He finally ended up at the bottom of the hill in a heap with the overturned buggy, Twinkies, and a soda spilled all over his lap.

The kids we grew up with were pretty "straight-arrow" kids who never got into serious trouble. However, there was one incident I still remember that might be considered a "minor" problem. When I was eight years old, there was a grocery store owned by two Filipino brothers, directly across the street, kitty-corner from the Beltran family's grocery store.

The brothers' store stayed open late and the cash register was usually manned by the oldest brother, who was partially blind. One night, after being sent to the store to purchase milk, I entered the store, looked around, didn't see anyone, then stuffed a package of sugar wafers down my shirt. Almost immediately, I heard the voice of the blind brother. "I caught you, Bobby. You took the cookie."

I turned around and there was the partially blind brother with his head pressed against the glass inside the cooler, looking at me. After that incident, whenever my aunt sent me for milk, I was too embarrassed to return to the store. Instead, I raced down to the market owned by a Chinese family, three blocks down on Yesler Way, then raced back to the apartment with the milk.

Maybe the closest to getting into serious trouble were Joe Yumal and Joe Gaudia. When these two were 11 years old, they found a truck tire in the hills below Yesler Terrace. They started to race the tire down the hill above Jackson Street where Conners Furniture Store once stood. The tire got away from them. They watched with amusement as the tire picked up speed and bounced down the hill past Main Street toward Jackson Street. Amusement turned to horror when the tire took a big bounce and landed straight into the back seat of a Packard convertible. No one was hurt, but the two kids prayed that they wouldn't be caught. Up until now, this had been their secret.

Playing sports was always a way for our neighborhood kids to live out their daydreams of being athletic heroes. We played all the sports even though organized team sports weren't as prominent then as they are today. After the Japanese American kids came back from internment camp, a basketball league was formed at the Buddhist Church gymnasium on Main

Street. Teams from the Japanese, Chinese, and Filipino communities were invited to participate. There were four Nisei (Japanese) teams, two from the Chinese community, and one from the Filipino community. Each community had its star athletes. Two of the prominent players from the Chinese community teams were college athletes Al Mar and Ray Soo. Stars of the Japanese community teams included Frank (Shobo) Fujii and the Otani brothers — Shig, Hod, and Ray.

Our team, the Filipino Cavaliers, was made up of neighborhood kids like George Lagasca, Jim Beltran, Leo and Bill Mamon, Bernie and Ray Cantil, Sal Del Fierro, Fred Cordova, Ed and Jerry Laigo, Bob Murray (an African American who we insisted had Filipino blood in his family), and me. We never won a league championship, but I remember winning a game against the great China Clipper team, when I stole the ball with five seconds left and scored on a shot from the half court line. It was just like my wildest dream, in which I won a national basketball championship game on a last second shot for the Cavaliers.

Football games were played on an open field between teams from the surrounding neighborhoods. We played two games a year with the Yesler Terrace kids. These kids from the projects were tougher than hell. They also had better football gear. When we showed up, George Lagasca was the only kid from our team with a complete uniform. The rest of us, 15 or so, had to pick from an equivalent of four complete uniforms. I usually ended up with just a set of rib pads. The kids from the projects usually won by three or four touchdowns.

Baseball games were pick-up games, and we roamed the parks in the Central Area looking for any team to play us. It was only later as young adults that we played organized baseball when my brother Sam recruited some of us to play for the Seattle Post Office Baseball team in the Seattle Park League. I was the second-string catcher, but only got to play when my brother Sam pitched. Sam was also the manager.

We played on Garfield, Broadway, Collins, and Liberty playfields. The Liberty playfield was our neighborhood playfield. During the 1962 Seattle World's Fair, the Liberty playfield was converted to accommodate a rodeo. Today, Seattle University's Connolly Center sits on the site of our old neighborhood playfield.

The Filipino community had its own tennis club. Its big tennis stars at that time were Frank Ortega and Victor Osoteo, who both taught tennis to us neighborhood kids on the tennis courts of Volunteer Park. It was one sport that we continued playing and teaching our own kids to play when we got older.

The best athlete in the community was Buddy Reyes, who grew up in Yesler Terrace. Buddy was a running back for Garfield High School, but was recruited by O'Dea High School in his junior year. He played one year for O'Dea, but quit school before his senior year. There's no telling how good he could have been if given the right coaching.

Buddy's father was Filipino and his mother was Indian. Today the term favored by the children of these marriages is "Indipino." The Reyes family was typical of many families in our community. Because of anti-miscegenation laws, Filipinos couldn't marry Caucasian women. With immigration laws limiting the flow of Filipinos to the United States, Filipino women had a very difficult time following their men to the States. That explains why it wasn't unusual to find mixed marriages between Filipino men and Indian women.

In many of the Pacific Northwest Filipino communities, Indipinos were not readily accepted by full-blooded Filipinos. Because of this widespread snub, many Indipinos followed their mothers' heritage by growing up and maintaining their Indian culture. Two of the more prominent Indipinos were the late Bernie Whitebear, CEO of the United Indians of All Tribes Foundation, and the late Joe Dela Cruz, who rose to chairman of the Quinault Indian Nation. My great grandmother, Caroline Gilbert, was a full-blooded Canadian Indian, so I qualified as an Indipino as well.

George Lagasca was our group leader. He was the quarterback on the ragtag football team, shortstop on the baseball team, the point and shooting guard on the basketball team, the best bowler, and the best tennis player. We often met at his house, shined our shoes in his basement, and lit up cigarettes that George stole from his dad. When his mom and dad, Amy and Joe, went upstairs to bed, George often took the keys to the family car, without permission, and we went cruising. One night, George took a turn too sharp and dented the door on the driver's side. Every night thereafter for about a week as we gathered at George's house, we heard Joe and Amy blaming each other for the dented car door.

The first girl I really liked was Helen Mamon, who lived with her parents, brothers, and sister just around the corner from Auntie Toni and Uncle Joe's apartment. Helen's brothers,

Leo and Bill, were members of our basketball team that played in the Buddhist League. Every Tuesday night in our teen years, we all ended up at the Mamon house on 15th Avenue and Spruce Street to watch Milton Berle on the Texaco Hour. They owned the only television set in the neighborhood. I was a freshman at O'Dea High at the time and often stayed at Helen's house after the "Milton Berle Show" to have her teach me how to dance. Helen was the best dancer in the group and actually taught the jitterbug, the swing, and the offbeat to both the young and the old. We didn't really go steady because her main steady was Jerry Laigo, who spent the school year at St. Edward's Seminary studying to be a priest.

At the weekly Saturday night dances sponsored by different Filipino organizations, the young teenagers kept up with all the new dance steps — thanks to Helen. One of the young teenagers was Cookie Delma, who was so good, he was recruited to be a dance instructor by the Arthur Murray dance studios. Cookie was tall and "Hollywood handsome." He not only made lots of money for the Arthur Murray people, he also made lots of little old ladies and not-so-little old ladies happy.

Hillary Clinton has said, "It takes a village to raise a child." Our "villagers" were Vince and Louise Flor, Pashong and Belen Braganza, and Serio and Lenora Josue. They were the ears and eyes of our neighborhood. When one of the kids got into trouble on the street in an accident or a fight, one of the "villagers" always knew about it and called our families to let them know. They were our uncles and aunts, even though we weren't blood relatives. Whatever we did as teenagers up until the time we reached young adulthood, our parents, aunts, uncles, and our friends' parents were never far away because all the young people in the Filipino community attended the same dances, picnics, church bazaars, and holiday parties.

Liking the Laigos

The Laigo family played a prominent role in my life. Uncle Joe once told me the story of the family patriarch, Valeriano Laigo, a successful businessman who had one of the few regular paying jobs during the Depression in the 1930s. Valeriano often drove his car loaded with bags of rice to the homes of families he knew were having a tough time making ends meet. It didn't matter to him (like it did to others) from what province in the Philippines you came. Mr. Laigo's life tragically ended in 1938, when he was shot by a man later found to be mentally insane.

Mrs. Bibiana Laigo later married Mike Castillano, who became a great father to Bibiana's five children — Val, Dorothy, Eddie, Ben, and Jerry. They raised a family and added four more children of their own — Michael Jr., Jeanette, Frances, and Marya — to the clan.

I was hired by Mike Castillano Sr. to clean the clam nectar pots at the original Ivar's Acres of Clams restaurant on the Seattle waterfront, where he was chef. In those teenage years, I also waited on tables at the Navy Officers' Club on Pier 91 and washed dishes at G.O. Guy Drugs on Third Avenue and Union Street. In August 1950, Seattle held its first annual Seafair week, a festival featuring parades, dances, water sports, and lots of fun events. I missed the whole celebration because I was working, but it felt good to have a couple of bucks in my wallet to spend.

Ed Laigo was my classmate from kindergarten at Maryknoll through graduation from O'Dea High. While attending O'Dea High, a Catholic school, I became very aware that Filipino kids were not popular with the Irish Christian Brothers and the school's coaches, unless we were athletes. I still remember when Wayne Ambrose, the football coach, told one of the Brothers, "There go the hot shot jitterbugs dressed in their zoot suit clothes." He was referring to the Laigos (Jerry, Eddie and Ben) and Albert Mendoza. They always wore clean white shirts with black trousers and black dress shoes, not because they were "hot shot jitterbugs," but because they all had jobs after school at downtown restaurants and didn't have lockers to change clothes.

Val Laigo was one of my first heroes because he was willing to share his life with us as a coach of our pathetic grade school basketball team. He wasn't your ordinary "jock" coach. Val was a very talented guy — an "artist." He sang, or rather crooned, at local talent shows. When I first met Val, he was also beginning to realize his talent as an oil painter, for which he later became internationally known. He became an art professor at Seattle University, where he taught until his death in 1992. Val's paintings are still shown in museums, art galleries, and exhibitions throughout the country.

Dorothy Laigo married Fred Cordova, a Seattle University graduate with a degree in journalism who had moved to Seattle from Stockton, California. Fred became a writer for the *Seattle Post-Intelligencer* and the *Northwest Progress*, the local Catholic newspaper. He later became the director for Information Services at the University of Washington. Dorothy later became prominent as a staff member of the Demonstration Project for Asian Americans, an organization which provided the research base for a national network of Asian American activists and social workers.

Keeping in Touch with the Old Gang

In 1975, I called together some of the guys I grew up with — Ben Laigo, Jim Beltran, George Lagasca, Bob Maxie, and my brother Sam, who played for the Cavaliers, our old neighborhood basketball team. We met for lunch at the Hong Kong restaurant and had a wonderful time reminiscing about old times and telling stories about the friends who didn't show up. We had such a good time at the lunches, we decided to call as many of the old neighborhood friends as we could find and hold a neighborhood reunion.

The first of many reunions was held in the Immaculate Church social hall with 50 people in attendance. As word got around about the fun everyone had at the first event, I started receiving calls from those who missed it, asking when the next event would be held. We waited a few years and held the second reunion at Ben Laigo and Ed Beltran's new restaurant, Edwardo's, at the corner of First Avenue and Marion Street. This time 120 people showed up. Eventually, the reunion became a biannual event. The reunion event usually started at 4 p.m., which gave people enough time to mingle before dinner at 6. After dinner, we would continue to party until the early evening or until the wine was gone. Ensuing reunions were held at the Harbor Club; Daybreak Star Indian Center, as guests of Bernie Whitebear; Caesar's; the Atrium; and South Seattle Community College.

The planning meetings for the reunion, held at the Bush Garden restaurant, were social events in themselves. As the years went by, the loss of more friends made the event that much more important for those of us who were left. The kids who grew up together, raised families and were now grandparents, even great grandparents, were always very close. We all really liked each other.

At first, it was just the guys who planned the neighborhood reunions. But as the years passed, the women took over the planning. Frankly, they were much more skilled at planning what had become very large and expanded neighborhood reunions. Death took a large chunk out of the planning committee, but those of us who are left — including Vi Matsuoka and her sister-in-law Carol Lagasca; Rose Rallos Damondon, her sister Shirley Rallos and their brother Sy Simon; Angie and Henry Gamido; Mich Matsudaira and his sister Pauline Yaguchi; Bill and Gloria Mamon; and myself — continue to look forward to seeing the old gang at the next reunion.

CHAPTER TWO

Growing as a Young Adult

Pursuing the American Dream — Family Life in the 50s

In 1952, when I was 18 years old, I joined the Marine Corps while the Korean War was still in progress. My basic training consisted of traveling to several different states where I attended military schools that taught aircraft engine maintenance. Despite this training, I wasn't a very good mechanic. If the outcome of the war had been left in my hands, the North Koreans would have won because I wouldn't have gotten our aircraft off the ground. Lucky for our side, the war was over just as I got to Korea.

I had joined the Marines to fight. Even though the war ended, I still wanted to fight. I joined the boxing team just after the armistice was signed and enjoyed the privileges of being an athlete in the service. There I was — Bobby Santos — the lean, mean, fighting machine. I won a few fights, but my overall boxing record convinced me to give up the notion of following my father into the ring. A prizefighter was not to be my profession. No cauliflower ears for me. I would be groomed to fight battles in other arenas. Besides, I didn't want to mess up my face.

While I was in the Marine Corps, my dad got remarried into a ready-made family. Her name was Viva. She had three small children of her own and together, Viva and my dad produced three more children — Ramona, Nori, and David. Their marriage was rough from the start. Having enough money was always a problem. My dad's only income came from Social Security. Viva didn't do much better as a night shift nurse. The marriage lasted 10 years. Viva eventually took the children and moved to Keyport, a small town in Kitsap County, across Puget Sound, to start a new life. Dad moved downtown to the St. Charles Hotel.

My dad died in 1971. I was sorry that I never got to be with him as often as when I was a kid. Over the years we had drifted apart. I had married and was raising my own family. Dad had his second family with kids much younger than me with whom he could spend time. But I was always grateful for the times I did spend with him. He had taught me to be a fighter, to never give up, even when the opponent was bigger and stronger than me. It was a lesson I took to heart, especially when our community of Davids later fought the Goliaths of government and downtown developers.

My brother Sam and I came home from the service, coincidentally on the same day in October 1955. We decided to live with Aunt Toni and Uncle Joe. After years of living in apartments, they finally had their own house with room to spare. Wherever they lived, it was home to me. It was Aunt Toni and Uncle Joe who raised me and who I really regarded as my parents. Even as I got older with a family of my own, I always kept in touch. Both Aunt Toni and Uncle Joe passed away just a few years apart in the late 1980s.

Sam and I spent a lot of time together. We had discussions about world events late into the night, watched the Tuesday Night and Friday Night fights, and played poker on weekends with Uncle Joe, who usually won most of our money. We often went together to Seattle Rainiers baseball games at Sick's Stadium (Emil Sick owned the Rainier Brewery, the baseball team and the stadium). The Seattle Rainiers were members of the Pacific Coast League and was a minor league feeder team which groomed prospects for the Major Leagues — Fred Hutchinson, a local star pitcher from Franklin High School, and Vada Pinson of the Cincinnati Reds — to name two. One of the most popular players was Bobby Balcena, one of the few Filipinos playing professional baseball.

Sam married Mary Goudeau. They were blessed with seven children. Sam worked first for the post office, then later worked for 15 years at Boeing in its vinyl upholstery department. Sam's greatest gift was coaching. He was player/manager for both the post office and Boeing's fast pitch and slow pitch baseball teams. He coached Little League football teams with four division titles and three city championships. He also coached Little League baseball at Rainier playfield for many years — almost to the day he died in 1982. Sam was only 49 years old.

There were some incidents which occurred during those young post-Marine Corps times that, looking back now, were totally embarrassing. For example, after a few months removed from active duty, I drove up Jackson Street with a car full of buddies who were also just separated from their military tours of duty. After a few beers, we got pretty rowdy. As we stopped for a red light at Maynard Avenue, the car behind us honked a few times. We had missed a few green lights because we were so busy slapping each other on the head to the beat of the music blaring from the car radio. The driver, a big White guy in a UW letterman's sweater, finally got out of his car and yelled at me while I lowered the window. Almost immediately, Bob Maxie, who was sitting in the back seat behind me, jumped out of the car and started to beat on the guy. Within seconds, the guys in our car were fighting the guys in the other car. Suddenly, we heard the sounds of sirens escalating louder, coming closer up the street. As we took off, Maxie asked what the guy had yelled at me. I replied, "He asked if we needed a push."

After my honorable discharge from the Marine Corps in 1955, I was hired by the Boeing Company. I was assigned to the hammer shop at Boeing's Renton plant. A year later, I met Anita Agbalog, a recent graduate of Franklin High School who was working through the summer at the Manila Cafe in Chinatown. Sound familiar? Just like my dad, I fell in love with a waitress. Less than a year after we met, I proposed, she agreed, and we settled into married life in a small apartment at 14th Avenue and Spring Street. Anita was also hired by Boeing. We did the things that young couples usually did — visited friends, attended Filipino community dances, and worked our way up in our new careers at Boeing. You might say we were pursuing the American dream.

Anita worked at Boeing as a graphics illustrator. In the late 50s, after receiving security clearance, she was added to the project team that designed the original Boeing 707 — which eventually became known as "Air Force One" — the plane designated for the exclusive use of the President of the United States. Anita was very conscientious and took her job seriously. As she worked on the plans for Air Force One, she was a stickler for detail, to the point of marking the famous red phone with an "R" on the schematics. This little detail received the attention of the FBI, who came to Boeing to check Anita out. In those days, there was widespread paranoia about communists infiltrating defense industries such as Boeing. The FBI didn't think it was a good idea to document the existence of the red phone. It was "top secret," after all.

My job wasn't so hush-hush. My shop foreman at Boeing was an old boxing fan and remembered my dad from his boxing days more than 25 years earlier. I rose quickly through the shop from hammer operator assistant to hammer operator in 16 months. At the hammer shop, metal was shaped and formed to the contours of a large shaped lead dye. It was the fork lift operator's job to move the dye into place on the bed of a ceco hammer. As a hammer operator, my job was to operate a lever, which controlled the hammer's pumping. I was always careful to avoid placing any part of my body under the hammer as it blasted the metal into shape.

One of the fork lift operators, a union shop steward, was jealous at my quick rise in the shop. He often ignored my repeated requests to move the heavy dyes to the bed of the ceco hammer I operated. One afternoon, I complained to the foreman that this fork lift operator was preventing me from doing my job. He then reprimanded the fork lift driver for not assisting me. Soon after, the driver rammed his fork lift into me. I knew he did it on purpose so I went after him, knocking him into a bin full of discarded metal scrap. When he got up, there were lacerations on his arms and face. He definitely looked beaten up, especially in the photos that were taken at the hospital.

I was arrested and charged with assault. The prosecutor was a young attorney named Anthony Savage, who later became one of Seattle's top criminal defense attorneys. As for me, not knowing any attorneys, Uncle Rudy Santos had his attorney take my case. Sylvester Garvin was one of the top defense attorneys in the Northwest. He advised me to bring half the staff of the hammer shop to testify on my behalf at the trial. Testimony was consistent — the driver provoked the incident. I was given a suspended sentence and kept my job. The fork lift driver was transferred to a different part of the plant. I became somewhat of a hero among the Filipinos in Chinatown because Uncle Rudy spread the word that I had beaten up a White man. Although I kept my job, I knew my days at Boeing were numbered.

The Laigo brothers, Eddie and Ben, and I went into business together, operating our own barbecue restaurant called the Rib Pit, located west of Rainier Avenue on South Dearborn Street, for a short time during the 1962 Seattle World's Fair. Actually, our business didn't do that badly. However, we got hammered financially, trying to promote a three-night jazz concert featuring the Dave Brubeck group at the Green Lake Aqua Theater. It was a fabulous concert with local talent like Teddy Ross, who years later won a Tony Award for his role as the Cowardly Lion in "The Wiz" on Broadway. The Joni Metcalf Trio also performed, but nobody came. We filed for bankruptcy under Chapter 11 and life went on.

In the mid-1960s, I left the Boeing Company to sell insurance for the Knights of Columbus. At the same time, I decided to channel my energy to something positive. I volunteered to coach a physical fitness program sponsored by the Knights of Columbus. Kids of the Knights' members and their neighborhood friends assembled each Saturday morning at the Knights' gymnasium. About 50 boys showed up every week. We put them through Marine Corps-style exercises, relay races with and without a basketball, and boxing.

As head coach, I was allowed to hire assistant coaches. I recruited basketball players from Seattle University such as Ernie Dunston, Tom Workman, Charlie Williams, and Peller Phillips. Ironically, Williams and Phillips ended up being examples to kids of what not to do. Williams and Phillips were implicated in a point-shaving scandal. They were kicked off the Seattle University basketball team. Workman and Williams later played professional basketball, Workman for the Atlanta Hawks in the National Basketball Association and Williams for several teams in the American Basketball Association.

One of the kids we had in the program was a skinny little White kid named Freddy. He didn't seem to be very athletic. He couldn't box. On some Saturday mornings, the kids were all there except for Freddy. I asked where he was and the kids replied, "Freddy had to caddy." We piled into the car and drove up to the Jefferson golf course. There was Freddy, lugging a set of golf clubs bigger than he was. The kids laughed and pointed at him. But I can tell you that no one laughed at who Freddy became. Who knew then that the skinny little White kid named Freddy would become the famous successful professional golfer Fred Couples? And no, we didn't teach golf.

After a few years, we bought our first house, a two-bedroom rambler which overlooked Sick's Stadium in the Mt. Baker neighborhood. Anita and I started a family. We got busy. Over a period of 10 years, the world welcomed Danny, Simone, Robin, Tom, John, and Nancy — three sons and three daughters. The first house we owned was too small to raise the family, so we purchased a seven-bedroom home on South Bradford Street in southeast Seattle, complete with four baths, two large fireplaces, and two wet bars. The kids finally had their own rooms and the house became the destination drop-in center for all the neighborhood kids and school chums.

All of the kids were involved in activities and athletics at school and at Rainier playfield. Each graduated from Franklin High, with Danny following my footsteps in and out of the Marine Corps. Tom earned All-Metro honors for two years in varsity football and basketball and lettered as a senior in varsity baseball. Robin and Nancy lettered for three years each in varsity basketball and baseball. Danny was a varsity soccer player for all his three years at Franklin. John played football and basketball for local teams in South Seattle. Simone was tougher than the other five combined.

Having and raising a family was both rewarding and fulfilling with more than a few memorable moments. Although both Anita and I had our own careers, we spent quality time raising the children. We shared the cooking, the laundry, and ironing duties. Because of my meetings and hearings that were scheduled throughout the week, Anita spent much of her after work hours delivering and picking up our active children from the art classes and sports events in which the Santos kids excelled.

Every so often on a Friday night after work, I first checked with Anita, then announced to the rest of the family to pack up because we were driving to Ocean Shores on the Pacific Coast to visit their grandfather. Godfrey Agbalog, Anita's dad, had moved to Ocean Shores in 1972 and opened the town's only barbershop. The kids headed directly to the sandy beach, collected driftwood and built their camp-like shelters. In the evening, the kids went with their granddad, an accomplished bowler, to the bowling alley to see if they could knock down any of the pins. Of course, as they grew older, they were better able to compete with him.

CHAPTER THREE

Civil Rights Activism

Civil Rights and Civil Wrongs

THE 1960S SAW THE RISE of the civil rights movement. Nationally, there were demonstrations, marches, and lunch counter sit-ins which brought attention to the rights of minorities. Seattle was no different. On July 1, 1963, a brief sit-in to promote the support of open housing by members of the Central District Youth Club, an African American community group, at the mayor's office compelled the Seattle City Council to form a human rights commission. Mayor Gordon Clinton appointed Phil Hayasaka to lead the commission. Under Phil's leadership, the commission proposed an open housing ordinance which was placed on the ballot in 1964. However, Seattle voters rejected the ordinance. Local civil rights groups continued to hold marches in support of open housing.

It was during my membership in the Knights of Columbus that I met Walt Hubbard. Walt, president of the local Catholic Interracial Council (CIC), invited me to join a march they were co-sponsoring in support of open housing. We met at St. James Cathedral, where I was handed a pole that held the CIC banner. The march went to the Seattle Center. The day was so stormy and cold, the wind battered the banner like it was a sail in rough seas. I fought hard against the wind to hold the banner up. It was an absolute no-no if I allowed the banner to hit the ground. No one asked if they could relieve me or take the banner because they all had been in my position before. This was an initiation rite of passage. I had to prove myself. It was after the march that I decided it was the last one I'd ever be in. But the next morning, there I was, on the front page of the Catholic newspaper, holding the banner.

I had my first taste of the civil rights struggle. While I was aware of racial discrimination — my experiences in the canneries taught me about that — I had never questioned it. I had assumed that life wasn't always fair. Discrimination was a fact of being non-White in America. However, being around the other civil rights activists, I found we could fight social injustice. There was a spirit of hope, but also the reality that no one was going to voluntarily open the door to equal opportunity for us. It was up to us to break the door down. Soon after, I joined the CIC and became heavily involved in the local civil rights struggle. The issues of the times were open housing, equal job opportunities, better educational opportunities, and the banning of Class H liquor licenses to private clubs that excluded non-Whites from joining.

Another civil rights organization I joined was the Coalition Against Discrimination (CAD). CAD was formed to fight private, racially exclusive clubs like the Elks Club, the Moose Club, and the Rainier Club, which received discounted liquor prices from state-owned liquor stores. CAD had a membership that included the Catholic Archdiocese of Seattle, the Anti Defamation League of B'nai B'rith, the American Jewish Committee, the Asian Coalition for Equality (ACE), the Filipino American Coalition for Equality, the Central Area Civil Rights Committee, and a dozen other groups. Due to our efforts and with such broad-based community support, the membership rules of these private clubs were eventually changed to allow membership regardless of race.

One day, out of the blue, Mayor Floyd Miller's office called to ask if I'd be interested in serving on the Seattle Human Rights Commission. I said yes. To this day, I have no idea who recommended my name to the Mayor's office. At about the same time, I was also elected president of the Catholic Interracial Council. Soon, I found myself going to meetings almost every night.

Walt Hubbard was my mentor during the early years of the civil rights struggle. I succeeded Walt as the chair of the Catholic Interracial Council. He had also been the executive director of CARITAS, a social service action agency. The name "CARITAS" came from putting the first letters of *C*ommunity *A*ction, *R*emedial *I*nstruction, *T*utorial, and *A*ssistance *S*ervice together. When Walt moved on to head the newly formed King County Office for Civil Rights, he expected me to take his place at CARITAS. I applied for the position, was interviewed by the CARITAS board of directors, and hired. My reasons for wanting to serve as the executive director of CARITAS were twofold — first, it was an opportunity to direct a wonderful program that served the needs of children and families; and second, it gave me the opportunity to work directly with newly-formed activist groups that used the St. Peter Claver Center facilities.

It was quite a coincidence that CARITAS was housed in the St. Peter Claver Center (owned by the Catholic Archdiocese of Seattle) because the building was originally the Maryknoll Church and School, which I attended so many years earlier. The services provided by CARITAS included one-on-one tutoring of students who had fallen behind in their class work. Individual tutors were recruited from local high schools, colleges, and universities. Counseling was also provided to students who needed it. The funding came through state grants.

St. Peter Claver — At the Heart of the Struggle

The director of St. Peter Claver Center was Father Harvey McIntyre, whose main job was pastor of the Immaculate Conception Church, a few blocks north. Because of the heavy workload at the Church, Father McIntyre designated me to manage the Center. St. Peter Claver Center became the springboard for many civil rights organizations and agencies — the Catholic Interracial Council; the Demonstration Project for Asian Americans; Project Equality; and the Central Area Civil Rights Committee. But its most important contribution to the fight for equality and justice was the network established among the multi-ethnic groups and the leaders who met there — people like Tyree Scott of the United Construction Workers Association; Dorothy Cordova of the Demonstration Project for Asian Americans; Bernie Whitebear of United Indians of All Tribes; Roberto Maestas of El Centro de la Raza; Larry Gossett, later executive director of the Central Area Motivation Program and a future King County councilman; and many others.

St. Peter Claver Center was a hub of activity. The auditorium was scheduled for meetings, two or three times a week, including weekends, by many activist groups and organizations. The social hall at the Center was provided at no cost to several organizations, including the Black Panthers, which used it daily for their free breakfast program. Regular meetings were held there by the Marion Club, a group of older Catholic women; the Blackfeet Indians of

Montana for tribal members in the Seattle area; CAD; the Asian Coalition for Equality; and the United Farm Workers.

I sat in on many of the meetings to show my support for issues presented by leaders of these diverse groups. On many occasions, I was the only Asian in attendance. But if our community support was needed on a march or rally, I passed the word on to our Asian activists. There were so many meetings and rallies at St. Peter Claver Center by the local activist organizations that complaints came in to the archbishop's office that the "left wing" had taken over church property. When questioned by the archbishop's staff, Father McIntyre always had an answer that seemed to cool things off at the chancery office.

I participated in the many rallies and marches because I believed in the important issues raised by the activist organizations in their meetings at the Center. Those issues dealt with equal opportunities and rights for minorities in employment, education, and housing. A national movement became a local one when the United Farm Workers (UFW) sent three staff members from Delano, California to Seattle to set up offices during the grape and lettuce boycotts. I used my newly formed network of business people and members of the Human Rights Commission to arrange meetings with the UFW staff to start a dialogue about farm worker rights. I brought my kids to Safeway boycott marches. I was proud that my family believed, as I did, in actually making a "political" statement about the rights of farm workers.

In 1970, representatives of tribes and organizations in the Native American community from throughout western Washington met at St. Peter Claver Center to plan the next move after their recent takeover of a surplused army base, Fort Lawton. The U.S. government had decided to consolidate its home-based military establishments and surplused several army bases, one of which was Fort Lawton, in the Magnolia neighborhood. When the government first acquired the land for Fort Lawton, there was an understanding that it would be returned to its "original owners" when the military no longer needed the land.

Seattle city officials believed that the city originally owned the land and stood to acquire the old fort with sweeping views of Elliott Bay and the Olympic mountain range. Native Americans, led by Bernie Whitebear, interpreted the "original owners" to be themselves, the indigenous people of the region — Native Americans of western Washington. When their claim to the land was ignored, they took matters into their own hands and occupied the fort.

The Indians regularly opened their meetings with traditional drumming and the ceremonial burning of sage. After one such meeting, one of the young Maryknoll sisters who lived in the convent next door ran up to me. "Uncle Bob," she exclaimed. "Those Indian kids are starting to smoke the sage."

"It's okay as long as they don't inhale," I said. She didn't think it was funny and walked away, shaking her head.

My involvement in these activities occurred during my administration of the CARITAS Program. I was able to run the program and expand my participation in the activist community. Not only did I have a young staff who knew the programs better than me, but it was a staff who earned the confidence and respect of students, parents, tutors, and the board of directors. I was extremely fortunate to have Alan Ogilvie, Richard Jones (later a lawyer, then a judge), Barney Gibson, Tandra DeCuir, and Judy Knoblauch on staff.

One of my young staff members was a young Theresa Fujiwara (later executive director of Asian Counseling and Referral Service, and then assistant to Seattle Mayor Paul Schell), just out of high school, who I hired as a receptionist. Theresa was uncompromisingly honest. There were times when somebody called with whom I didn't want to talk. I told Theresa to say I was out of the office. Theresa, however, insisted. "But you're here. I'm not going to lie and say you're not." From then on, when Theresa buzzed me to say so-and-so was on the phone, someone I didn't want to talk to, I'd get up and physically leave the office. Theresa then informed the caller that I was out of the office. Then I'd return.

The expanded network brought together by the meetings, rallies, and demonstrations coordinated at St. Peter Claver Center was most beneficial to leaders of the young Asian American community. Alliances and working relationships were formed between the different civil rights activists; the minority rights organizations; activists from the local college campuses, the Filipino community, and the Alaska cannery union reform movement; the new groups forming in the International District; and Asian American peace activists. These alliances and working relationships were very important when broad support was needed to take on the developers planning the construction of the Kingdome and other large-scale construction projects in the International District community.

Four people in particular served as inspirations to me — Tyree Scott, Bernie Whitebear, Roberto Maestas, and Larry Gossett.

Tyree Scott — The Live Wire

In the early 1970s, Tyree Scott, a black electrician, organized Black and other minority construction workers to fight discrimination in the construction trades. Tyree was one of the founders of the United Construction Workers Association (UCWA). UCWA held their meetings in our social hall early in the mornings when they planned the shut down of construction jobs without minorities on the work force. Up to that time, the construction unions only hired friends of friends and sons of fathers in the trades. Minorities and women were left out. Tyree kept tabs on new job sites under construction, then often approached the construction company's superintendent or foreman to hire and train minority apprentices for the skilled and unskilled jobs needed at the job site. When the superintendent didn't hire minorities, Tyree and his association of unemployed minority construction workers undertook a coordinated campaign to close the site down.

Tyree looked for projects which used federal funds because they were subject to enforcement under the Civil Rights Act. Tyree often led a group of 10 to 20 unemployed minority workers to a site before the all-White work crews showed up. Tyree's group would close the site down and send the all-White work crews home with the promise to reopen the construction work site when minorities were hired. Construction job sites were shut down at Seattle Central Community College (SCCC), the University of Washington, and Seattle-Tacoma (Sea-Tac) Airport. To be fair, the construction site at the largely African American Mt. Zion Baptist Church was also closed down because the construction company and work crews hired to build the church were all-White.

Construction sites were shut down all over the city, from highway construction to the University of Washington's new campus buildings. One of the largest demonstrations held by UCWA targeted the new administration building under construction at SCCC. Tyree led about 70 activists on the first of several days of demonstrations which started out from the St. Peter Claver Center. Seattle Central's old administration building was the target on the first day. Demonstrators trashed the first floor by breaking windows and furniture. Several were arrested, but most got away before the police "tac" (tactical) squad arrived.

The next day, 150 demonstrators marched in force to the college. I went along with them as an official representative, the vice chair of the Seattle Human Rights Commission. The goal on that day was to negotiate more jobs for minorities with the construction site superintendent. I joined the demonstrators with the thought that I should be there in support of job opportunities for minorities, but also in my capacity as vice chair. I thought being a member of the Commission had some clout. I learned later that my membership there meant absolutely nothing to the police.

As we entered past the eight-foot high fence which enclosed the construction site, we started walking to the superintendent's trailer. Several White workers, working on the second floor of the building, threw chunks of wood and metal down at us from above. Tyree yelled to us not to retaliate, that this was a nonviolent demonstration, but his words fell on deaf ears. The demonstrators became incensed by the abuse. They climbed the ladders to the second story of the newly erected metal-framed skeleton of the four-story building where the White workers stood.

Demonstrators and construction workers met head on at the second floor level. Violence erupted as fights broke out. Then someone yelled, "The tac squad is coming." The demonstrators ran quickly down the ladders and out beyond the fence. I stayed behind to assist one of the White foremen, a middle-aged balding guy, who earlier yelled, "You'll come up here over my dead body." To no one's surprise, the foreman was trampled and lay injured. I stayed with him until the aid crew arrived.

I proceeded alone, down the ladder, and started walking past the fence. I stopped. To my right, under a tree, were Tyree and three other Black demonstrators — Michael Ross, Sylvester Carter, and Todd Hawkins. They were surrounded by police. Michael Ross pointed at me and said, "He's with us," to the cops. A cop yelled to me, "Are you with them?"

"I guess so," I answered, and I was handcuffed along with the rest and sent to jail.

Down at the King County Jail, they put us two to a cell. My cellmate was Todd Hawkins. Todd, a plumber by trade, was very laid back in demeanor. He always wore overalls to demonstrations and marches. Nothing fazed him. For Todd, being arrested was no big deal.

The first thing he did was flop on the cot, his back to me, while I paced back and forth, trying to figure out what I got into. I thought about the police brutality I had seen on the network news during demonstrations in the South. Images of getting struck by clubs and sticks flashed in my mind. Todd, on the other hand, began to snore.

I started to hum, "We Shall Overcome." I felt quite noble in being arrested. With his back still turned toward me, Todd snorted, "Will you shut the fuck up?" I continued pacing back and forth in the cell until the arresting officer came in and announced, "Okay guys, you need to sign these citations. Then, you can go." I jumped to grab the citation when behind me, Todd, still with his back to me, sternly said, "Hold it. We are here to give a message. We may stay a week. We may even go on a hunger strike." Hunger strike? I grabbed the pen and whined, "But I have a wife and kids at home. They don't know I'm here and it's my turn to cook dinner." I left the cell before Todd had a chance to pull me back.

The next day at the St. Peter Claver Center, there was a large group of demonstrators ready to march back to the college. As I came into the social hall, the people clapped their hands. Someone yelled, "You're on the front page of *The Seattle Times.* We saw you busted on TV." To which I bravely responded, "Yes, we were willing to stay a week. We were even willing to go on a hunger strike." God, it was great to be a hero!

A few days later, I received a call from Mayor Wes Uhlman's office to "get your butt up here." Uhlman was Floyd Miller's successor. I walked in. Sitting beside the mayor was Seattle Police Chief Frank Ramon. The mayor, in his "Father Knows Best" tone, said, "You're a human rights commissioner! How in the hell did you get arrested? And why were you in the no-trespass zone?"

"How else can I observe what's happening on the other side of an eight-foot fence?" I answered.

Mayor Uhlman then produced a yellow hard hat with the city logo and the inscription, "SEATTLE HUMAN RIGHTS COMMISSION," in bold letters. Handing it to me, he said, "You'll wear this from now on when you represent this city." I immediately stored it in a box so it wouldn't get dirty. I never took it out of the box and there it remains to this day.

Another major site targeted by the demonstrators was Sea-Tac Airport, where a parking structure was under construction. About 150 people rallied at the airport and disrupted the travel schedule of some airlines by clogging up the waiting lines at check-in counters. One tactic used for disrupting business, for example, was to purchase airline tickets by credit card at different airline counters, then cancel the ticket a few days later. Demonstrators marched from concourse to concourse with the airport police in close pursuit to keep us off the tarmac.

A sit-in at a centralized location within the airport produced several arrests, among them Dolores Sibonga, later a Seattle city councilwoman, and the Rev. Michael Holland, pastor of St. Mary's Church in the Central Area. Father Harvey McIntyre, pastor of the Immaculate Conception Church and director of St. Peter Claver Center, was livid when Father Holland was led away. Father McIntyre yelled at the police, "Hey! You can't arrest him! I'm the civil rights priest! You gotta arrest me first!"

A short time after the airport demonstrations, a national human rights conference was held in Denver. The Seattle Human Rights Commission was invited to participate. Three of us went to represent the Commission — Phil Hayasaka, director; Father Harvey McIntyre, chairman; and myself, vice chair. While there, we learned that Tyree and four other Seattle Black construction workers were in Denver to support local Black workers who were fighting the trade unions to open up jobs to minorities and women as in Seattle. We decided to visit them.

As we expected, Tyree and the others had spent time in the Denver jail for their activities on that city's streets. But they had been released from jail. As we walked up the pathway to their rented brick home, we heard music blaring from the house. After ringing the doorbell five or six times with no answer, we let ourselves in. We took three steps inside and saw Tyree conducting the other four, singing at the top of their voices "Jesus Christ Superstar" while the album played in the background.

Back in Seattle, acting upon a complaint which UCWA filed in federal court, Federal District Court Judge William Lindbergh ordered the skilled trade unions to open up their apprenticeship programs to minority job applicants. It was a sweet victory for our cause.

Tyree Scott, more than anyone else, had a profound effect on my life. As people looked to Mahatma Gandhi or Martin Luther King Jr. for inspiration on an international level, we in Seattle had Tyree. And yet, Tyree has never sought recognition. Hundreds of other activists followed him as he forced the construction industry to follow the letter of the law. It wasn't easy. Those in the building trades were tough, rough people not open to equal opportunity. The "old boys" union leadership did not like Tyree because he didn't play their game by their rules. It didn't matter to Tyree how he dealt with the union. He sat down at the negotiation table or he stood outside the fence demanding that people of color be placed on their job sites.

The last protest I shared with Tyree was in 1985. On a cold November morning, about 20 demonstrators — including Tyree, Roberto Maestas, Larry Gossett, Debbie Ross, and I — showed up at a recycling company where large dump trucks were being dispatched. Roberto of El Centro de la Raza had organized us to come out because the company had fired a Latino employee who questioned working conditions. Our group formed a human barricade at the entrance of the yard that held the trucks. As the first truck approached, we stood our ground. The truck stopped with about a dozen trucks backed up behind it. The driver and his helper jumped out of the lead truck and confronted us in front of the bumper. A long diatribe of profanity was reserved for Roberto who was trying to reason with the crowd of drivers who had formed behind the lead driver and his helper.

After half an hour passed without agreement between the two sides, tensions got ugly. The drivers threatened to get back in their trucks and run us over. While the yelling and screaming continued, Tyree walked around the back of the truck toward the driver's side and jumped into the cab. In less than a minute, Tyree slid out of the cab and told me he was going to take a nap in his car. Off he went. A few minutes later, the driver of the first truck and his helper decided to drive through our group. As they got in the cab, the driver yelled to his helper, "Hey, Willy. Do you have the keys?"

"No," Willy answered. "I thought you had them." The driver then yelled to the other drivers heading to their trucks.

"Hey! Who's got the key to my truck?" No answer. During the next hour, the drivers and their helpers looked unsuccessfully, on their hands and knees, for the keys that Tyree had in his pocket while he slept in his car.

Tyree remained involved with the Northwest Labor Employment Law Office (LELO), an organization fighting for justice. When Mt. Zion started construction of the federally financed Samuel B. McKinney Manor, Tyree found an all-White construction crew and struck again. He brought a group of demonstrators to force closure of yet another job at the Mt. Zion Church. Rev. McKinney, with robes flowing, flew across Madison Street to see what sins Tyree had committed that day. The next day brought more protesters. Eventually, there were workers of color on the job site. Tyree, more than anyone else, brought our communities of color together. We marched, we got arrested and the message was loud and clear, "You don't change, we're closing you down."

Bernie Whitebear — Storming the Fort

Bernie White "Grizzly" Bear had been a Boeing engineer. He shortened his last name to "Whitebear" because the name didn't fit on his Boeing ID card. At about the same time Tyree was closing down construction sites, Bernie and Bob Satiacum led a group of Native American activists in a takeover of the Fort Lawton Army Base in the Magnolia neighborhood. When the federal government surplused Fort Lawton, Bernie, a member of the Colville Confederated Tribes, and Bob Satiacum, chairman of the Puyallup tribe, gathered tribal leaders and members across the Pacific Northwest. Despite traditional tribal differences, they were in agreement that Native Americans should be at the head of the line when the land was surplused. They presented their claim to city officials. The mayor, Seattle City Council and business leaders from throughout the city rejected the Native American community's claim on the Fort Lawton site.

In response, Bernie and Bob Satiacum led a group of Native Americans and "attacked the fort" on March 8, 1970. They were joined by actress Jane Fonda, who at the time was in her radical activist-chic period, and her celebrity status drew attention to Bernie's cause. They occupied Fort Lawton for a few weeks until local and military police took action. They arrested Bernie and dozens of other protesters. Bernie had done his homework, uncovering treaties and other documents that proved Native Americans were, in fact, the original owners of the land. In 1977, after gaining the support of U.S. senators Warren Magnuson and Henry Jackson, a deal was struck which gave 30 acres of land to the United Indians of All Tribes, under a 99-year lease, where they built the Daybreak Star Cultural and Education Center.

Bernie Whitebear became the voice and inspiration of the urban Native American community for more than 30 years. No one fought for Native Americans as hard as Bernie.

Under Bernie's leadership, United Indians of All Tribes implemented cultural and art programs; an early childhood education program; a Head Start program; an employment program; a housing and education program for troubled Indian youth; and the annual Pow Wow, a Seafair event that draws thousands of participants and spectators. He traveled the nation to share his experiences about developing programs that served the needs of Native Americans.

Bernie was born with the name "Bernie Reyes." His mother was a Colville Indian and his father was Filipino. After Bernie's father died, his mother married Harry Wong. Of a family with six siblings, three children were part Filipino and three children were part Chinese.

Bernie wanted to know more about his Filipino heritage. He began to spend more time in the International District trying to keep up with me. We spent many evenings together at the Four Seas restaurant; the Silver Dragon restaurant where we celebrated his 50th birthday; China Gate, where the hostesses loved to dance with "Barney" Whitebear; the Quong Tuck Bar and Grill, our "private" club managed by Wilma Woo who just loved Bernie; and Bush Garden's karaoke bar, where when the mood was right, he treated us with the Elvis tune, "Don't Be Cruel."

When the International District Improvement Association (Inter*Im) built the I.D. Community Garden in 1975, we put out the call for help. Every week, I recruited a different agency to assist in spreading truckloads of topsoil from the Longacres racetrack (it was actually steaming horse manure). Roberto Maestas brought his staff from El Centro de la Raza. Larry Gossett came with his staff from the Central Area Motivation Program (CAMP). Silme Domingo and Gene Viernes brought volunteers from the Alaska Cannery Workers Association. The Asian Counseling and Referral Service sent its staff. When Bernie brought the folks from Daybreak Star, they didn't come alone. The local media came along as well. Bernie's crew worked all day. On the front page of next morning's *Post-Intelligencer* was a photo with the headline, "Indians Build Garden for Asian Elderly." Bernie Whitebear was shrewd enough to know when a great photo opportunity presented itself.

Bernie often testified at hearings in support of our housing and social service programs in the Asian community and always offered the support of Native Americans who stood in solidarity with the Asian community for vital resources. But what I liked most about Bernie was that even when we dealt with serious issues or demonstrations, he never took himself seriously. I remember when the Inter*Im celebrated its 15th anniversary at the Wing Luke Asian Museum, then located on Eighth Avenue South. After the reception, the party moved across King Street to the Quong Tuck Bar and Grill. After half an hour, I got a call. Wilma said it was Bernie, which I thought was weird because I thought he was with us. I took the phone. "Bernie, where are you?" I asked.

"I'm still here at the Wing Luke Museum because just before you left, I went to take a pee. And when I came out, it was dark and I couldn't find the lights or the door or the phone until now. Come get me." And so I did.

After years of successfully championing the Native American cause, Bernie's final achievement, before his death in 2000, was planning the People's Lodge at Discovery Park. In 1997, Bernie learned he had colon cancer. The doctors gave him six months to live. Bernie didn't take this news lying down. He held on for three years. When he went through chemotherapy, he still went to his office at Daybreak Star. Bernie kept his spirits up until the end and he insisted that we keep our spirits up as well. Bernie's goal to build the People's Lodge at the Daybreak Star Center kept him going for more than two years. The People's Lodge was a project supported by communities of color, but faced opposition from Bernie's Magnolia neighbors who challenged the project on "environmental" grounds.

Bernie's Magnolia neighbors argued that the People's Lodge would upset their peace and quiet, add unwanted traffic, and create security problems. These were concerns I understood. We had used the same arguments to protect the International District from unwanted development. Bernie understood these concerns as well and compromised. The original plan for the People's Lodge reached a height of 65 feet, but Bernie, working with his architects, lowered the plan by 20 feet. He also cut the square footage significantly.

However, no matter what Bernie did, it wasn't enough to satisfy his Magnolia neighbors. In his effort to build the great lodge that would seat 1,500 people for large gatherings, he was beaten back time and time again by the environmentalists from the Magnolia community who felt the lodge was too large for the exclusive neighborhood. He worked daily to design a facility that would be accepted by the community and fill the needs of Native Americans throughout the region. Unfortunately, Bernie did not live to see his People's Lodge built.

Bernie's illness hit the Gang of Four (Larry Gossett, Roberto Maestas, Bernie, and myself) very hard. Knowing that time with Bernie was very precious, we arranged to have lunch together every few months. When Bernie was hospitalized in March of 2000 and his radiation and chemotherapy treatments were halted, we kept close tabs on his condition. I called him soon after he was sent home in April. When I asked how he was feeling, Bernie replied, "Don't call me for two months." A few minutes later, Lawney Reyes, Bernie's brother, called me to explain that Bernie was not in a good mood because of the pain medication he was taking. I called back two days later and said, "Hey, Bernie. This is Uncle Bob."

"How time flies when you're having fun," he replied.

Sharon Tomiko Santos (whom I married in 1992) and I spent as much time as we could with Bernie and his family. On Sundays, I would cook for whoever showed up at the Whitebear house. Bernie's favorite dish was my chicken *adobo*, which I think kept him going longer than the medical experts predicted back in 1997. On July 9, 2000, Bernie put together a barbecue and invited Roberto Maestas, Larry Gossett, a few staff from Daybreak Star, his family (brothers Lawney Reyes and Harry Wong and sisters Laura Wong, Theresa Wong, and Luana Reyes), Sharon Tomiko, and me. We ate, we laughed, we all had our pictures taken with Bernie, and then we left, never to see him alive again. He knew the end was very near.

One week later, on July 16, 2000, Bernie died. The day after he died, both of the city's major metropolitan newspapers ran editorials in support of the People's Lodge, that it should be built as a legacy to Bernie Whitebear. That was Bernie's gift, still persuading people to his way of thinking, even after he died.

On Thursday, July 20, more than 500 people attended his wake at the Daybreak Star Center. The following day, 1,600 people attended the funeral services at the Washington State Trade and Convention Center. Speakers included Sen. Patty Murray; Sen. Daniel Inouye of Hawaii, chairman of the Senate Committee on Indian Affairs; Congressman Jay Inslee; Governor Gary Locke; former Governor Mike Lowry; King County Executive Ron Sims; Seattle Mayor Paul Schell; Bernie's family; and the staff of the United Indians of All Tribes Foundation. After the pallbearers — which included Roberto Maestas, Larry Gossett, and myself — placed the pine casket in the hearse, the door was closed. Suddenly, a large gust of wind whipped through the corridor and lifted the 20-foot canvas covering the construction site for the convention center's expansion, blowing over wooden planks and extra building material. Everyone muttered simultaneously, "There goes Bernie."

The Gang of Four, minus one, served as honorary co-chairs of a fund-raising campaign dedicated to build Bernie's dream — the People's Lodge — that will become this great man's legacy to his people and to all people of this land. With the consent of his family, we have renamed the People's Lodge. The name of the facility will be the Bernie Whitebear Memorial People's Lodge.

Roberto Maestas — Compadre and Caballero

Roberto Maestas was an angry Mexican kid, raised by his grandparents in New Mexico, who grew up working the cropfields in the American Southwest. He was also a bright inquisitive student who always asked the tough questions of authority figures, including parents, older siblings, teachers, professors, elected officials, and police chiefs. Roberto found his way to Washington state, where he attended and later graduated from the University of Washington.

I first met Roberto at a meeting at St. Peter Claver Center when he and the long-time feminist activist Clara Fraser were heatedly arguing. Fraser was a tough, opinionated woman, a co-founder of Seattle Radical Women, one of the country's first feminist organizations. She was also known locally because of her successful lawsuit against Seattle City Light, which improperly fired Fraser because of her sex and politics. The argument ended with Clara calling Roberto an insensitive, macho pig, or words to that effect. She wasn't necessarily wrong.

Influenced no doubt by Bernie's success, Roberto and a handful of mostly Chicano and Chicana supporters began occupying the old Beacon Hill Elementary School on North Beacon Hill in October 1972. They demanded that the vacant structure be turned over by the Seattle School District to the Latino/Chicano community for use as a much-needed cultural education and social service center. Roberto and a cohort of compadres — Juan Bocanegra, Roberto Gallegos, and Stella Ortega, to name a few — called the old school "home" for the next few months. After weathering the cold winter months, negotiations with city officials and the Seattle School District bore fruit. The building was leased to the Latino/Chicano community and El Centro de la Raza was created.

Roberto and his Spanish-speaking staff set up bilingual classes; provided social services and health education; established a much needed food bank; and opened a day care center for families. El Centro became a place where politics, domestic and international, were discussed and debated. The center grew.

From the mid-1970s into the 1980s, the El Centro staff became engulfed in an international struggle, aligning itself with the Sandinista government of Nicaragua. The U.S. government, under the leadership of President Ronald Reagan, was supporting an illegal war through the Contras in Nicaragua. Roberto and El Centro staff, working with prominent civic and elected officials, helped form the Seattle-Managua Sister-City Association. The Association recruited supporters, politicians, clergy, students, leaders of color, and anyone else who sought the truth to join fact-finding delegations to Nicaragua to see and learn whether the revolutionary government was accepted by the Nicaraguan people.

In 1983, I went with Roberto on one of El Centro's fact-finding missions to Nicaragua. I was a member of a delegation of 21 people, including a crew from KING-TV headed by television commentator Bob Simmons, who spent one week in Nicaragua. The delegation included Ricardo Sanchez, editor of *La Voz* (a Latino newspaper); Harold Bellemont, spiritual leader of the Sammish tribe; Sam and Carol Goldberg, representing the Seattle Chapter of the United Nations Association; and Rev. David Bloom. El Centro sent several members of its staff — Sam Martinez and his daughter, Alma; Roy Wilson, Patricia Jones, Stella Ortega, and Ramon Soliz, among others. Some observers branded our group a left-wing support operation. Others thought of us as a tourist-oriented fun group. But the presence of the TV crew legitimized our mission as a fact-finding tour.

We spent three days in Managua, the capital. The mayor of Managua, I was amazed to find, was named Samuel Santos. When I told him my father and brother shared his name, he insisted we must be related. The Sandinistas went out of their way to make us feel comfortable. They put us up in a resort named Ticomo, in the rolling hills on the outskirts of Managua, and we dined at the best restaurants in the area. The Sandinistas were trying to prove to the delegation that the country, under the revolutionary government, was becoming more self-sufficient and on the way to recovery from a devastating earthquake in 1972.

Even though money, food, and equipment had been sent to Nicaragua, the former dictator, General Anastasio Somoza, diverted the resources for his personal use. More than 10 years after the earthquake, the people of Managua were still recovering. We visited the barrios where running water was piped in, sewers were being laid, streets and sidewalks were under construction, and families were rebuilding their homes, replacing wood and sheet metal siding with concrete construction blocks.

Our government led us to believe that Nicaragua was ruled by an oppressive, Marxist, totalitarian regime. What we found were a people besieged by U.S. military-backed Contras. We visited one village, Pantazama, where 47 Sandinistas and civilians had been massacred just two weeks before our arrival. The Contras, CIA-trained and equipped mercenaries, attacked many villages in Nicaragua from their Honduran-based camps. The people we met in Nicaragua were more fearful of an invasion of their country by the Contras and the U.S. military than they were of the Sandinistas. Resources which should have gone to rebuilding the country's infrastructure had to be spent on military defense.

When we came to Nicaragua, the Sandinistas had been in power for almost four years after Somoza was overthrown in 1979. Our trip was important because it allowed delegation members the opportunity to talk freely with the Nicaraguan people about the need for a truly democratic and honest national election. Later, when elections were announced, our government continued to spew out its propaganda that such elections could never be honest while the Sandinistas were in power. When President Daniel Ortega, leader of the Sandinistas, lost the national election for President to Ms. Violeta Barrios de Chamorro, publisher of the national newspaper, our government called it a victory for democracy.

Despite its political stances, El Centro de la Raza was designated as one of President George H. Bush's "Thousand Points of Light" for its service to the community. (What a pair of strange bedfellows: George H. and Roberto.) In 1999, after many years of negotiations, the Seattle School Board formally transferred ownership of the old Beacon Hill School to the agency. Roberto continued to serve as the executive director of El Centro.

Ironically, Roberto and El Centro later became embroiled in a complaint filed with the National Labor Relations Board by the Office and Professional Employees International,

Local 8 over unionizing the El Centro staff. After months of divisive negotiations, El Centro and the union mediated the dispute, allowing El Centro's employees to organize in the future if they so wanted. I always felt it was difficult to unionize a non-profit organization because, at least in my case, staff were virtually on-call 24 hours a day, seven days a week. My staff typically worked beyond a 40-hour workweek.

Larry Gossett — CAMP Director

On March 29, 1968, Larry Gossett — a young college student activist — and several other young Black community activists staged a sit-in at Franklin High School to protest the expulsion of a Black student. Larry and the others were arrested. The next day, attorney William Dwyer, who later became a federal court judge, secured their release. Larry and the others flew to San Francisco where they met Bobby Seale, head of the Black Panther Party, at a conference for Black youth. After meeting Seale and attending a funeral for Panther Bobby Hutton, who had been shot by police officers, Larry and the Dixon brothers — Elmer and Aaron — among others, decided to form a Black Panther chapter in Seattle. In June of 1968, Larry and the others were convicted of criminal trespass for their sit-in at Franklin High School. Riots broke out in the Central Area after the verdicts were announced.

While the Dixons led the Black Panthers, Larry focused on student activism at the University of Washington. As one of the original leaders of the local Black Student Union, Larry pressured the University of Washington to initiate the Black Studies Program. After graduating from the university, he joined the Vista Volunteer Program and was sent to work in New York City's Harlem neighborhood. There, he learned about the real world in the biggest of big cities.

Larry first earned a reputation as a social activist. Then he got involved in the UCWA demonstrations. Later, he joined the ranks of those with "real responsibility" when he was hired as executive director of the Central Area Motivation Program (CAMP), a social service agency riddled with mismanagement. Larry's first challenge was getting his staff to recommit in serving the evergrowing needs of the Central Area community. Solvable issues were first on the priority list. More long-term issues were handled by task forces. CAMP became alive once more. Larry began to network with the other heads of agencies. From the alliance among Maestas, Gossett, Whitebear, and myself, the "Gang of Four" was formed. We not only had much in common, with growing professional and community responsibilities, but we liked each other's company and became close friends.

Larry yearned for a larger and more influential leadership position in the African American community which had been headed by older, wiser, but not necessarily progressive political leaders. In 1993, Larry decided to run for a seat on the King County Council. Because of Larry's many years of service to the diverse community in the 10th county district, which included the Central Area and the International District, a large multi-racial campaign steering committee was established for Larry's campaign.

One of the first tasks the committee undertook was a massive voter registration program in the minority communities where, traditionally, voter turnout was low. When the final votes were tallied in the general election, Larry won by a landslide. Larry's council office, ironically, was located at the same site as the old King County Jail cell where he was held during his young militant days. As a measure of his reputation and effectiveness, when Larry ran successfully for re-election in 1997, he was unopposed.

The Gang of Four

There was a time when it seemed there were sufficient public resources for use in urban communities. But as resources dwindled due to funding cutbacks and as more agencies were created, competition for those resources became more intense. By the mid-1970s, Larry Gossett was the executive director of the Central Area Motivation Program, Bernie Whitebear was the executive director of United Indians of All Tribes, Roberto Maestas was the executive director of El Centro de la Raza, and I was the executive director of Inter*Im. The four of us attended finance committee meetings of the Seattle City Council, not only to present funding requests for our own agencies, but to support proposals submitted by other agencies. We refused to be divided in our quest for funding from the pool.

Recognizing this show of unity, several people began to refer to this cooperation as a coalition. Activists and other executive directors joined the four of us at those hearings. Joe Garcia, former assistant director of El Centro de la Raza, coined the moniker, "Minority Executive Directors Coalition," and community leaders Ike Ikeda and Dave

Okimoto promoted the idea of a working coalition of community-based organizations.

In 1981, the Minority Executive Directors Coalition of King County (MEDC), an organized network of executive directors and administrators of color from community-based organizations, was born. The purpose of MEDC was to track legislation that impacted on ethnic and minority communities. For the first few years, MEDC was an ad-hoc committee of a few community-based organizations. As the years went by, more organizations joined. By the early 1990s, an executive committee was formed with regular membership meetings. After intense debate among the member organizations about structure, a part-time staff coordinator, Richard (Dicky) Mar, was hired.

Under Dicky's leadership, MEDC was represented at more Seattle City Council hearings and King County Council hearings. He coordinated travel for minority representatives of our agencies to testify at important legislative hearings and meetings in Olympia. He recruited new members and developed the MEDC position on proposed legislation in education and social services.

After a few years of success and personal burnout, Dicky stepped down, and Dorry Elias took over as a full-time executive director. Dorry was able to bring MEDC to new heights with her energy and bubbly enthusiasm. Under Dorry's leadership, MEDC established partnership relationships with such established entities as United Way, the Seattle Human Services Coalition, and the Family Leadership Fund, which coincidentally was staffed by Dicky Mar. By the end of 2000, there were more than 70 community-based member organizations in MEDC. Dorry has grown into a very successful advocate for social service agencies and has attracted a long list of supporters for MEDC causes, including elected state officials, local officials, and heads of private companies and foundations.

Our success at forming coalitions gave us an international reputation. One of the greatest trips I ever took overseas was in 1990 when Roberto, Larry, Bernie, and I were invited as guests of Japan's Ministry of Foreign Affairs and the Japanese Foundation Center for Global Partnership. We were asked by the Japanese government to share our experiences in grassroots organizing in our respective communities. The official name for the trip was the Multi-Cultural Exchange and Education Tour. The Japanese Foundation Center for Global Partnership coordinated the itinerary for our delegation, scheduling stops for presentations in Tokyo, Kyoto, and Kobe. We were joined on this trip by Theresa Fujiwara, the foundation representative in Seattle; Alice Ito, a Seattle-based foundation consultant; Cheryl Ellsworth, a feminist who gave the activist women's perspective; and Don Williamson, editorial writer for *The Seattle Times,* who was sent to cover our trip.

The trip was "red carpet" all the way, with first-class hotel accommodations and meals in gourmet restaurants. At one of the best restaurants in Kobe, Roberto kept asking for more *wasabe* (a type of hot mustard) with his meal. After three trips back and forth from the kitchen, the waiter finally brought a medium-sized bowl filled with *wasabe*. The kitchen's chefs watched in amazement as Roberto poured the *wasabe* over his rice like it was gravy. The chefs returned to the kitchen shaking their heads. I'm sure as Roberto tells it, the *wasabe* probably gets hotter as the years go by.

In 1982, city officials were prepared to choose among a small number of companies that showed interest in the acquisition for a cable franchise covering the Central Area, Capital Hill, Downtown, and Beacon Hill. Dolores Sibonga, chairperson of the City Council committee holding hearings on the cable franchise legislation, strongly suggested that city officials award the franchise to a local, minority-owned company rather than a wealthy national firm.

Roberto, Larry, and I were approached by Bill Johnson, a former Ohio State University football player who played under legendary coach Woody Hayes. Johnson owned a cable television franchise in his hometown of Columbus, Ohio. Johnson, an African American, promised Inter*Im, CAMP, El Centro, and the Seattle Opportunity Industrialization Center (SOIC) a 20 percent stake as a group (he would be the majority owner with the remaining 80 percent interest) in his newly formed SeaCom Communications, a cable service company.

At the City Council hearing before the Personnel and Property Management Committee chaired by Dolores Sibonga, Johnson introduced the formation of SeaCom with an ownership that included our four non-profit agencies representing local minority-based participation. SeaCom was awarded the franchise and just like that, we were in the cable television business.

Johnson formed a board of directors which included him and his wife as president and vice president. Larry Gossett served as our representative on the executive committee. Visible signs of trouble began after a year, when Larry was excluded from SeaCom's board meetings. Our repeated requests for a meeting with Johnson to discuss our concerns were met with complete silence. The honeymoon was over. We had been used. After another year passed, Johnson decided to sell the company at a huge profit without telling us and left town. The two SeaCom checks sent to Inter*Im, as part of its share from the sale of the company, bounced.

As it turned out, Johnson did a lot of things without telling us. He paid himself a $364,000 "franchise acquisition fee" and a $101,000 "management consulting fee" in 1984 after SeaCom was awarded the cable franchise. He also paid himself or his wife a $78,000 "management consulting fee" in 1985. We didn't learn about these irregularities until after Johnson had decided to sell his rights to Summit Communications. In a last ditch effort to block the sale, Larry had brought in a financial analyst, John Schlosser, to review SeaCom's financial records. His review showed that SeaCom had no assets and listed liabilities of more than $800,000. After three years, Johnson had failed to deliver. Whole areas of the city, particularly downtown Seattle, still had no cable access. The sale went through.

But what goes around, comes around. In 1993, I received a call from a community organizer in Chicago who heard that minority community agencies in Seattle had a problem 10 years earlier with a person named Bill Johnson, the same Bill Johnson who owned the SeaCom Cable company. I was informed that Bill Johnson was the principal of a group of investors negotiating for the acquisition of a Chicago-based bank, the largest African American bank in the Midwest. Activists from Chicago's African American community were seeking our help to block Johnson's takeover of the bank. A reporter from a Chicago newspaper interviewed Larry Gossett and me to get our perspectives on Johnson. We told the reporter how Johnson had exploited the good faith of our agencies for his personal gain. A few months passed when we learned that Johnson failed in his bid to acquire the bank in Chicago. Did our problems with Johnson derail his attempts to buy the bank? I'd like to think so. Pay back.

From Filipino to Asian

One of the first Asian American groups to focus on ethnic consciousness in the 1960s was the Filipino Youth Activities (FYA). Founded by Fred and Dorothy Cordova, FYA became a nationally-known and honored youth program. Dorothy and Fred were obsessive in their dedication to build FYA. Their work resulted in providing many positive youth activities for hundreds of our Filipino youth. FYA became a way of life for many Filipino kids and their families with the drill team at the center of the activities. The FYA drill team, a unique and ethnically outfitted precision marching team, is very popular in the Pacific Northwest, especially during the two-week Seattle Seafair summer celebration. It has thrilled thousands of fans in parades, community shows, and community events all over the nation for more than 40 years. It was the first of very few "straight" participating organizations which performed in Seattle's Gay Pride parades.

Long before "Black is beautiful" became a popular catchphrase, Dorothy and Fred preached "brown is beautiful" to hundreds of Filipino kids. The students and young adults who emerged as leaders from the drill team became involved in the new Civil Rights Movement, demanding new educational programs and equal rights for all minorities in housing and jobs. They marched in demonstrations and spoke at rallies. Some of the older FYA alumni like Anthony Ogilvie, Roy Flores, Angie Quintero, and the Castillano sisters worked with Fred and Dorothy in 1971 to plan and sponsor the first Filipino Young People's Far West Convention in Seattle. This convention brought several hundred activists together from cities along the Pacific Coast. Workshops were held on a variety of issues, including educational opportunities, low-income housing, and the rising political tension in the Philippines under President Ferdinand Marcos.

It was about this time that Pete and Terri Jamero moved to Seattle from Washington, D.C., where Pete had worked as a high-level official with the Department of Health, Education, and Welfare (HEW). Pete, a social worker with a Master's degree, brought a new prospective to the Seattle scene, a knowledge of and experience in federal programs and funding sources.

As the 1970s rolled around, many of the "Young Turks" ran for office on the Filipino Community Council. Those elected to the board included Anthony Ogilvie, Andres Tangalin, Dorothy Cordova, Fred Cordova, Pete Jamero, Terri Jamero, Bob Flor, and the Domingo brothers, Nemesio and Silme. The "Young Turks" was a slang term which the older generation of the Filipino community gave to us American-born Filipino activists.

All the candidates campaigned for better Filipino youth programs, housing for the elderly, and raising funds for the renovation of the community center. But after being elected, it was usually just talk for most of the council. The Young Turks were sincere in wanting to see these campaign promises fulfilled, but more time and energy were usually spent by the council on arguments over the operation of the annual Filipino community queen contest (the council's biggest fund raiser) and other frivolous issues. After two terms on the Filipino Community Council, the Young Turks decided to serve out their terms and not run for re-election.

Asian American Activism — Yellow Power/Brown Power

The late 1960s and early 1970s saw the emergence of the Asian American community as a strong political force. Prior to the civil rights movement, the term "Oriental" was used to identify ethnic groups with roots from Asia and the Far East. But the term "Oriental" excluded Filipino Americans and Pacific Islanders. On the other hand, the term "Asian American" became a politically acceptable term which Filipino American and Pacific Islanders agreed was more inclusive. I was among the many local activist leaders — including Fred and Dorothy Cordova, Anthony Ogilvie, Nemesio Domingo Jr, Lois Hayasaka, and Andres Tangalin — all Filipino Americans, at the time who spearheaded the use of the "Asian American" political label.

My interest in the Asian American movement began in 1965 when I met Philip Vera Cruz and Larry Itliong, who were then organizing Filipino farm workers in the fields around Delano, California. My kids still remember when I brought them to a demonstration or boycott march at the Safeway stores. In those early days, we supported the United Farm Workers' boycott of table grapes and lettuce. There was a family tie-in with the leadership of the United Farm Workers. Anita's aunts and uncles, one of whom was Philip Vera Cruz, had settled in Delano. Vera Cruz was vice president of the United Farm Workers, second in command to Cesar Chavez, and the highest ranking Filipino in the UFW. During his visits to the Pacific Northwest, he often stopped by our house where we talked about the great farm worker movement until the wee hours of the morning when the bottle of "Old Grand Dad" was empty.

Vera Cruz often brought Larry Itliong with him. Itliong had earned a national reputation as a labor rights organizer, involved in workers' rights struggles in California and Alaska. In 1956, he founded the Filipino Farm Labor Union in California, one of the first unions to organize farm workers. In 1959, Itliong worked with the AFL-CIO to form the Agricultural

Workers Organizing Committee (AWOC). AWOC was composed mostly of older Filipino workers, with some Chicano, Anglo, and Black workers as well.

While many people believe that Cesar Chavez led the first grape boycott, a few of us know better. Larry Itliong carved his immortal place in the history of the farm workers when as the area director of the AWOC, he led a strike of several hundred Filipino American farm workers in the grape vineyards of Delano on September 8, 1965. Several days later, the United Farm Workers, led by Cesar Chavez, joined Itliong and led his Chicano workers out of the fields. A national farm workers movement was born.

When Vera Cruz and Itliong visited Seattle, they ended up at the home of my in-laws, Mildred and Godfrey Agbalog, and we talked about organizing Filipino farm workers. They were also interested in the development of a local Asian American movement in the Seattle area.

Vic Bacho was another Filipino community leader who made a strong impression on my interest in civil rights. Vic was one of the few Asian leaders who became an outspoken advocate for the open housing bill. When I saw him on the local television news speaking before the City Council, arguing passionately for equal housing, his words stirred me to act. I joined the Catholic Interracial Council and participated in their sponsored marches in support of the legislation.

At the time, there were only a few Asian Americans involved in the Catholic Interracial Council of Seattle, Dorothy and Fred Cordova among them. I rose to leadership within the Council quickly after I chaired the successful CIC banquet in 1968, which drew 2,500 people to honor Archbishop Harold Perry of New Orleans, the first Black archbishop in the nation. I was elected president of CIC in 1969, then followed Walt Hubbard as executive director of CARITAS.

The Catholic Interracial Council and CARITAS shared the same offices in St. Peter Claver Center on Jefferson Street. Part of my duties as executive director of CARITAS and president of the Catholic Interracial Council was to manage the St. Peter Claver Center facilities. I was able to persuade Filipino Youth Activities (FYA) to move from their cramped space at Seattle University to St. Peter Claver Center. I also found space at the Center for the newly formed Asian Multi-Media Center. Other Asian American groups formed to fight discrimination found their way to St. Peter Claver Center, where I offered meeting space at "no cost." It was through this connection that I became a participant in almost every Asian American organization that came along. The flurry of activity attracted virtually every civil rights leader in the Pacific Northwest to meetings and rallies held at the Center.

The "Asian Movement" was not only a constant struggle for civil rights and equality, but also a search for ethnic identity and pride. The Asian Coalition for Equality (ACE) was one of the earliest Asian American advocacy groups in Seattle, if not the nation, and was particularly ground breaking because it was the first political advocacy group which crossed Asian ethnic lines. ACE was formed by a group of young Asian professionals, including Phil Hayasaka, Lois Fleming, Joe Okimoto, John Eng, Joan Kis, Larry Matsuda, Don Kazama, Sonny Tangalin, and Anthony Ogilvie. I joined members of ACE when they picketed the Everett Elks Club, which barred non-Whites from membership, during a fund raiser for Sen. Henry Jackson.

ACE wanted to send a message to Sen. Jackson that racial discrimination was not accepted in our community. It helped that support in the Asian American community came from mature leaders like Don and Sally Kazama, Min Masuda, the Rev. Mineo Katagiri, and Aki Kurose. ACE protested negative stereotyping of Asian Americans in the media, minimum height requirements for policemen and firemen, and fraternal clubs which excluded Asians and other minorities from membership. ACE members also picked up protest signs and joined the United Construction Workers Association in demonstrations at various job sites.

In the spring of 1969, ACE members challenged admission policies at the University of Washington's Educational Opportunity Program (EOP), which denied "minority status" to Asian Americans. After many meetings, ACE members convinced the University of Washington to change its policies, leading to the creation of the Asian Division in EOP, soon to become the University of Washington's largest ethnic division. Bringing Asian American students into the EOP may have been one of the major accomplishments for Asian Americans in the 1970s. Without the program, many Asian Americans would have been denied a college education.

Meanwhile, over at Seattle Central Community College (SCCC), Asian American students organized the "Oriental Student Union" and demanded more Asian American faculty and an Asian American history class. In the early 1970s, I marched with the Oriental Student Union — headed by Dick Sugiyama, Alan Sugiyama, and Mike Tagawa — into the administrative offices at SCCC. There ensued a six-hour takeover of the administration building where walls were "decorated" with yellow paper (symbolizing "yellow power"). The demonstrators overturned office furniture and poured White Out into electric typewriters, shattering preconceived stereotypes about a "quiet, submissive model minority." After the demonstration was over, five Asian American demonstrators were charged with theft. It took one year for all to be cleared of the charges. But the demonstration proved to be successful. Frank Fujii was hired as SCCC's first Asian American administrator.

Meanwhile, Asian students from the University of Washington formed the "Asian American Student Coalition" and became active in campus politics. Asian students also volunteered in the community. Ruthann Kurose, for example, helped establish the Asian Drop-In Center as a place for young Asians to hang out. Other Asian college students such as Susan Tomita, May Lee, and Al and Keith Muramoto started "Young Asians for Action," one of the first groups concerned with the welfare of Asian elderly.

Nemesio Domingo, Jr. and Sabino Cabildo, among others, started the *Kapisanan,* a Filipino student newspaper. Other Asian American college students became involved with the paper. One year later, the *Kapisanan* became the *Asian Family Affair (AFA).* Under the leadership of Frank Irigon, Alan Sugiyama, and Silme Domingo, the *AFA* became a "voice," first for Asian American students, then for all Asian American activists. *AFA* was instrumental in organizing Asian American activists around civil rights and ethnic pride, and there was no greater source of ethnic pride than the fight to preserve the International District.

In fact, many of the activists such as Frank Irigon, Alan and Dick Sugiyama, Elaine (Ikoma) Ko, Shari Woo, Silme Domingo, and Doug Chin were active both in the struggle to preserve the International District and in writing, selling ads, layout, and distribution of the *Asian Family Affair. AFA* members were very involved in the well-publicized demonstration at the Kingdome during ground breaking ceremonies in 1972.

The 1971 White House Conference on Aging brought together a network of Asian American social workers who demanded official minority status on par with African Americans, Latinos/Chicanos and Native Americans/American Indians. The network was coordinated by Toyo Biddle, a social worker from Washington, D.C. She did a wonderful job bringing together a group that included Sharon Fujii, Donna Yee, Louise Kamikawa, Pete Jamero, and myself, as well as social workers from Los Angeles and San Francisco.

Several people from this group established the Demonstration Project for Asian Americans (DPAA), based in Los Angeles. Jim Miyano of Los Angeles was hired as its national director. DPAA offices were opened in Seattle, staffed by Dorothy Cordova, and in San Francisco. The National Board was made up of Donna Yee, Louise Kamikawa, Pete Jamero and myself from Seattle; Royal Morales and Paul Chikahisa from LA; and George Woo from the Bay Area. To combat the stereotype that Asian Americans were "the model minority," we needed cold hard facts. DPAA began to gather data and conduct studies about the socio-economic status of Asian Americans. We may have shared the same concerns and issues with other communities of color, but we also had the added problems of language and immigration status.

In 1972, Asian American activism became "politically correct" when Governor Dan Evans formed the Washington State Asian American Advisory Council which two years later became the Commission on Asian American Affairs. Martin "Mich" Matsudaira, from the old neighborhood at 16th Avenue and Jefferson Street next to the old Maryknoll church and school, was appointed to serve as executive director. That summer, the Commission held public hearings to document problems Asian Americans faced in the canneries, employment discrimination, access to higher education, negative stereotypes, treatment in the military, and access to social services.

I was honored to be selected as one of the original commissioners. Among my fellow commissioners were Roy Flores, who helped link students from the community college system to the community; Min Masuda, one of my role models, a founding member of Asian Americans for Political Action, and a Japanese American community leader who supported all of the young activist-led causes through the years; and Don Kazama, an older Japanese American activist who helped form the National Pacific Asian Center On Aging and always got a kick out of "pissing off the establishment."

CHAPTER FOUR

Preserving and Developing the International District

THE JACKSON STREET COMMUNITY COUNCIL

MEANWHILE, A LOT HAD happened in the old Chinatown neighborhood that I grew up in. The end of World War II saw an emergence of community activism in Chinatown. One of the first organizations concerned with living conditions in what we now call the International District was the Jackson Street Community Council (JSCC), formed in 1946. JSCC was the forerunner to the International District Improvement Association (Inter*Im). It was a grassroots self-help organization, one of the first neighborhood improvement organizations in the city. JSCC members were active — clearing vacant lots, planting trees on the hillside below Yesler Terrace, sponsoring community events, replacing the wooden sidewalks on Jackson with cement sidewalks, convincing the U.S. Postal Service to establish a branch at Sixth Avenue South and King, and creating a children's playground at Bailey Gatzert Elementary School.

JSCC became a model for inter-ethnic cooperation. Among its early members were Toru Sakahara, Japanese American attorney; Fred Cordova, Filipino American journalist and community activist; Rev. Pio Daba; Alex Bishop, African American pharmacist; James Matsuoka of International Realty; Jimmy Mar, Chinese American funeral director; Dr. Henry Luke, physician; William Mimbu, Japanese American attorney; Don Chin, Chinese American merchant and community activist; Tak Kubota, Japanese American community activist; Frank Hattori, Japanese American community activist; and later, Ben Woo, Chinese American architect; all of whom were active participants in the later development of the International District.

It was JSCC which first recognized that Chinatown wasn't restricted to the Chinese community. Reflecting the diversity of its membership, JSCC lobbied city officials to designate Chinatown and its surrounding areas as the "International Center." Responding to pressure, Seattle Mayor William A. Devin issued a proclamation designating Chinatown as "Seattle's International Center." His proclamation recognized that the area's "Chinese, Japanese, Filipino, and Negro" ancestry had made outstanding contributions to the city's civic and cultural life.

Despite this proclamation, the "International Center" did not catch on with the public. Most people still referred to the area as "Chinatown." By the mid-1950s, newspapers referred to the area as "the Jackson Street District." Tourist guides referred to the area as the "International Settlement." A notice in the 1962 JSCC newsletter referred to the "First International Rickshaw Race" in the "International District." Gradually, more people began referring to the area as the "International District."

In 1952, the state Highway Commission announced its plans to build a Seattle freeway. Plans were then made to construct the freeway through downtown. There was some opposition from a few downtown business operators who felt the proposed construction would bring more congestion to the central core where parking was already inadequate. However, public pressure on city leaders to do something about the increasing traffic congestion was relentless. The downtown path had the support of Governor Albert Rosellini, Seattle Mayor Gordon Clinton, the Seattle City Council, and the majority of Seattle's residents whose properties were not affected by the proposed construction.

When the downtown route was announced, the Jackson Street Community Council argued that the construction of the freeway, later known as Interstate 5, would divide the International District in half. The original plans for the freeway cut off all access through the International District except South Jackson Street. Weller, Lane, and King streets and Yesler Way were completely blocked at Ninth Avenue South, where the freeway would be built. JSCC pointed out that under the original plan, to get from Yesler to Jackson, access was available only at Third Avenue South or 12th Avenue South. JSCC proposed an overpass on Yesler Way to allow vehicular traffic to go through on King Street under the freeway. This proposal was accepted.

However, actual construction was delayed for several years until funding became available under the 1956 federal highway program. Buildings were bulldozed to make space for the new freeway. By 1965, the construction of Interstate 5 had physically divided the area and eliminated businesses, homes, and churches, further contributing to the overall deterioration of the area.

By 1968, the Jackson Street Community Council no longer had a presence in the International District. Many of the Asians who had served on the Council left. JSCC had moved their office to Rainier Avenue South and turned its attention toward improving conditions in the Central District, merging with the Central Area Community Council to become the Central Seattle Community Council.

INTER*IM — LEADING THE WAY

The District hit a low point in the mid-1960s, when assaults and shootings were common occurrences. Tough looking streetwalkers had replaced the call girls of the past whose services had been an accepted necessity for thousands of single male District residents. Lines of cars circled the block from Jackson Street to King Street and Seventh Avenue South to Maynard Avenue to pick up the women who ran in and out of the taverns, alleys, and doorways. The streets were dark and mean. The International District was in serious decline. It was a ghetto.

By 1968, nearly all of the housing was substandard and dilapidated. Because of increasingly stringent fire and housing codes, many hotels were closed and abandoned. Social services were few. For example, health services for the District's residents were offered at the Pioneer Square Health Station, outside the District. There were no counseling services, day care facilities, or nutrition programs. There were no sitting areas for the District's elderly. Streets, sidewalks, alleys, and parking lots were used for socializing. After years of neglect, conditions in the International District had deteriorated to a point where no one wanted to live there. Between 1950 and 1978, approximately half of the existing hotels and apartment buildings closed. The District's population dropped substantially from nearly 5,000 in 1950 to 1,300 in 1978.

The residential base in the International District had declined. As the children of Asian immigrants grew up, racial tolerance and the passage of civil rights laws opened up housing opportunities in other parts of the city. Upward mobility allowed many younger

Asian Americans to leave the International District and purchase their own single family houses in the nearby Central Area, Beacon Hill, and Rainier Valley neighborhoods.

In 1968, a group of business owners and activists, some of whom were former JSCC members such as Don Chin, Alex Bishop, and Ben Woo, formed the International District Improvement Association ("Inter*Im") to revitalize and promote the commercial potential of the International District. The original Inter*Im board was made up of a diverse group including Don Chin, a small business owner from the Chinatown Chamber of Commerce; Carlos Young, a civil engineer with his own firm on Jackson Street; Shigeko Uno, manager of Rainier Heat and Power Co.; Hong Chin, a property owner; Abie Label, a low-income housing developer; Ben Woo, an architect; Alex Bishop, a local pharmacist and owner of Bishop Drugs; Wesley Tao, an insuranceman; Donna Yee, a graduate student; and Tomio Moriguchi, chairman of his family's business, Uwajimaya.

Tomio has been one of the most successful businessmen in the International District. His store, Uwajimaya, was the commercial anchor for economic development in the District. Tomio's father, Fujimatsu Moriguchi, started Uwajimaya as a small Tacoma fish market in 1928. Ironically, as many Japanese Americans moved from the International District after World War II, Tomio's father brought Uwajimaya from Tacoma to the heart of Seattle's International District. By 1970, Tomio was in charge of the family business. Uwajimaya became the largest Asian grocery and gift store in the Pacific Northwest. Tomio's presence gave Inter*Im credibility with both the downtown business establishment and City Hall.

Inter*Im received start-up funding under Seattle's Model Cities Program and began developing community improvement plans. The Model Cities Program was President Lyndon Johnson's major domestic program, the showcase of his "Great Society," the domestic war on poverty, discrimination, and inadequate housing. Under the Model Cities Program, many social service programs were established, including day care, community health services, recreational facilities, vocational rehabilitation, residential rehabilitation, employment, elderly care, and drug abuse prevention.

Inter*Im opened an office in a storefront in the N.P. Hotel. Mike Conlan, a Model Cities staff person, was assigned to Inter*Im to get it off the ground. In its first two years, Inter*Im, with Conlan's assistance, lobbied successfully for better lighting, resulting in new florescent street lamps installed along Jackson Street and King Street, and for increased police patrols to help minimize crime.

In 1970, Inter*Im's Board of Directors applied for full funding from Model Cities to hire a full-time staff person. Eric Inouye, a Model Cities staffer who had replaced Mike Conlan, and Donna Yee, Inter*Im board member, wrote a proposal to Model Cities to fund a full-time director, support staff, and operating capital. As executive director of CARITAS, I had been elected as a voting member of the Model Cities Board of Directors. When the Model Cities Board met to vote on the proposal, there was a 14 to 14 tie. Board Chair Judge Charles V. Johnson, an African American, broke the tie and voted against the motion to fund Inter*Im.

This decision didn't sit well with the I.D. representatives who attended the meeting. They felt the decision was a vote against the Asian American community. There was still a perception that Asian Americans had no problems. I knew we had to invest time to educate the rest of the minority communities about our community's unique problems. We had to work to prevent communities of color from fighting each other for scarce resources. Fortunately, Inter*Im submitted a second proposal to the Model Cities Board in 1971, which gained the necessary support for full funding.

The Inter*Im Board found it difficult to retain staff as it went through two coordinators and two directors in three years. Although new to the Inter*Im Board, I was recruited in 1971 to apply for the open executive director's position by board members Shigeko Uno and Jacquie Kay. Because of my history of activism, Tomio and some others had reservations about my ability to work with a business-oriented board of directors. With the support of activists who pressured Model Cities and the Mayor's office on my behalf, my appointment was accepted and I began my long career working in the International District.

The Kingdome — Casting a Giant Shadow

In November of 1971, King County officials decided to build a multi-purpose domed stadium at King Street after voters had rejected a proposed Seattle Center site. This decision caused great concern in the International District. How could the District survive the increased traffic which would undoubtedly come from the stadium? How would the stadium affect property values for low-income housing? Would the stadium bring more crime to the District? How many housing units were going to be torn down for parking and fast food restaurants? Given the fragile state of its residents, many community activists feared the worst.

Sabino Cabildo, a Filipino activist with the Revolutionary Communist Party, announced at a Filipino community meeting in early 1972 that construction of the domed stadium near the International District would force the elderly Filipino residents out of the community. Peter Bacho, a law student who later became an accomplished author, worked with Evergreen Legal Services to file a lawsuit on behalf of the "Concerned Filipino Residents of the International District," charging violations of the State Environmental Policy Act. However, the lawsuit was thrown out of court on September 15, 1972.

An ad hoc group of activists attended Inter*Im board meetings to press for action against the construction of the domed stadium. The activists believed the domed stadium would increase traffic congestion, parking problems, and noise. They argued that the escalation of property values and raises in rents would ultimately drive the low-income residents out of their single room occupancy units. I criss-crossed the District, talking with merchants, property owners, and residents about their feelings toward the domed stadium. The reaction was mixed, with some merchants worried about parking, but also delighted with the prospect of gaining lots and lots of new customers. Property owners expressed concern about escalating property taxes. Residents were very worried about being forced out of their homes.

Inter*Im sponsored a series of public meetings to identify problems which the stadium would bring to our community. At one of these meetings, Seattle City Councilman Bruce Chapman suggested the possibility of an Asian cultural center. Chapman, a conservative Republican who later served in the Reagan White House, felt that an Asian cultural center was a good way to attract tourists, similar to the developments in San Francisco's Chinatown and Nihonmachi, an idea we didn't like. He was a little surprised when his proposal received only a lukewarm response from our group. His examples were ones we used in explaining what we wanted to avoid in the International District — serving tourists at the expense of residents.

The International District was not the only neighborhood affected by the stadium. The

Pioneer Square neighborhood was also concerned about the stadium's impact on its community. A Citizens Action Force was formed with members appointed jointly by Mayor Wes Uhlman and County Executive John Spellman. Three members were also added from the International District, all from Inter*Im.

Recommendations from the group entitled, "Stadium Impact Resolutions," were incorporated into a set of 20 resolutions passed by the Seattle City Council in September and October 1972 to mitigate the stadium's impacts on Pioneer Square and the International District. These resolutions called for a variety of measures, one of which was a multi-purpose Asian community cultural and trade center to serve as a center for meetings and projects, a cultural center for traditional and new forms of art and education, and a trade center for both offices and commerce. Other recommendations called for more street improvements (such as trees, planters, lighting, park benches), traffic control, housing, social and health services, and public bathrooms.

The Party Is Crashed

Concern over the proposed domed stadium energized the young Asian student activists. They, as I, did not like the idea of Kingdome fans trudging through the community without acknowledging that this was a residential neighborhood. While Inter*Im was working behind the scenes with the City Council to mitigate the stadium's impacts, the young activists wanted to focus the public's attention on living conditions in the International District.

On November 2, 1972, the ground breaking ceremony for the Kingdome drew almost every major officeholder in the state. A nearby restaurant, Gasperetti's, provided tasty treats for the dignitaries. A small group of uninvited guests from the Asian American community showed up as well. King County Executive John Spellman kicked a ceremonial football through a makeshift goal post. Then, as the officials mounted the makeshift stage, Asian activists yelled, "Down with the Dome."

When no one noticed, the young activists threw little mud balls. With the rain came nice firm, snowball-sized mud balls that more often than not found a target. Spellman was splattered. There was an angry confrontation between the young Asian activists and City Council

President Liem Tuai. The demonstrators accused Tuai, a Chinese American, of being a "traitor" and a "pawn of the establishment." (Ironically, it was Tuai who, before he was elected to the City Council, drafted the incorporation papers for Inter*Im in 1969.)

Deputies from the Sheriff's office were called in. Nemesio Domingo, Jr. was arrested and led away in handcuffs on charges of disorderly conduct for shouting obscenities and giving the "finger" to a policeman. The charges were later dropped, and he was released on $50 bail, which was paid so fast he didn't serve a day in jail. The headline in the next morning's newspaper read, "Mudslinging Incident at Stadium Site." The activists got the desired media attention. We had sent a message to our political leaders: you may have your Kingdome, but don't forget about the I.D. Yet, when Spellman was interviewed about the incident, he told a reporter, in response to a question about the stadium's impacts on the International District, that the stadium "in no way jeopardizes that area. I don't think they have a legitimate case at all."

Gearing Up — The March to HUD

After the demonstration, we met that night at St. Peter Claver Center. It was a foregone conclusion the domed stadium would be built. We wouldn't be able to stop it. King County officials had invested too much money in it. Seattle wanted professional baseball and professional football. One possible course of action was having a series of demonstrations at the domed stadium site. This idea was rejected because most of us felt media attention had peaked at the ground breaking ceremony.

Instead, there was general agreement that the community effort should be directed toward building more elderly low-income housing in the I.D. We called our group, "Concerned Asians for the International District." I was among those who suggested that a visit by residents and supporters to the local HUD (U.S. Department of Housing and Urban Development) office might be appropriate. HUD was the federal agency that provided housing programs and resources.

Twelve days later, on November 14, 1972, a rally was held at the site of what would later be Hing Hay Park. Speakers explained the gist of the proposals we were presenting to HUD officials, who had agreed beforehand to meet with a small I.D. delegation. Those chosen to meet with HUD included Peter Bacho; Dawn Canton, an elderly resident of the Frye Apartments; Norma Asis, another student activist and one of the founders of the International Drop-In Center; Ben Woo, board president of Inter*Im; and I.

More than 150 demonstrators gathered for the march. We were joined by other minority groups led by Roberto Maestas and Larry Gossett, who were there to support us. The demonstrators marched down Jackson Street to a site overlooking the vacant Kingdome site, then north on Second Avenue to Union Street, where HUD offices were located in the Arcade Plaza. The march traveled slowly, led by the community's elderly residents. Frank Irigon chanted into a bullhorn, "The people united, will never be defeated." The crowd picked up the chant.

There were many signs with unique messages: "Save the I.D.," "Doom the Dome," "A Parking Lot is Not a Home." The sign that received the attention of the Associated Press wire service was the now famous, "HUM BOWS NOT HOT DOGS!" When Larry Gossett saw the sign, he went up to the elderly Filipino resident carrying the cardboard placard and asked, "Hum bows, what's that?" Somebody shouted, "Asian soul food." Larry smiled and said, "I can dig it."

The march proceeded to the HUD offices at the Arcade Plaza. Groups of 20 took the elevators up to the fourth floor. When we arrived at the secretary's desk, I told her we were there for our appointment with Marshall Majors, HUD's regional administrator. The five of us went into the conference room while the rest of our group milled around the outer office. Our delegation met with Majors and other HUD officials and discussed our housing priorities. Peter Bacho listed a number of I.D. hotels we wanted to see rehabilitated — the Atlas, Panama, Eastern, and N.P. hotels.

Suddenly, the door opened and our people rushed in. Everyone wanted to hear what the HUD officials had to say. The group crowded around the table and grabbed every available chair. Some stood, lined up against the wall. Others crowded around the door, straining to hear every word. Soon, there were more than 75 of us packed into HUD's small conference room. We called for order. The crowd quieted down.

HUD officials mentioned some of their programs that could benefit our low-income residents. Majors pointed to the Kawabe House, outside the International District, as a place where the elderly residents could relocate. In response, Ben Woo replied, "You're not facing the real problem, which is the breaking up of an ethnic social order. These are people who want to stay right where they are — where they have been for 30, 40, 50 years."

Others complained that housing codes were being selectively enforced near the stadium site, forcing old men and women into the street while "deplorable disease-breeding conditions" were allowed to persist in other structures like the Milwaukee Hotel. One HUD official told us that we should find builders and developers to rehabilitate the old buildings. Roy Flores, representing the Governor's Asian American Advisory Council, declared, "That's the old run-around again. We can't get commitments from builders without the HUD money and you won't give us the money unless we have the builder first."

Majors advised us that Seattle city officials had to include the I.D. in its comprehensive plan for housing development before HUD could allocate its resources to the International District. He further advised us to work with the Mayor to have him prioritize the I.D. as a targeted neighborhood for new elderly low-income housing. The discussion became very heated. This is not what the crowd wanted to hear. We weren't getting anywhere. Our crowd called for action. Majors promised more meetings to discuss specific programs. I was chosen to continue with the ongoing discussions. (It should also be noted that in 1972, the Nixon administration froze funding for several housing programs promised for I.D. developers.) After the meeting with HUD, the crowd quietly dispersed. We had our work cut out for us.

Getting Busy — The Effort to Get More Housing

Shortly after the march on HUD, Ben Woo and I met with Barbara Dingfield, the city's director of the Department of Community Development, and several members of Mayor Uhlman's staff to talk about the housing needs of the International District's low-income residents. When Dingfield said the city was not in the housing business, Ben firmly replied, "Then the city better start getting concerned about housing."

Dingfield suggested to us that the International District follow the example of Pioneer Square and other urban neighborhoods — develop a strong retail-commercial core and worry about housing later. Ben Woo explained, "We're doing it backward." Pioneer Square was not a good example to follow. It had a resident base of extreme opposites — shelters for very low-income transients remained while new high-income condominiums were built for more affluent professionals. It was a neighborhood where residents were forced out of old turn-of-the-century brick buildings that were sandblasted and completely renovated into architecture award-winning design models for modern professional offices and commercial space. Its residents had to find housing elsewhere.

The mayor's staff insisted that Inter*Im show evidence of broad community support before city officials prioritized low-income housing for the International District. I knew this would not be easy. Some property owners and shopkeepers insisted that commercial revitalization be the top priority. I criss-crossed the I.D. day and night to gather broad-based support. I enlisted Phil Hayasaka, who brought me around the Nisei (second generation Japanese American) business community during the day. At night, I was on my own.

Phil introduced me to his friends at insurance agencies, law offices, drug stores, restaurants, and the local hotels and apartments. Most of the Nisei community didn't think there were any problems that needed solving. Many of these professionals were in the service business with a middle class clientele and didn't work with low-income residents anyway. They didn't care if the buildings were renovated to maintain the residential base.

On the other hand, the Chinese businesses in the King Street core, such as the restaurants and shops, depended more on the residents for their patronage. Although they didn't become politically active in our efforts to bring more affordable housing to the District, Chinese business owners, also aware that many of their parents lived in the International District, were more supportive of housing renovation. The most active support for decent, affordable housing came from the mostly Filipino residents, many of whom were Alaskeros who, with their recent history of advocating for cannery labor reform, relished in the activism they were asked to participate in.

Property owners had the most to gain if they decided to renovate their property, especially if they took advantage of public resources available through government grants, low interest loans, and rent subsidies for elderly low-income residents. Rent subsidies allowed the elderly residents to pay only one-third of their income for rent with the balance of the rent guaranteed by HUD through a voucher or certificate program.

LAYING THE FOUNDATION — MAKING THE CASE FOR MORE HOUSING

Inter*Im studied similar urban neighborhoods in major cities along the Pacific Coast. San Francisco's Chinatown, Nihonmachi, and Manilatown were slowly losing housing stock. In those communities, large money interests, many of whom were foreign-based, competed for space, which caused a sharp rise in rent and property values. One example told to me was of a San Francisco herb store operated by an elderly couple. The couple paid $400 a month in rent, but were forced out of business when the building owner demanded and later got $2,500 a month for their space from a gem shop featuring exotic jade from the Orient.

In 1974, Ben Woo and I traveled to Los Angeles to talk with Kango Kunitsugu, director of the Community Development Agency in Little Tokyo, about their redevelopment. Los Angeles' Asian American community, which already lost part of its Chinatown and Little Tokyo, was undergoing massive change from a residential neighborhood to almost a strictly retail and commercial center, showcased by the New Otani Hotel, a first class tourist-oriented hotel built with Japanese money. We found out that preservation of their retail core was the number one priority. Their plans for development of a greater commercial base with office space and a first class hotel were on schedule. When we asked him about housing, Kunitsugu said the housing would be addressed later.

My testimony at the Seattle City Council hearings began with this: "Urban centers all across the nation are losing downtown neighborhoods to progress at the expense of the pioneers who built these cities. And we in the International District refuse to follow this trend. The preservation of the International District is our number one priority."

No one disagreed that the I.D. housing stock needed upgrading. But there were very few building owners who wanted to reinvest in their buildings for any kind of renovation if it meant giving up complete control over tenant selection or losing the option to sell to commercial developers. The young activists decided to take action. Inter*Im, the International District Youth Council (IDYC), and the newly formed International District Housing Alliance (IDHA) were at the forefront of organizing the elderly residents to fight for decent affordable housing. Tenant organizing was a cause close to my heart, based on my experience of having lived in room 306, a single room occupancy (SRO) unit, with my dad at the N.P. Hotel. In my dad's day, no one looked out for the residents. I was determined to change that.

A year later, in 1973, the federal government lifted the freeze on funds for developing low-income elderly housing. The International District became a natural place for housing developers to acquire property and develop housing, using combinations of federal government low interest loans, grants, and rent subsidies. Meanwhile, city officials placed the International District on a high priority list for HUD-subsidized low-income elderly housing.

Abie Label, an early Inter*Im board member, acquired the Union Apartments building and used HUD funds to remodel it into the International Apartments. The Seattle Housing Authority acquired the land at Sixth Avenue South and Main Street and used HUD funds to build the International Terrace, a 99-unit building. Orville Cohen acquired property on the northwest corner of Sixth Avenue South and Main Street from Danny Woo and built the Imperial House. Security Pacific built the International House on the Banchero property at Maynard Avenue South and Weller Street. Barry Mar was one of the first Chinese hotel owners in the King Street core to apply for public funds and developed the Atlas Apartments.

There was an organized effort by the International District Housing Alliance to make sure that neighborhood residents had a fair chance at getting the new housing units. The Housing Alliance held meetings to inform the elderly about the availability of new housing and the process for determining eligibility to live in these new units. The working combination of young activists such as Elaine (Ikoma) Ko and Shari Woo from Inter*Im, Andy Mizuki and Rick Furukawa from the Housing Alliance staff, Silme Domingo and Gene Viernes from the Alaska Cannery Workers Association, and elderly residents, such as Housing Alliance board members Al Masigat, Clark Robinett, Sammy Esperanza, Dawn Canton, Richard Bartelle, and Pantel Cabuena, was very effective in organizing the elderly who showed up at the popular International Drop-In Center (IDIC).

Housing developers approached Inter*Im because of our long list of elderly tenants in need of these new federally subsidized modern apartments. Word went out among the elderly in the District that Inter*Im staff were signing up residents for the new apartments under construction. Elderly Chinese ladies who signed up for housing brought in pastries and lots of cookies to show their appreciation for our role in finding them better places to live.

Concerned Asians for the International District — Listing the Demands

The impact from the Kingdome construction continued to be an issue with the International District community. Although city officials had taken steps to mitigate the impacts of the domed stadium (through the "Stadium Impact Resolutions" passed by the City Council), county officials had been slow to respond. Many of the activists who had been at the ground breaking ceremonies demanded a commitment from King County Executive John Spellman to lessen the impacts on the International District. The group, first called "Concerned Asians for the International District," then later the "Committee for Corrective Action in the International District," presented Spellman with six demands.

These demands included: 1) setting aside a percentage of profits from the stadium to fund I.D. social and health services; 2) having a community representative in the selection of the stadium's manager; 3) appointing an Asian American to an administrative position on the stadium staff; 4) giving I.D. residents preference in hiring; 5) setting aside a percentage of jobs at the stadium for Asian Americans; and 6) allowing the elderly I.D. residents free admission to any stadium event.

Spellman gave us a verbal commitment that all six demands would be met. We should have known better. Always get commitments in writing, especially from politicians. Variations of the demands were implemented, but not necessarily as a direct result of anything Spellman did. For example, King County officials provided the original seed money to establish the International District Community Health Center, but major grants came from the state and federal governments.

Similarly, International District residents were hired as part-time ticket takers, but only one Asian American was hired on the construction crew which built the Kingdome. Elderly District residents didn't get free admission to events, but did get senior citizen discounts, which all senior citizens got for some events. When the Kingdome opened, several Asian Americans such as Jerry Laigo were hired in key administrative positions for the county. The last director of the Kingdome before its implosion in the spring of 2000 was Ann Kawasaki, but she had been hired by Gary Locke when he was King County Executive.

Selecting the Director of the Kingdome — Aloha Means Goodbye

One demand made by the Committee for Corrective Action to County Executive John Spellman was the appointment of an Asian to the committee to select the Kingdome director. Spellman appointed me to the committee, which included: Bob Bratton, assistant to Spellman; Zollie Volchok, an events promoter; Chuck Collins, director of METRO; and County Executive Spellman himself.

After going through all of the resumes, the managerial selection committee ranked the candidates. We requested interviews of the top three candidates. The person who most impressed the committee was the director of the Hawaii Convention Center. That seemed okay to me. After all, if he worked in Hawaii, I assumed he had experience working with Asian Americans.

During the oral interview, I asked the candidate why he would leave that paradise to move to Seattle. The *haole* (Caucasian) replied, "My daughter just turned 16. Boys are starting to come over to the house. But they're those *Chinese* boys. We thought it was a good time to move."

His response didn't sit well with me. It showed a racist attitude. But other members of our committee still considered him the top candidate. After much debate, I finally threatened the committee. I declared, "If you hire this man, I promise you, there will be protesters to greet him every morning he comes to work." I think Spellman, who later became governor, had his fill of stadium protests. This was one headache he could avoid. Needless to say, that guy wasn't hired. Ted Bowsfield, a former major league baseball player, was selected as director of the Kingdome. As it turned out, Bowsfield and I got along.

Diana Bower — The Compassionate Consultant

Diana Bower, a local architect, urban planner, and an outside consultant with Model Cities experience, had been hired by the city in 1973 to coordinate actions in response to the City Council's "Stadium Impact Resolutions." As coordinator, Bower served as a liaison between city departments (such as Engineering, Human Resources, Parks, Community Development, and Building) and both Pioneer Square and the International District. She worked closely with Inter*Im staff.

Diana was a perfect fit for this position. She worked for several years on the staff of the Model Cities Program in Seattle's Central Area, a predominantly African American neighborhood. In her role there, she worked with residents, property owners, community activists and owners of commercial businesses to coordinate Model Cities resources from the city to the community. She was also an artist who studied and was influenced by Asian art, which helped her transition into the International District culture.

Diana was the first proponent for the creation of the International District Community Garden. After talking with a number of International District residents about their needs, she came to the conclusion that after meeting housing, health care, and nutritional needs, residents wanted the ability to garden and raise their own vegetables. A proposal to construct a community garden for the community's elderly was presented to the Inter*Im board. After board approval, a hunt started to identify a garden site.

One day, Diana, Ed Hidano, and I set out to take soil samples in the overgrown hillside above Main Street. Ed and I, armed with two car tires, threw them to weigh down the thick blackberry bushes that were growing seven to 10 feet above ground. Diana would point to a section and we would throw the tires in that direction. Diana would step on the tires and bend down to test the soil in the designated spot. She would then point to another section. Ed and I would pick up the tires and throw them again at Diana's direction. After four separate areas were tested, I thought we had enough samples to establish a pretty fair idea of the hillside's soil make up. Diana had a different idea. She felt as long as we were there, we might as well test the whole hillside. After three hours of Diana's pointing and our heaving the tires, we had over a dozen jars of soil. Finally, Diana called it a day. Ed and I, sweating, scratched, and bloodied, spent the rest of the afternoon replenishing our body liquids with Olympia beer with Wilma Woo at the friendly confines of the Quong Tuck Bar and Grill. Diana eventually had the soil tested. The soil experts suggested that soil from the hill mixed with pea gravel, topsoil, and fertilizer from Longacres racetrack would make ideal growing soil for produce to grow.

Diana attended most of our many community meetings. She was able to pinpoint county or city resources to resolve particular problems. Diana worked effectively with city and county department heads to address the needs of the communities she was assigned to, not only the International District, but Pioneer Square and the social service agencies which worked with that neighborhood's low-income tenants. But many of us who worked with her in the International District felt she dedicated more time to our issues than the other groups she was assigned to assist.

Diana's work facilitated the development of many positive improvements in the I.D. These included: the establishment of Hing Hay and Kobe Terrace parks; the creation of the International Special Review District Board; the extension of the "Magic Carpet" Metro bus transportation free zone to the International District; bus stop shelters in the I.D.; translation of bus schedules into Japanese and Chinese; and the development of an Asian medical center which became the International District Community Health Center and later, International Community Health Services.

The Health Clinic — Patients and Patience

One of the positive outcomes from the Kingdome fight was funding for a health clinic. An Inter*Im survey of residents, shopkeepers, and activists identified health care as the second most mentioned need in the International District. Housing was first. Bruce Miyahara, who had a Master's degree in health administration, and who later served as the state director of health, was hired to coordinate the clinic project.

Activists such as Miyahara, Shiz Sata, Sister Heide Parreno, Dr. Alan Muramoto, Dr. Ken Mayeda, and Lonnie Bayagawan helped plan strategies to address health issues. Funding was desperately needed to build and maintain a multi-lingual clinic in the I.D. Our strategy for raising public attention focused on sending out press releases and bringing 50 sign waving (sign waving was always a sure way to get the news cameras involved) "concerned citizens" to the office of my "dear friend," King County Executive John Spellman.

After several unannounced and unsuccessful visits to see Spellman (which often resulted in the County Executive fleeing out the back door), a simple call in late 1973 to an old childhood friend, Jerry Laigo, a Spellman aide, finally produced a meeting. When we met, our group of sign waving, vocal protesters submitted a list to Spellman, demanding the county's support and funding for a health clinic. Maybe it was pressure from our protesters, maybe it was the news media, but Spellman agreed to support a health clinic. With a positive response from Spellman, the now courteous group accepted the promise of a $25,000 matching grant and all left peacefully. For some unexplained reason, however, the County Executive was left with an empty display case which once held the "golden spike," symbolizing the last railroad spike pulled up at the ground breaking ceremony at the Kingdome, built on the site of old railroad tracks. Someone in the group took the spike, but no one ever stepped forward to take credit. Its whereabouts are a mystery to this day.

Later, after a meeting unrelated to the Kingdome with a county official, I passed by Jerry Laigo's office, popped my head in, and announced, "Hey, Jerry. We came back."

"Oh, shit," he yelled. "How many are there this time?" When he finally came out and saw I was alone, he said, "Hell, Bob, you almost gave me a heart attack. Can you wait a second because I need to call security off."

After the county provided its support, matching grants were secured from the Seattle City Council and the state of Washington with assistance from Pete Jamero, now director of the Washington state Department of Vocational Rehabilitation, who arranged a key meeting with his counterpart at the state health department. The state, in fact, surprised us with a $40,000 grant (almost $15,000 more than what we had asked for) from a "discretionary account," allowing us to bypass the long arduous legislative process normally involved with a state funding request.

The $90,000 we pooled from the different governments allowed Inter*Im to shop around for the ideal space to establish the clinic and hire staff. The preferred location for the clinic was around the Hing Hay Park area. Barry Mar, owner of the Atlas Hotel, pointed to 416 Maynard Avenue, a storefront across the street from the park. He didn't have to say anything. I approached King Monillas, proprietor of a Filipino fraternal social club and after-hours gambling club which rented the downstairs space. I winked at King, which let him know I knew what was happening behind closed doors and to assure him I wouldn't tell Barry or the vice squad if he moved his "operation" upstairs. Shortly thereafter, we received a long-term lease from Barry. The sound of dominos tinkling from the second floor added a little flavor to the clinic's ambiance.

Diana Bower helped us move the clinic project through the permit process maze. Joey Ing, Vera Ing's husband and a well-known architect, took time from his busy schedule and designed the physical layout for the clinic. Kaz Ishimitsu, a contractor, took on the construction work. Both worked tirelessly. I don't think Joey or Kaz made money on the project.

After Inter*Im secured funding for the health center and the construction was complete, the clinic formed a board of directors. The health clinic's original board came from the health professionals who assisted with the planning of the clinic, activists who put the pressure on county government, business owners, and low-income residents who were also the clients. For a short time, there were two boards overseeing the clinic — the clinic board and the Inter*Im board. It had been so much easier to get things done for the contractors, planners, and bureaucrats when they had only the Inter*Im board to deal with.

Soon after, a multi-lingual health professional staff was hired which reflected the multi-cultural clients being served. Bruce Miyahara, who assisted in almost every phase of the initial development from demonstrations to writing proposals, transferred from Inter*Im and was hired as the health center's first executive director.

Bruce was paid under the Comprehensive Employment Training Act (CETA) Program administered through the city of Seattle by John Franklin, director, and Nelson Park, assistant director, one of 13 International District staff positions which John and Nelson worked their magic to have CETA fund through Inter*Im. Susie Chin, then Inter*Im's office manager, and I were also funded under the CETA Program for several months. John and Nelson should be proud to know just how valuable these funds were in developing our future careers as community activists.

Food and Nutrition Programs — I Can Vouch for It

In addition to health, there was also concern over nutrition. Donnie Chin, director of the International District Emergency Center (IDEC), and young activists from IDYC opened a food bank for residents at the site of the old Inter*Im office in the storefront of the N.P. Hotel. It was a common sight in the mornings to see long lines of elderly waiting for the food bank to open. But a food bank was not enough to meet the needs of our residents.

We discovered there was $20,000 in unspent city funds allocated for elderly nutrition programs in the downtown area. I met with Rick Locke, executive director of the First Avenue Service Center (FASC) in Pioneer Square. We decided to share the $20,000 for completely different elderly nutrition programs. FASC incorporated the money into a kitchen planned for the Morrison Hotel, a low-income housing project across the street from the downtown King County Courthouse.

We decided on a voucher distribution program. With $10,000, there wasn't enough money to start our own kitchen. In addition, we didn't want to compete with the local restaurants. The critical time for fixed income elderly was the last week of every month when pension money ran low. We met with five local restaurants that agreed to accept $2 food vouchers during the last week of every month. These vouchers allowed the elderly residents to purchase hot nutritious meals. Once a month, the elderly streamed into our office to receive five vouchers for their trips to their favorite restaurants.

Another food program started by Inter*Im was the Food Buying Club. Through membership in this club, coordinated by Doralinn Jung, the low-income elderly purchased dry food and canned goods at rates cheaper than offered at grocery stores. Doralinn bought the food wholesale. Club members joined by paying a one-time $1 fee. Doralinn recruited volunteers like me who, once a month, assisted in delivering the groceries. I always dreaded delivering to the Eastern Hotel because it had four floors with steep stairs and no working elevators. It seemed like everyone who ordered 100-pound sacks of rice lived on the top floor of the Eastern.

These elderly food and nutrition programs turned out to be the greatest organizing tool we could have invented. This "captive" audience was extremely grateful to us. Their gratitude was expressed whenever we had to show government leaders and foundations evidence of elderly support. Although we brought the elderly on trips to shopping malls and other places they were interested in, we also brought them to meetings and City Council hearings. We always had those willing to testify, in their own language, about their support for whatever project we had before the City Council. Sometimes, we embellished their testimony.

For example, Mrs. Chin, an elderly resident, stepped up to the mike and testified in Chinese that she "would really like to bring her cat to an apartment with her own bath." Our translator, usually Maxine Chan, "translated" these words into, "Mrs. Chin said she was being displaced by the Kingdome and is dying of malnutrition." After such heart-wrenching testimony, the City Council members dried their eyes and gave us their support and their vote.

This was not a usual occurrence, but there were times our translators were "creative" when testimony strayed from the point we wanted to make.

The Legal Clinic — Storefront Lawyers

Over the years, Inter*Im moved its offices to several sites within the International District. First, our office was in the N.P. Hotel on Sixth Avenue South between Jackson and Main streets. Then we moved to space in the International Realty office on the corner of Sixth Avenue South and Jackson while the Toda & Chin ("T & C") Building space underwent renovation for occupancy by our staff. After a few years hidden away on the second floor of the T & C Building between Maynard and Seventh Avenue South on Jackson, where few elderly found their way to the office, we moved to the old United Savings and Loan Bank site in the corner space of the Bush Hotel at the corner of Maynard and Jackson. The staff was crammed into the old bank, but they loved the action of the streets.

Having a street level office also encouraged walk-in traffic. Being able to connect with the community was very important to maintain our credibility. During this active time in the mid-1970s, a group of young Asian American attorneys and law students including Tony Lee, Bob Yamagiwa, Diane Wong, and Rod Kawakami opened up a free volunteer legal clinic every Tuesday at the Inter*Im office. Tony, Bob, and Diane were Evergreen Legal Service lawyers while Rod was fresh out of law school.

Unfortunately, during this time, Inter*Im temporarily lost its funding with the breakup of the Model Cities Program, which ended in 1974. Fortunately, the Asian Counseling and Referral Service (ACRS) was sharing office space with us and paid the rent which allowed Inter*Im to continue operating. The Inter*Im staff, consisting of Susie Chin, our office manager, and me, went on unemployment to make ends meet while volunteering to keep the agency open.

Working the Foundation Madness

After losing our funding, I knew that in order for Inter*Im to survive, we had to learn how to play the game called, "Please Fund Our Agency Before the World Comes to an End."

This game was played in every agency office funded by foundations and government programs. Those who were good at playing the game were rewarded with a grant.

Our fund-raising team consisted of Dan Rounds, team captain; Dan Rounds, quarterback; Dan Rounds, batting cleanup; Dan Rounds, playing center, forward, and point guard; and I was the coach. Dan came to Inter*Im in the mid-1970s. He had gone to college with Tony Ishisaka. One day, he just showed up with Tony while we were working on the hillside community garden. After learning about our activities and programs in the International District, he asked if he could help us in some way. Dan had a keen analytical mind with the innate ability to put technical jargon on paper. Words like "self sufficiency," "economic viability," "in-kind funds," "matching funds," "consolidation profit margin," "accelerated depreciation (for those developing housing)," and "networking" were popular with foundations and government programs.

Having a well-written proposal was just the first step. Some agencies submitted their proposals to all foundations, sat back, and prayed for divine intervention. The most productive formula for us was to invite staff members or board members from foundations to the International District for lunch and a tour of our programs. We felt that once a representative from a foundation could actually learn and see the rich history and development of the International District, we then had more than half a chance for serious consideration. In some instances, it took a little money (lunch, no bribes) to make a lot of money. It also took a good sales pitch and above all, a successful program to show off. Everyone liked a winner and success so it didn't necessarily mean that the most needy and worthwhile programs got the attention.

ACRS — Solving Our Own Problems

The Asian Counseling and Referral Service grew up with Inter*Im and the International District Community Health Center. There had always been a need for mental health services in the Asian American/Pacific Islander community, but the general perception was that Asian Americans didn't have problems. When there were problems, Asian American families tried to hide them from other family members and the community. There were growing numbers of Asian American clients with mental illness, alcohol and drug abuse, and domestic violence. It wasn't easy for families in our communities to seek out professional help. Families in crisis had only the mainstream social services to turn to. But mainstream social services weren't sensitive to the cultural differences between Asian Americans and the general community.

A few Asian American professionals did something about it. Counseling sessions were held in private offices by volunteer social workers. In 1972, a national network of social work professionals met in Seattle for the National Conference for the Council of Social Work Education held at the Olympic Hotel. It was a great opportunity for Asian American social workers from around the country to meet with local social workers and community activists to develop strategies that led to funding for national Asian American research grants. Prominent at the national conference were local social work professionals such as: Pete Jamero, Min Masuda, Sharon Fujii, Don Kazama, Tony Ishisaka, Sam Shoji, and social work students Donna Yee and Louise Kamikawa.

In 1973, these local mental health professionals decided to establish a formal counseling service in the Asian American community. The Asian Counseling and Referral Service (ACRS) took shape and formed a board of directors. George Hom was hired as its first executive director. We agreed to provide space and George soon moved in with the Inter*Im staff in our offices in the Toda & Chin Building on Jackson Street. What started off as a short stint turned into a two-year stay. Supervised by Tony Ishisaka, a social work professor at the University of Washington, and social workers Sue Tomita and Bob Krisologo, student interns Theresa Fujiwara, Jerry Shigaki, and Y.K. Kuniyuki worked out of the Inter*Im office. They provided limited counseling and did a whole lot of research.

When Inter*Im was forced to move its offices to the Bush Hotel, ACRS moved with us, too. When Inter*Im lost its Model Cities funding, it depended on ACRS to pay the office rent. After Inter*Im regained full funding, ACRS, with an infusion of newly allocated grants, moved out on its own into its new office space in a storefront in the Evergreen Apartments on Jackson Street. ACRS eventually grew into a multi-service agency that became one of the largest Asian American/Pacific Islander non-profit community-based social service agencies in the nation.

THE INTERNATIONAL EXAMINER — READ ALL ABOUT IT

Another I.D. community-based organization which Inter*Im helped was the *International Examiner*. The *International Examiner* was established in 1974 when Larry Imamura, the owner of Officemporium, an office supply company, and Gerry Yuasa, the bank manager of Seafirst's I.D. branch, decided to publish a newspaper to highlight businesses in the International District. Larry became the newspaper's publisher. After a year, the newspaper became too much of a full-time effort for Larry to handle. The Officemporium was right across the street from the Alaska Cannery Workers Association office. When Nemesio Domingo, Jr. heard that Larry wanted someone else to publish the newspaper, he crossed the street and told Larry he was willing to take the newspaper over. Larry sold the *International Examiner* to Nemesio for $1.

When I heard Nemesio had bought the *Examiner*, I immediately called him to offer my support. Larry Imamura did an excellent job of promoting the International District business community, but there was so much more going on in the community that needed to be documented and hadn't been covered. The *Examiner* soon became the voice of young activists who were more interested in the preservation of a neighborhood than the promotion of business.

The focus of the paper shifted from promoting I.D. businesses to covering the social and political issues affecting the District, reflecting the political activism of its young, college age student staff. Nemesio recruited writers such as Gary Iwamoto and Elaine (Ikoma) Ko, two journalism students from another local Asian American newspaper, the *Asian Family Affair*, to write news stories for the *Examiner*. Articles about low-income housing, the Asian elderly, and distrust of redevelopment soon began to appear regularly on its pages. As the newspaper grew, the community's best writers such as Mayumi Tsutakawa, Doug Chin, Gary Iwamoto, Ken Mochizuki, and Ron Chew wrote regularly for the *Examiner*.

The *Examiner* depended on volunteers to write stories, take pictures, solicit ads, and distribute the newspaper. Funding was always scarce. The newspaper needed to hire a full-time editor. Facing the loss of the *Examiner* as a valuable community resource, I was able to find a source for funding the newspaper. I hired Ron Chew as an Inter*Im staff member with funding through, once again, the CETA Program, and assigned him to work as the editor of the newspaper. I even persuaded our funding source, the Community Services Administration, to allow Inter*Im to publish our own column, Inter*Im's Corner, in the *International Examiner* instead of sending out a regular newsletter. In addition to our column, I contributed several opinion pieces on a variety of local and international issues, whenever the mood to write hit me.

The newspaper evolved into a diverse mixture of political, human interest, and cultural stories. Donnie Chin wrote a column that provided a firsthand account of fires, accidents, and emergency situations in the District. Doug Chin detailed the history of the Chinese in Washington state. Gene Viernes wrote a series of articles on the Alaska canneries. Alan Lau coordinated coverage of book reviews, art shows, and cultural events.

After the federal funding ended, the *Examiner* was able to pay its editors out of its own efforts. The *Examiner* continued to grow. What started out as a four-page monthly newspaper eventually became a 16-page bi-weekly news/magazine. The *International Examiner* was read widely, not only throughout the Asian American community, but also in the larger community and by almost every elected official in city and county government. Because the *Examiner* was now more of a community-based newspaper than a business, its editors such as Ron Chew, Mayumi Tsutakawa, and Bob Shimabukuro always gave us favorable coverage and supported our activities.

Inter*Im's Parking Lot — Housing for Cars

During Kingdome events, especially on Sundays when the Seattle Seahawks played at home to capacity crowds, the International District became an extended parking lot for stadium fans. The I.D. became a ghost town because regular customers went elsewhere. Originally, city officials alleviated this problem by extending the hours for on-street parking meter use during Kingdome events. On Seahawk Sunday, parking meters were in force one hour before the 1 p.m. start of the event. The fans who attended the games did not park at parking meters because the two-hour parking limit was much shorter than the length of the game.

Problems occurred when customers who came to the International District to eat and stick around in the lounge for a few hours on Sunday became very upset when they found overtime parking tickets on their cars. Street parking had previously been free. Some restaurant owners had a habit of parking after hours in front of their establishments which also resulted in overtime parking tickets for them. These owners pleaded with city officials to resume the traditional free parking on Sunday. Because the fans knew street parking was free again, competition became fierce for International District on-street parking. Parking continued to be a lose-lose situation.

To address the parking problem, Inter*Im negotiated with the state Department of Transportation to lease the space under the I-5 freeway on Jackson Street between Eighth Avenue South and Ninth Avenue South, for a parking lot to serve District customers, employees, and residents. A long-term lease was signed and Inter*Im was in the parking lot business. The state Department of Transportation leveled the site, laid the blacktop, and painted the strips for 234 stalls. A monthly rate of $6 was charged, but the lot stood empty. Business owners felt the parking lot was too far away to be effective and even pressed to have their customers park for free.

To fill the lot, we had to be creative. Mayor Uhlman's staff had drafted a proposal to provide free bus service in the "Magic Carpet Zone" in downtown Seattle. This proposal allowed bus riders free access anywhere downtown south from Virginia Street to north of Yesler Way with I-5 the eastern boundary, but excluded the I.D. from the Magic Carpet Zone. Inter*Im packed the City Council hearing with elderly from the I.D. I testified in favor of expanding the Magic Carpet Zone to Eighth Avenue South and Jackson Street to allow the elderly residents of our community the opportunity to shop downtown. This proposal was also key to the success of filling the Inter*Im parking lot under the freeway. The City Council accepted the amendment to expand the Magic Carpet Zone to include the I.D. You might say that Inter*Im invented "Park and Ride."

Ed Hidano, a recent graduate of Washington State University, had run out of money and was ready to return to Hawaii when he was hired by Inter*Im to market the "Park and Ride" concept to downtown workers. Ed, with Betty Terada's help, produced a flier and went floor to floor in downtown office buildings, handing out the "Park and Ride" announcement. He was eventually forced to promote the parking program from street corners. But the parking lot began to fill and the revenue was used to subsidize Inter*Im's programs.

In the late 1970s, Inter*Im, with Glenn Chinn playing a key role, took the lead in establishing the Merchants Parking Association. Merchants Parking managed almost every off-street parking lot in the I.D. Because the parking was managed by non-profit corporations, we were able to keep parking affordable for I.D. workers, residents, and customers.

The I.D. Emergency Center — The First Line of Defense

Any description about the history of the International District would be incomplete without mentioning Donnie Chin and the International District Emergency Center (IDEC). When you hear the sound of sirens in the I.D., Donnie will be first on the scene, emergency aid kit in hand. For more than 30, I repeat, 30 years, Donnie has responded to thousands of emergencies within the District — medical, emotional, and personal traumas; fires; shootings; assaults; car accidents; and water leaks. You name it, Donnie was probably right in the middle of it. Donnie was the District's paramedic, the first line of defense. People active in the community knew when something bad happened, call Donnie.

IDEC was started in 1967 in a storefront on the west side of Canton Alley by Donnie with some assistance from Dean Wong and Michael Kozu. They were still in their teens and wanted to make a difference in our community at a time when the International District was a deteriorating, neglected neighborhood. They called themselves the "Asians for Unity Emergency Squad" and patrolled the streets. The service they provided was simple — if anyone in the community needed immediate help, they were there.

Donnie's world had been the IDEC since junior high school days. Donnie, Dean, Michael, and others made regular rounds of the hotels, apartments, and stores in the International District and removed discarded cardboard, garbage, and other material that blocked safe passage to fire exits. After a few years, many left to join other causes, raise families, or attend school. Donnie remained to carry out the mission of the Emergency Center. He made sure he knew what he was doing. He took training classes and studied emergency first aid techniques. He installed a police radio to monitor the action on the streets. What started off as a simple act of community self-determination became an all-volunteer effort to assist the fire department when it came into the District. It took some time, but Donnie earned the complete respect and cooperation of both the Seattle fire and police departments.

Even as a child, Donnie spent long hours in the District. His father, Don Chin, was active in community politics. Donnie's mother, Myra, ran the Sun May novelty store and was a fixture behind the counter. Donnie and his sister Connie helped out at the family store. Donnie knew all of the old-timers, many with no families to speak of. He looked out for them while they were alive. And when they died alone, Donnie was often there to see them off to the funeral home or the morgue.

A tour of a lifetime was a Donnie Chin-led tour of the I.D. because you only went once. You didn't want to go back. He took you to places where he had saved somebody's life or dressed a knife wound. He pointed to where Andrew Maderas hung himself and where the body fell when it was cut down. He told you to put your finger in the bullet hole on the wall that first went through some guy. He explained that blood on the wall came from a fight with some guy swinging a broken bottle. As you followed his flashlight beam, he showed how a guy fell head over heels down the flight of stairs and broke his neck right there at the bottom of the landing.

IDEC is tucked away in Canton Alley behind a heavily secured locked door. If you were among the privileged few who gained his confidence, the first thing you noticed as you walked in were several types of emergency kits that Donnie and the staff grabbed as they ran out the Center on their way to a call. Each kit was stocked with special equipment, depending on the type of call they got. Once they got the call, they instantly grabbed a kit and off they went. IDEC operated on a shoestring budget, depending on donations and contributions from the community. The Seattle Firefighters Union has contributed annually to IDEC because its members appreciated what Donnie and IDEC has done to help them do their jobs in the community. Donnie Chin may be the most dedicated hard-core individual I have ever known. He has taken the spirit of community service to its zenith, on call 24 hours a day, seven days a week.

Community Garden — From Bushes to Bok Choy

In 1975, as new housing units and the health clinic were under construction, the elderly voiced a need to be more physically active. The idea of building a garden in the International District designed specifically for the elderly gained lots of support. It was natural to look at the hillside property above Main Street. It was vacant and available.

Danny and Wilma Woo owned the hillside property. Danny was a descendent of one of the oldest Chinese families in Seattle. His grandfather, Woo Quan Bing, was associated with the Quong Tuck Company, one of the pioneer Chinese businesses in Seattle. Danny and his wife Wilma were successful in owning and operating several restaurants in the International District. Their New Chinatown Supper Club was a popular jazz club and dance hall in the mid-1950s during and after the Korean War. Later, they sold the New Chinatown and built the Quong Tuck Bar and Grill on South King Street. The "QT" soon became the hangout for local activists.

I approached Danny one day at his restaurant about using this property for a community garden. He listened intently, puffing on a pipe as I told him how much we wanted to build a vegetable garden for the elderly and how we wanted to acquire the land on a long-term lease. "How much you can afford?" he asked.

"Well, you know, Danny, we are a non-profit agency."

"And Bob, you know I'm a businessman."

"We could probably afford $1 a year." He almost choked on his pipe. Danny told me he'd have to think about that.

The next week, he called me in and agreed to donate the use of the land. He insisted, however, that a long-term lease was not an option. Danny didn't want to commit to a long term because the possibility existed that some developer might come along and offer huge sums of money for his property. He also wanted the flexibility because one day, he might have other ideas for the property. Luckily for us, that day never came. No such developer stepped forward or if one did, Danny never told us about it. After a few years, Inter*Im paid the Woo family the equivalent of their property taxes for rent. When Danny died, the garden was renamed the "Danny Woo International District Community Garden" in his honor.

To start the garden on the right foot, we called around to see who had the experience to help us. Those in the know recommended we hire Darlyn Rundberg, who started the city's much honored Community P-Patch Program. The Community P-Patch Program gave neighborhoods the opportunity to grow vegetable gardens on vacant city property. Darlyn jumped at the idea of working with the I.D. activists and residents to build a community garden. The first task was to clear Danny's hillside property, a jungle overgrown with blackberry vines, four-foot high weeds, and piles of trash that had built up over the years. It wasn't hard to recruit the young activists who showed their great energy in marching up and down the streets just a few years before. We harnessed those energies to good use. Our hardy crew of volunteers chopped and hacked away at weeds and overbrush with their trusty machetes.

As the hillside became cleared of the growth and trash, plans were drawn up so easy to read that even we, the Inter*Im staff, could follow the drawings and build the project from the ground up. Natch and Yosh Ohno from the Ohno Landscaping Company volunteered their time, equipment and labor to cut four terraces into the hillside. Darlyn set up meetings with officials of railroad companies who had mixed feelings about donating railroad ties to the community. We reminded them that Chinese and Japanese workers had played a major role in building the railroad system in the West, including Washington state. Eventually, we hustled more than 1,200 railroad ties from Burlington Northern.

Volunteer crews showed up for weekend marathon work parties while a small crew which included Denise Louie, Lorraine Sako, and I worked throughout the week. Lorraine was a landscape design student whose expertise was very helpful. With the growing season fast approaching, it became imperative to finish the garden. We recruited volunteers from social service agencies to work alongside the regular crews. On a typical Saturday, the hillside was filled with hard working, sweat-soaked bodies. I can't speak for the others, but for me, it always felt good to work up a sweat and get my hands dirty.

The Alaska Cannery Workers Association sent several crews to the garden work parties. I will always remember the sight of Gene Viernes, a farm boy from Wapato, running up and down the hillside with loads of heavy gravel, hardly taking a break, until the entire load was spread. I will always remember the sight of Silme Domingo backing down the narrow road to the staging area in his maroon Monte Carlo, stepping out on a rock, wearing his black Italian shoes, and directing truck traffic to the dump site while never working up a sweat.

Working like those chain gangs in the old movies, we dug four deep trenches in which we laid an intricate drainage system. Then, we meticulously installed an irrigation system. To shore up the garden, a crew of landscape architecture graduate students headed by Glenn Takagi from the University of Washington built the walls from railroad ties and utility poles.

We used the top terrace as the staging area where trucks backed down a makeshift road made of railroad ties, dumped their loads, and went off for another load. Work teams of four, male and female, picked up the ties, weighing as much as 200 pounds, and carried them downhill. Other dump trucks made regular trips with full loads of fertilizer dirt from the Longacres racetrack. When they dumped the dirt, work teams were ready with rakes and shovels to spread the fertilizer and topsoil. Other work teams constructed makeshift bridges, which allowed our sweaty group of volunteers to maneuver wheelbarrows, loaded with dirt or sand or gravel, out and back.

The first phase of the garden, resulting in 40 terraced garden plots, was completed in 1975 with a ribbon cutting ceremony and a pig roast. The second phase of the garden expansion began in 1980 with our request to the city Board of Parks Commissioners to use Kobe Terrace Park for the community garden. We were accompanied to a city Board of Parks Commissioners hearing by 30 elderly gardeners who came in support of our request. The Parks board was concerned that this transfer of parkland would start a dangerous precedent, allowing other communities to build gardens on park property in their neighborhoods. Prior to our request, the Community P-Patch Program had been limited to vacant city property. We testified that the community garden enhanced Kobe Park, and they agreed. The Commission granted us the use of land on the lower portion of Kobe Terrace Park and the expansion proceeded.

Funds for the expansion came from HUD's Neighborhood Self-Help Development Project Grant Program. The grant, prepared by Dan Rounds, included the entire history of the I.D. from the Great Seattle Fire in 1889 when the original Chinatown was destroyed to the construction of the first phase of the garden in 1975. The proposal was 160 pages, with a narrative, photos, and maps. On page 80 of this massive proposal, we inserted an envelope that read, "You are halfway through. Take a break on us," and inside the envelope was a tea bag. We had local and headquarters staff visit the site after we learned our proposal was the only non-housing application out of 700 submitted to be considered.

One key supporter was Gerry Johnson, a high ranking staff member in U.S. Senator Warren Magnuson's office. Gerry, legislative aide to Seattle City Councilman John Miller for many years, was well-acquainted with both Inter*Im and the I.D. Nothing was as impressive as calling Gerry for help when I was in Washington, D.C.. I had made the rounds lobbying with HUD staff for the garden expansion funds without much success, just curt denials to requests for meetings while in their offices. A call from Gerry of the "Chairman's Office" (Magnuson was chairman of the Appropriations Committee) would result in a meeting within the half-hour. Needless to say, we were awarded the grant funds plus a few thousand more because our funding application scored high enough to earn bonus points.

Unlike the first phase of the garden development when Inter*Im used only a part-time staff person, the second phase allowed us to hire a full-time construction crew headed by Ben Masaoka. I helped operate heavy equipment such as bulldozers and fork lifts. Dan Rounds, who had a degree in architecture, drew up the design. Once again, the call went out for volunteers. Six days a week, Monday through Saturday, young activists, older professionals, and elderly gardeners formed work crews who attacked the blackberry vines, dug trenches, and carried the railroad ties. The expansion of the garden took six months to complete and resulted in an additional 60 terraced garden plots. Once again, the ribbon-cutting ceremony was concluded with a pig roast and picnic.

The hillside flourished. The garden gave the land back to the old folks who left it in the old country to strike it rich here. They never realized just how much they missed the earth. The elderly residents who lived in the I.D. took an active role in developing and maintaining the garden. Cappy Capistrano was the in-house carpenter. Leo Lebree built the pig roast pit. Others built planter boxes and a cold frame, brought in their own composting material, and purchased seedlings and seeds for their own use. These gardeners meticulously cultivated their plots, yielding a bountiful crop of herbs and plants such as bok choy, shiso (beefsteak plant), garlic chives, chrysanthemum greens, scarlet runners (beans), minaly (watercress), mustard greens, and garlic.

One of the most involved was Jack Takayama. Jack was a familiar sight every day in the garden until he died at the age of 79 in 1981. Jack was one of the first tenants of the International Terrace when it opened in 1973. He had spent most of his adult life operating a farm, east of the Cascade Mountains, in the Yakima Valley. Jack was also known for his design and construction of scenic parks in Yakima (a city in central Washington). He generously shared his expertise, particularly in the redesign of Kobe Terrace Park, where he directed the planting of trees and shrubs around the four-ton stone lantern and the planting of trees in the expanded orchard area.

The four-ton stone lantern in Kobe Terrace Park was a gift from the mayor of Kobe, Japan, the sister city of Seattle. It had been originally hand-carved in 1916 and for years, stood in the "Garden of Seattle" in the Kobe Municipal Arboretum. In 1976, it was transported to Seattle and reassembled in Kobe Terrace Park by a delegation of 10 artisans from the Stoneworkers Guild of Japan. The accompanying tablet was engraved from granite found only in Japan and traditionally reserved for the Emperor. The inscription on the lantern reads, "May the Lantern shed light on the Friendship between the Peoples of Kobe and Seattle."

The garden provided the community with many benefits: nutritional, because the residents grew their own vegetables to eat; aesthetic, because the garden provided a green landscaped area with trees and walking paths; social, because residents and community volunteers could work together; economic, because the previously vacant lots were used in a productive manner; and political, because the garden was pointed to with pride by civic leaders and elected officials as an example of what can happen with strong community involvement.

Turning the Pig — The Annual Pig Roast

To celebrate the kickoff of the Danny Woo International District Community Garden, we roasted a pig. Actually, the pig roast had been an annual event at our family home in Rainier Valley, but after the celebration and the great reception we received in the community, we moved the annual pig roast to the garden. No one was happier than my wife Anita and our Rainier Valley neighbors. Pete Jamero and Tony Ishisaka, a college professor of social work and one of the founders of Asian Counseling and Referral Service, started the tradition — killing the pig and dressing it (gutting its intestines), using their *lechon* (Filipino pig roast) experiences growing up on farms in California's Central Valley.

The pig roast rules were simple. A big yard (or in this case extra garden space) was necessary to dig the pit wide and deep enough for a fire to barbecue a 140-pound pig. Logs or briquettes were placed in a circle along the edge of the pit. The pig was shaved, then fitted with a metal pipe which traveled from the pig's mouth through the body and out just below its tail. The pipe, with holes drilled through it, was lined up so a metal dowel could be placed through the holes to secure the pig. The pig was then wrapped with chicken wire and tied down with bailing wire. It was stuffed with onion, celery, lemon grass, and garlic, then sewed and placed on the metal pegs above the fire and turned slowly throughout the night. Teams of two or three people took shifts for the steady turning of the pig, periodically basting the sizzling porker with water. The pig was turned until it was tender.

The annual ritual of the pig roast served as a get-together time for the old and new activists. It also gave the elderly gardeners a chance to meet the people who built their beloved garden. The event normally started at 6 p.m. on a Friday night in July with the preparation of the pig. At midnight, as many as 40 to 50 people were there to enjoy the late night breakfast cooked by "His Honor" Doug Luna (so named because Doug, who was part Filipino and part Tlingit, is a tribal judge) during their shift as pig roast turners. At noon the following day, the cooked pig was butchered and served as part of a potluck for the gardeners, activists, and community supporters.

The first three pigs acquired for the roast were purchased live at a pig farm in Auburn. During the first two years, our crew, made up of Doralinn Jung, Tony Ishisaka, Dan Rounds, Frank Irigon, my son Danny, and I arrived at the farm at 7 a.m. on a Saturday. After we picked out the pig, the big bad adults cornered it so Danny could wrestle it to the ground. Then we hog-tied the pig's feet and laid it on the butcher table. Tony, a farm boy who grew up with Filipino migrant farm workers, learned how to kill the pig while saving the blood for *dinuguan*, a Filipino delicacy. Tony stuck the sharp knife into the center of the pig's throat and twisted his wrist in such a way that the knife sliced through the jugular vein. When done right, the kill took no more that seven or eight minutes. The porker was then shaved and readied for the steel pipe that was used as a rotator.

The third year Tony was unable to attend the ritual. Dan Rounds felt he could handle the responsibility of killing the pig. After the pig was hog-tied, Dan, dressed in yellow rain gear from head to toe, branded the sharp knives. He inserted the long blade into the pig's throat and did the quick twist of the wrist. Nothing happened, no blood squirted out, nothing. Dan withdrew the knife, then plunged it in again and twisted. Again, nothing. After about nine times of being stabbed, the pig, with its eyes bugging out, squealed. The farmer rushed over and wanted to know if we wanted him to shoot the critter. The last thrust did the trick and victory was ours. From then on, we decided to purchase our pigs all dressed-out from International District barbecue restaurants. It was a lot easier to buy the pig dressed-out. No muss, no fuss. Then all we needed to do was roast it in the garden barbecue pit.

Someone to Watch over Me — Denise Louie Day Care Center

One day, a five-year-old girl playing with matches started a fire in a room at the Milwaukee Hotel. Luckily, the fire was extinguished shortly after it was started. The little girl had been locked in her room by her single mother who worked in a garment factory. The next day, my staff assistant, Susie Chin, brought the child to the Inter*Im office because there was no place else in the District to watch over her. Several activists had previously mentioned the need for a childcare center for the I.D. This little girl was a living example of that need. There and then, the idea for the Inter*Im childcare center was born. We formed a task force, chaired by Inter*Im board member Denise Louie, to coordinate the planning effort. The task force found several potential sites, developed a budget and identified potential funding sources such as the federal Head Start Program.

Denise Louie was a young college student I first met when she worked as a part-time secretary receptionist for the Asian Multi-Media Center at the St. Peter Claver Center. She was just a high school student then, but Denise was wise beyond her years. Whenever we needed volunteers, we could count on her. Denise loved working in the Asian American community. People liked being around her. She was the type of person who reached out to others, expecting nothing in return. Denise cared when no one else did. Her concern for people didn't stop with those she knew. She even worried about the winos on the street. Her belief that Asians were beautiful people was unshakable. She got mad at Charlie Chan movies and wrote protest letters to television stations, telling them to present Asians as beautiful people rather than slant-eyed fools.

In 1977, Denise was killed in a crossfire during an ongoing gang war between the Wah Ching and the Joe Boys which erupted in the Golden Dragon restaurant in San Francisco's Chinatown. Denise was visiting San Francisco on Labor Day weekend when she, two friends from Seattle — Janis Imanishi and Wendy Suto — and Paul Wada, a law student from the

Bay Area, went to the restaurant for late night noodles. Three masked members of the Joe Boys, a Chinese gang, barged in and sprayed the restaurant with bullets from a revolver, a shotgun, and a semi-automatic rifle. One gunman went to the table where Denise and her friends were sitting and fired at Paul, mistakenly believing that Paul, who was unarmed, was pulling out a gun. Denise, Paul, and three other innocent bystanders died instantly. Janis and Wendy were among 11 others who were also shot, but survived.

After Denise died, we continued to work on the day care center project. We were determined to finish the project that was so dear to her. Funds were raised from a variety of foundations, government grants, and the community to open the day care center. A site was found in the annex of the old Chinese Baptist Church on 10th Avenue South and King Street.

One day, I brought the managers of the three local banks, United Savings and Loan, Seafirst National Bank, and Rainier Bank, to lunch. I requested their assistance to help raise $1,000 each for the purchase of needed furniture for the childcare center. Within two weeks, United Savings and Loan donated furniture and money. Gerry Yuasa, the manager of the District's Seafirst branch, called me to say their corporate offices downtown would handle the request.

The next day, a Seafirst Bank vice president called to ask me about the childcare center. He fired a series of questions in rapid succession: What is the total cost of the project? What was the 10-year projection of participants served? What was the 10-year projection of income? What was the source of the funding?

After 10 minutes of grilling, I stopped him and said, "Sir, we are only requesting a lousy $1,000, so why don't you just stick these questions up your ass. While we're at it, we'll withdraw the Inter*Im account...the parking lot account...and the health clinic account from your bank, and we'll see that every elderly resident in the community withdraws their savings account from your bank." I paused, then added, "Oh, yeah, then we'll picket and boycott your bank...daily." I then hung up the phone, wondering if I had screwed up.

Two days later, Norm Rice, a Rainier Bank corporate official and later mayor of Seattle, took me to lunch and handed me an envelope with a check for $1,500. "Hey Bob," he said. "Heard you had a little run in with Seafirst."

The next week, Gerry Yuasa called. "The funniest thing happened," he anounced. "Corporate headquarters decided I can make the decision here. So why don't you swing by and pick up a check?"

Whenever I think of Denise Louie, I remember her big, radiant smile. She made you feel good because she touched you with a warmth that doesn't leave easily. Yes, she died young. As she used to say to me, "It isn't the quantity, it's the quality." Denise's life had a hellava lot of quality. To honor her memory, we named the day care center the "Denise Louie Early Childhood Education Center." It was our way of saying, "Thanks, Denise."

Back to Basics — A Community Cultural Center

In 1973, the Seattle City Council, due to the perceived impact from the domed stadium, authorized $200,000 as seed money to develop an Asian cultural center in the International District. While there were many other established community groups, such as the Japanese American Citizens League, the Chong Wa Benevolent Association, and the Filipino Community of Seattle, these groups had not opposed the domed stadium. So, city officials looked to Inter*Im because we had raised the most issues.

As Inter*Im's director, I felt that any center in the District must have enough space for social service agencies as well as cultural activities, but $200,000 was far short of what was needed to build a community center. We negotiated with the city's Department of Community Development to increase the amount of the funding. In response, city officials kicked in an additional $185,000 for a total of $385,000. However, state law prohibited city officials from giving money directly to Inter*Im or any other I.D. group. On the other hand, state law permitted city officials to give money to a public corporation.

Being Our Own Developer — The Public Development Authority

In 1974, Norris Bacho, one of the original Kingdome protest organizers, had become a legislative aide for Seattle City Councilman Paul Kraabel. He called and kept bugging me to start a public corporation to develop our own low-income housing. I learned that a public corporation was a quasi-municipal non-profit corporation chartered by the city.

Perhaps the best way to describe a public corporation is that it is a formal partnership between the community and city government. In many ways, a public corporation was like any non-profit corporation because it was tax-exempt with a volunteer board of directors; but city officials had oversight control, appointed members, and audited the books. In other ways, a public corporation was like a government agency because it provided governmental services such as low-income housing and neighborhood preservation; but it was also community-based, answerable to a public constituency. A public corporation was also a convenient means by which the International District could tap into the city's resources such as block grants. After discussing this idea with the Inter*Im board, we realized that it made good sense to start our own public corporation.

Inter*Im organized a working group to draft language for the International District Preservation and Development Authority. This group included: Yale Lewis, an attorney with years of experience creating public authorities, having drafted the charters for the Seattle Indian Services Commission and the Pike Place Market Preservation and Development Authority; Ben Woo, president of the Inter*Im board and the chairman of the committee; Paul Woo, an International District property owner and the representative of the Chong Wa Benevolent Association; and Tomio Moriguchi, businessman and civic leader.

After the draft was completed, the committee held several meetings with community groups, including the Chinatown Chamber of Commerce; the International District Economic Association; the International Drop-In Center; and the residents. Changes were made and the final charter was submitted in the name of the "International District Preservation and Development Authority" to Mayor Wes Uhlman's office with a long list of signatures supporting the charter.

At the very same time, Paul Woo shared the draft charter with Ruby Chow and others from Chong Wa. Ruby was the King County council member who represented the International District, but never worked well with our diverse group of Asian American activists. A few days after we submitted our charter, another charter was submitted by Chong Wa in the name of the "Chinatown Preservation and Development Authority" to Mayor Uhlman, an exact word-for-word version of our charter, except for its title, along with a petition signed by restaurant workers, garment factory workers, shopkeepers, and members of Chong Wa.

The second PDA charter was a blatant attempt by Chong Wa to take credit for all of the hard work we had put into the original document. I believed Ruby Chow and her faction were concerned that the activists from Inter*Im, the International District Housing Alliance, and the International District Economic Association threatened her perceived control over Chinatown. From our perspective, she hadn't done enough to make her Chinatown a viable, thriving community. I'm sure she viewed us as a bunch of wild-eyed radicals up to no good. In reality, it was our intention to make the entire District, including the King Street core, a better place to live, do business and enjoy each other's cultures.

Mayor Wes Uhlman, not wanting to offend his good friend Ruby Chow, decided to merge the two charters and appointed a combination of individuals recommended by one side or the other. Even the title reflected the merger. In late September of 1975, the public corporation was finally named the Seattle Chinatown-International District Preservation and Development Authority (PDA). Well, the merger might have looked good to Uhlman as a political compromise, but it was a very bad idea.

The original board included Ben Woo, Roy Mar, Ted Choi, Tomio Moriguchi, Paul Woo, Howard Dong, Tak Kubota, and Jo Pepita Ignacio. In its early stages, the PDA was marked by dissension and distrust between the two competing factions. The animosity was so bad that the Chong Wa faction voted to remove two of our appointees, Tomio Moriguchi and banker James Young, from the PDA's executive committee. Very little was accomplished. One of our board members, Jo Pepita Ignacio, couldn't always be counted on to vote in favor of our position. She had a habit of voting the same way as the person she sat next to, whether it was a Chong Wa-backed board member or one of our board members. We had to make sure that our board members sat on either of Jo Pepita to get her vote.

We created the PDA to exercise community control over developing and maintaining low-income housing in the I.D., but all of our attention and energy were spent on political infighting instead. The Chong Wa members made no secret of their motives. They resented references to the area as the International District, preferring to call the area Chinatown. By this, they meant "Chinatown for Chinese only." While Chong Wa tried to take over the PDA, we were not intimidated. Eventually, when it was clear that there was no political support for their position, most of the Chong Wa members quietly resigned from the PDA board. Others left when their four-year terms expired.

The first order of business was to hire an executive director. We decided to hire McDonald

Sullivan. Sullivan came from the Ramada Inn Corporation with little, if any, background in dealing with such a diverse racial community as the I.D. He was accepted by the business community, but did little to gain credibility with the young activists.

Fortunately, Ben Woo agreed to be the first chair of the PDA board, providing the PDA with credibility among the delicate balance of players such as Executive Director Sullivan, the Chong Wa faction, the business community, and the activists. Later, in 1983, the PDA board lost confidence in McDonald Sullivan, and he resigned. Once again, Ben Woo was called upon, this time to serve as the executive director of the PDA, to restore credibility and order to the agency.

First Things First — The Bush Hotel

When the PDA was exploring sites for the community center, the Chong Wa faction insisted on a site which was owned by one of its members. The PDA commissioned feasibility studies, however, that identified the Bush Hotel as the best site. The decision to place the community center at the Bush Hotel struck the final blow to Chong Wa's attempt to control the PDA.

The Bush Hotel was owned by the Rainier Heat and Power Company. Established by William Chappell, the Rainier Heat and Power Company had been one of the largest property owners in the International District. Chappell had made his fortune as a successful prospector in the Alaska Gold Rush. Reportedly, he was one of the first men at the Klondike site when gold was discovered. In 1912, Chappell invested his fortune and established the Rainier Heat and Power Company as a family trust. He acquired a large section of land in and around the International District.

Among the properties which Chappell acquired were the Bush Hotel, the Publix Hotel, the Welcome Hotel (later the site of the local Bank of America branch), and the Dreamland Hotel (later the site of the local post office). These properties remained as the property of the Rainier Heat and Power Company long after Chappell's death in 1923. Chappell left specific instructions to dispose of all properties held by the trust. By the late 1970s, all of the properties were sold, the proceeds distributed to Chappell's heirs who were spread throughout the country, and the trust was dissolved. The Bush Hotel was one of the last properties which remained in the trust.

The Bush-Asia Center was the PDA's first big renovation project. Built in 1916, the Bush Hotel had been, during the early 1920s and 1930s, one of the largest railroad hotels in Chinatown. However, in the years following World War II, the Bush Hotel deteriorated from a "first class hotel" into a seedy, but comfortable home for transients and elderly. The PDA acquired the Bush Hotel from the Rainier Heat and Power Trust in 1978 through funding awarded under the federal Urban Development Action Grant Program (UDAG) with strong support from Sen. Warren Magnuson. The Urban Development Action Grant provided federal "seed money" for housing renovation and urban renewal projects to stimulate economic development and private investment in "distressed" or low-income communities.

The renovation took three years. I took an active role, serving as a member of the demolition crew, using a pickaxe to break up the old concrete floor in the basement of the Bush Hotel. However, there were construction delays and cost overruns which pushed back the date of completion. The PDA had to make additional funding requests to city officials who responded by granting community block grant funds to retire the PDA's liabilities. City officials tightened their oversight role by assigning Karen Gordon, a staff person with the Department of Community Development, to work with the PDA. Finally, the Bush-Asia Center opened in September 1981 with a ceremony which included top government leaders like Sen. Henry Jackson and Mayor Charles Royer.

The newly renovated Bush Hotel housed more than 200 low-income residents through a variety of rent subsidy programs. The three lower floors became the center for all kinds of agencies and programs. In the basement, called the park level, a mid-sized dining room with a commercial kitchen was built. Inter*Im's Food Buying Club, Inter*Im's Meal Voucher Program, and International Drop-In Center's lunch program were consolidated into one Congregate Meal Program with funding provided by the city's Division on Aging Nutrition Program. By 1985, the International District Elderly Congregate Meal Program was serving 35,000 lunches annually. We also added a home delivery component for shut-in residents which provided 10,000 meals annually.

A bakery and the International Drop-In Center, a hangout for Filipino seniors, moved into newly renovated space in other parts of the basement. Retail space was created on the street level, anchored by the Hanil restaurant. The second floor was divided into office space which housed Inter*Im, ACRS, Chinese Information & Service Center, and the PDA offices.

After we moved into the Bush Hotel, we continued making the building more accessible to the community and its elderly residents. One example was the rooftop garden project. When the hillside community garden was completed, there was a long list of gardeners signed up for plots, but only a few, if any, were from the Bush Hotel. John Foz, a veteran cannery union activist, had been hired as the community center coordinator, a liaison between PDA and the Bush residents. He suggested a rooftop garden for the Bush Hotel residents, some of whom had expressed an interest in having a garden. We developed a proposal for a rooftop garden.

However, there were issues raised by city officials about the structural integrity of the roof, which was more than 70 years old. There were questions whether it could support the added weight of a garden. We contacted Environmental Works, who sent a structural engineer to look at the roof. Based on the structural engineer's report, we revised our proposal. Instead of a traditional garden, our proposal called for all-weather cold frame planter boxes, a small greenhouse where plant sprouts could be nurtured then transferred to the planter boxes, and a wooden deck for drainage. Thanks to grant money from the Neighborhood Technology Coalition and the expertise of Environmental Works, we transformed the roof of the hotel into a greenhouse where tenants grew vegetables up the stairs from their rooms. Our greenhouse was the first of its kind in a low-income housing project in the city.

The New Central — The Short End of the Stick

In 1978, as work began on the renovation of the Bush Hotel, HUD designated the International District as a "Neighborhood Strategy Area" (NSA). This designation allowed HUD to prioritize the I.D. for government resources to develop elderly low-income housing programs. The PDA looked for projects in the District to develop housing. Building owners were contacted to determine their interest in developing their properties. One promising site was the New Central Hotel. Ironically, Ben Woo, the PDA's chair, had grown up in the New Central Hotel in the 1930s, where his family ran a laundry.

In 1979, the PDA acquired the New Central Hotel from the Nishimura family under a 49-year ground lease agreement. Under this arrangement, the Nishimura family owned the land, but leased the building to the PDA. Because of the length of this lease, the PDA was able to receive HUD funds under the Section Eight rent subsidy program to rehabilitate the New Central Hotel's top three floors for low-income elderly housing.

The Section Eight rent subsidy program gave incentives to private developers to build low-income housing because it provided a guaranteed source of income. Low-income residents paid rent based on a percentage of household income. HUD then subsidized the rent by paying the owners of Section Eight housing the difference between the actual rent paid by the low-income tenant and the fair market rent. The rent subsidy program gave low-income residents more choices for housing.

Unfortunately, HUD funds only covered a portion of the renovation of the New Central. Funding to complete the renovation was hard to come by. City officials wouldn't help. There was a group of New York investors who were willing to put up the funding in exchange for tax credits. These investors got a sweetheart deal. They put up $338,000 and got a $2,000,000 building plus the tax credits. They also got an off-site management fee that paid back their original investment.

Under the terms of the agreement, which our attorney, Jon Schorr, negotiated, the investors had 40 years to pay off the balance of the $2,000,000. Our attorney told us we had a good deal and charged us $200,000 for negotiating this deal. As it turned out, the investors had no intention of paying off the balance. When the 40-year period ended, the investors could just walk away from the agreement without paying. It was our attorney who brought the New York investors to the PDA. The money from the investors wasn't enough to pay for the renovation. The PDA had to borrow $700,000 to complete the renovation. We also fired our attorney.

After the renovation, the New Central Hotel was home to 28 low-income elderly. It also served as the temporary home to the Inter*Im staff during the renovation of the Bush-Asia Center. While the New Central project was underway, the PDA assisted in the renovation of and obtained a management contract for 17 units in the Jackson Apartments. These two projects added 45 units of low-income housing to the International District.

Keeping the Culture — The Bush-Asia Annex

In 1978, Bea Kiyohara, the long-time artistic director of Northwest Asian American Theatre (NWAAT), joined the PDA board and lobbied tirelessly for theater space. As the Bush Hotel was being renovated, the PDA acquired a large two-story garage on Seventh Avenue South and named it the Bush-Asia Annex. Plans were devised to convert the lower story of the garage into a theater. Like most PDA projects, funding to complete the renovation was hard to come by. In fact, for two years, there was no construction activity at all and the PDA carried the Bush-Asia Annex as a liability. The financial situation became so desperate that the PDA board considered operating a bingo game at the Annex to raise funds.

It wasn't until the Wing Luke Asian Museum, named for the first Chinese American Seattle city councilman who was tragically killed in a plane crash, became a tenant that the project could be marketed as a cultural center. The museum had been looking for more space. Its board decided to move from a small storefront on Eighth Avenue South and lease the upstairs of the renovated garage.

Discussions with Ron Sims (later a King County councilman and King County executive), legislative aide to state Senator George Fleming, and Joan Yoshitomi, legislative aide to state Senator Jim McDermott, led to a state legislative capital appropriations bill sponsored by senators Fleming, McDermott, and Phil Talmadge, granting the PDA construction money from the state bicentennial fund. State Representative Gary Locke, chair of the House Appropriations Committee (later Washington state governor), was instrumental in getting the legislative bill through the state House of Representatives. Strong letter writing campaigns were conducted by museum and theater supporters. Governor Booth Gardner signed the $200,000 appropriations bill in June of 1985.

The Bush-Asia Center was the only minority cultural preservation project given funding as the state celebrated its 100th birthday. At the same time, financial support came from the City Council, thanks to Dolores Sibonga and Paul Kraabel, in the form of a $40,000 weatherization grant to complete the exterior and to connect the electrical wiring. I can't say enough how nice it was to have friends in high places.

The popular Wing Luke Asian Museum became the showcase for many Asian American artists. Later, with Ron Chew as the executive director, the museum expanded to become what I believe is the premier Asian American museum in the country. It expanded not only as a museum, but an audio/visual center for a wide range of historical collections and cultural exhibits on our Asian American experience.

Acting Up — Northwest Asian American Theatre

The second tenant for the Bush-Asia Annex was the Northwest Asian American Theatre (NWAAT). For many years, NWAAT's productions took place on a rented stage at the renovated Nippon Kan Theater. Bea Kiyohara, artistic director of NWAAT, needed a home for the actors' group and theater space for its productions. The Bush-Asia Annex proved to be the ideal spot. The completed theater, named "Theater Off Jackson," had the capacity to seat 150 people, with every seat having a good view of the stage. In January 1987, the new theater opened with the premiere of "Miss Minidoka," a musical written by long-time community activist/writer Gary Iwamoto, about a beauty contest held in a Japanese American internment camp. The musical was a hit, the theater was a hit, and NWAAT took off.

The success of Gary's play got me involved with NWAAT. At the time, I lived in the District at the Freedman Building. I spent a lot of time at the theater which was just down the block on Seventh Avenue South, and got to know Kathy Hsieh and Manuel Cawaling, two of NWAAT's very committed staff members. Many of NWAAT's regular troupe of actors — Stan Asis, Maria Batayola, Ken Mochizuki, and Tama Tokuda were also community activists I had known outside of the stage.

When I was growing up, I used to dance the tinikling, an old Filipino folk dance using long bamboo poles, with other Filipino kids in the local nightclubs. It was a kick to be on stage, a feeling I never forgot. Years later, NWAAT provided me with the first opportunity as an adult to perform on stage. NWAAT produced the Holiday Community Show-Off as its annual fund raiser. The Showoff allowed members of the community, with or without talent, an excuse to perform on stage.

One of the headline acts for the Showoff was the Gang of Four — Bernie Whitebear, Roberto Maestas, Larry Gossett, and yours truly, Bob Santos. Even though the four of us were hams at heart, Bernie always stole the show. While we all thought we were knockout performers, Bernie was really the only one who actually had talent, the best singer and dancer of the four of us. He was a master of timing, with an uncanny knack of hitting the punch lines.

Each year, we met beforehand at the Quong Tuck restaurant where we tossed ideas for our act. We had Gary Iwamoto write a skit and made time to rehearse for the fund raiser. One year, we played Seattle City Council members in a committee meeting. The next year, we sang and danced to "Heard It Through the Grapevine." We played the Pips while Annie Galorosa lip-synched Gladys Knight. Another time, we dressed up like *mariachis* (Mexican troubadours) with guitars like the "Three Amigos." Once, I dressed up as a woman with a fright wig in a parody of the "Dating Game" with the others as the "eligible bachelors." Another year, we played kids at a day care center.

I was flattered when asked to join the NWAAT board. Every board member was asked to volunteer in some role with the theater. Some assisted with mailings; others took tickets during productions or sold coffee and cookies during intermission; but I took the job as "Supreme Commander of Janitorial Services." Twice a week, I got to clean the four restrooms. Starting with Miss Minidoka, I warmed up the audience prior to each NWAAT production. I welcomed the audience, told a few jokes, and plugged the refreshments. Let's face it, I was a frustrated actor who loved being on stage, but couldn't memorize lines. Doing the warm-ups before shows gave me the confidence to be more willing to emcee community dinners and other large gatherings.

At about the same time, community groups, schools, and universities called me to give speeches about the International District from the Kingdome demonstrations to its economic development. I developed a before-and-after slide show of the International District, which I updated several times a year, to illustrate my lectures. Knowing how trying it was to keep audiences awake during a slide show featuring old buildings, I decided to spice up the presentations with anecdotes and personal stories growing up and working in the neighborhood. The more I spoke, the better I got, and the lectures became informative, fun, and very entertaining. The more lectures I gave, the more material I had.

Finally, in 1994, I incorporated these lectures into a script and developed what became my one-man show, "Uncle Bob's Neighborhood." Gary Iwamoto wrote an outline for me to follow and Bea Kiyohara gave me directions where I should stand on stage. "Hit your marks,

Uncle Bob," she'd say. The sound of people clapping was addictive. There's nothing more satisfying than audience appreciation. I was a little nervous performing lectures that people were now paying to enjoy, but since I really relished the chance to perform on stage, no one had to push me into the spotlight. I enjoyed being on stage.

"Uncle Bob's Neighborhood" was produced by NWAAT with the proceeds shared with other non-profit agencies in the International District. The shows drew enough interest to make a tidy little profit with several standing room only audiences. These presentations served not only as an educational tool, but as a history of the struggle of people to survive racism and later, development pressures from the encroachment of sports stadiums, freeways, transportation centers, and an ongoing building boom that continues today.

The Best Causes Are the Lost Causes — The Milwaukee Hotel

In early September of 1977, Donnie Chin rushed into the Inter*Im office and told us Municipal Court Judge Barbara Yanick had ordered the closure of the Milwaukee Hotel on Seventh Avenue South and King Street. Judge Yanick cited 60 ongoing fire code violations which had not been addressed, six of which posed serious life-threatening dangers. The fire department had filed a complaint against the hotel's owners, who had refused to pay for repairs to bring the building into compliance with the fire code. Acting on the complaint, Judge Yanick also called for the removal of the hotel's tenants within seven days.

The Milwaukee Hotel, built in 1911, and one of the first buildings in Seattle to be constructed by a Chinese person, was designed to suit the style and specifications of Goon Dip, one of the wealthiest merchants in Seattle. He had constructed the first buildings in the King Street core after the Jackson Street Regrade. Until the time of his death in 1933, the hotel's entire third floor was occupied exclusively by Goon Dip, his family, bodyguard, and servants. Furnishings were made of carved teak and ebony, in-laid with mother-of-pearl. Exquisite silk, cloisonné, and porcelain were found throughout the building. The entrance to the hotel still bears his name.

The owners had taken possession of the Milwaukee Hotel in 1965. At that time, the Milwaukee was still in relatively good condition. However, by the time of Judge Yanick's order, only 50 of 145 rooms were habitable and occupied. The fire department noted that it took about 10 years for a building without maintenance or repairs to get in as bad condition as the Milwaukee Hotel.

The owners said they had spent far too much money to bring the building up to code and were not going to contest the hotel's closure. We knew better because the tenants told us. The hotel fell into a state of squalor because the owners did not pay for simple repairs. For example, when a tenant complained about plumbing to the hotel manager, he moved the complaining tenant to another room where the plumbing worked instead of fixing it. A few months before we took over the management of the building, there was a fire in the back stairwell leading from the alley. The owners received a fairly substantial insurance settlement, but very little of the proceeds went back into the building.

Inter*Im, the International District Housing Alliance, and IDEC organized the Milwaukee tenants to fight the closure. Attorneys Tony Lee, Diane Wong, and Rod Kawakami represented our grassroots group and asked Judge Yanick to reconsider her order to close the hotel. The fire department drew up a list of critical violations which needed to be addressed immediately before the department could even consider supporting our request to rescind the order. These violations included defective plumbing and sanitation, inadequate building security and maintenance, defective electrical wiring, broken windows, defective heating equipment, and inadequate door locks.

We called volunteers to help us keep the hotel open. More than 180 friends, activists and community workers responded to our call for help. We worked diligently at the hotel through the next 72 hours to clean and make repairs. As we went from floor to floor, room to room, an army of cockroaches, fleas, and spiders of varying shapes, colors, and sizes scurried away in retreat. The stench was so bad we had to cover our noses and mouths with surgical masks to breathe. There were rooms so deteriorated there was nothing we could do. We simply marked the doors with a taped "X" and went on to the next room.

Impressed with our effort; the fire department petitioned the judge to extend the order for another week. During that week, volunteers and tenants hauled away more than 20 tons of trash in health department trucks (courtesy of Health Inspector Perry Lee), built fire walls, installed new electric wires, made $8,000 worth of repairs, put up exit signs, and relocated tenants to other rooms while theirs were being repaired. Inter*Im and the Housing Alliance took over the management of the Milwaukee.

The fire department urged Judge Yanick to allow the hotel to remain open. Fire department officials wrote a letter in support of our efforts. They wrote, "the Fire Department applauds the International District Improvement Association (Inter*Im) and the International District Housing Alliance for their superior effort at what had to be a most impossible task. In a period of eight days, they were able to complete the requirements which (included) the removal of 20 tons of debris. We believe that the owner, who was ultimately responsible, has benefited considerably, although he has not helped in any way."

Judge Yanick lifted the order to the cheers of the volunteers who showed up that morning in her court. She thanked the group and asked us to extend the 24-hour fire watch until a fire alarm system was installed. The fire watch lasted for a year and a half. The activists stayed in the building and walked through the hotel, provided fire protection and personal security seven days a week, 24 hours a day for 18 months to make sure the residents, mostly elderly Chinese and Caucasians, lived in a safe environment.

Many work parties of professional tradesmen and volunteers were formed. For example, Tyree Scott, an electrician, installed and upgraded all the electrical work to bring the building up to code. Volunteers brought tools from home, but some tools disappeared into the rooms of tenants. Steve Lock built a toolbox that measured 4'x4'x4'. The trouble was, some workers couldn't bend over far enough to retrieve tools at the bottom of the toolbox. Oh, well. At least the tools were safe.

Fire watch volunteers took two- to four-hour shifts, staffed the hotel office, made periodic rounds through the dark creaky halls to check for hints of smoke and fire, checked on tenants for medical assistance, repaired leaky roofs, changed and fixed lights, scraped walls, and painted rooms. The prospect of spending two to four hours (depending on who followed you on shift) doing fire watch duty at the Milwaukee Hotel was a lonely chore at 6 a.m., my assigned time slot. I discovered a large red journal that was virtually untouched. I began to write down some personal comments about the hotel, the I.D., politics, whatever came into my mind, in what became known as the Milwaukee Hotel Journal.

In the late night and early morning hours, fire watch volunteers listened to the radio, snacked, played mah jong or wrote thoughts in the journal, often responding to other entries in the old red book. I had no idea that anyone else would write entries, but the idea took off and the journal became a forum for creative writing and gross story telling. A core group of fire watch volunteers emerged from Inter*Im staff Dan Rounds, Doralinn Jung, and myself; International District Housing Alliance staff Andy Mizuki and Rick Furukawa; International District Emergency Center volunteers Donnie Chin, Dicky Mar, Tim Otani, Gary Iwamoto, Susie Chin, and Mark Della; ACWA leaders Silme Domingo and Gene Viernes; the *International Examiner's* Ron Chew and Steve Goon; and others like Dale Borgeson and Cissy Asis. But the champion of all fire watchers was Maxine Chan, who not only walked the halls, but looked through the keyholes, too. The best way to describe Max is to picture Mae West as a Chinese American. Maxine didn't just walk, she sashayed. She was colorful and earthy (meaning she swore a lot). Maxine entered these remarks in the fire watch journal:

"3rd floor — everything was okay. 4th floor — Mr. Ennis' room unlocked, roaches surrounded his cheeseburger; Mr. Lister's room unlocked, looks like he was sleeping with Betty from third floor; everything else was okay."

One morning, a father of two small children who lived in the Milwaukee Hotel anxiously met the Inter*Im staff at the office as we opened the doors for the day. He said, "You better come to the hotel right away. Mr. Maderas is sick and maybe die."

As I rushed to the hotel, I stopped at the health center and yelled at Edna Arias, a nurse, to follow me to the hotel because Maderas was having a problem. When we climbed to the third floor, Donnie Chin and Tim Otani were already there. As we rounded the corner at the top of the stairs, there was Mr. Maderas, sort of blue, hanging from a rope secured from a water pipe that ran the length of the hallway 10 feet above the hall floor.

Donnie and Tim stood a few feet away from Maderas. Tim's face was turning green. Donnie urged Tim to snap a photo. Tim answered, "Hell no. Do it yourself." I suggested to Edna to feel for his pulse. Edna shot back, "I'm not getting my fingerprints on him. They'll think I killed him." Donnie said, "I guess Maderas won't be hanging around the Milwaukee anymore." This was a tragic situation, but we all cracked up.

One afternoon, I received a visit to my Inter*Im office by an agent from the Federal Bureau of Investigation. He looked like any fresh, clean, athletic type college graduate. I wanted him to know I was intrigued in his line of work in what could have been an exciting, movie-like career. I asked, "What kind of interesting cases have you been assigned to, sir?"

"The bureau pulled me off refrigerator-smuggling duty up near the border," he answered. I didn't pursue this. "I was called to investigate the theft of social security checks by the former manager of the Milwaukee Hotel," he continued. "Do you have any idea where we could find him?"

"No, sir," I answered. "He never left a forwarding address." I felt bad I couldn't come up with a lead for him to follow.

Eventually, problems developed in the building's heating plant, the electrical system, and plumbing. Without legal title to the Milwaukee under a long-term lease or sale, it became impossible to receive grants from public and private resources for a complete renovation. After many months of negotiations, the PDA offered to purchase the Milwaukee from its owners for $325,000 on a long-term contract that gave the owners yearly "tax free" interest of six to eight percent of the purchase price. We gave the owners a golden opportunity to sell the property, make some money, and keep the hotel open. But the owners rejected our offer. We had no choice but to end the fire watch.

The fight to save the Milwaukee Hotel was a cause that symbolized our efforts to preserve the International District as a place to live. We were too late to save many of the hotels which had closed because of housing and fire code violations, but at least with the Milwaukee Hotel, we tried to keep it open. Ultimately, it was a lost cause. The owners had other ideas for the building, but whatever ideas they had weren't shared with us. However, a decade later, the FBI and the Seattle police department closed portions of the building where illegal mini-gambling casinos were discovered. When the Milwaukee closed its doors in 1978, the 35 remaining residents were displaced from their homes. We found other places for them to live. The closure brought the total number of hotels and apartment buildings in the International District which closed since the mid-1960s to 30.

Two Plans for a Jail in the I.D. — Do Not Pass Go

The Immigration and Naturalization Service (INS) building is a large one-block building located on Airport Way, just south of the International District. For years, the old brick building served as the processing center for newly arriving immigrants. Any immigrant who had to get a "green card" (signifying permanent resident status) was well-acquainted with the building.

In the late 1970s and early 1980s, two different government agencies had similar ideas for the future use of the INS building. The first proposal came in 1979 from King County Executive John Spellman, who proposed conversion of the INS building into an 85-bed work release center with potential expansion to 300 beds. We protested the county's proposal. No neighborhood wanted a work release facility in its backyard. The International District was no exception. With the King County Jail less than a mile north from the International District, placing a county work release facility at the INS building just south of the District would have put jails on both ends of the I.D.

When we first learned of this proposal, county officials had already undertaken months of planning. County officials had originally decided that an environmental assessment was not required. Since the INS building space had been used for detention of illegal aliens, the county determined that its use of the INS building as a work release facility was not a "change in use."

At this point, Seattle city officials responded to the outcry from the International District property owners, shopkeepers, social service agencies, residents, and local elected officials, including King County Council member Ruby Chow, by determining that the county plan was a "change of use" requiring City Council approval. After several months of maneuvering for its case to use the INS building as a work release center, county officials backed off because the pressure from the International District community and Seattle city officials was too great. County officials, instead, found an alternative downtown site for its work release program at the expanded King County Jail.

A second plan for the INS building emerged in 1980. The Justice Department, faced with the prospect of the closure of its federal prison at McNeil Island (off the shores of south Puget Sound) looked at the INS building to house its minimum security prisoners. The initial plan called for the renovation of the top floor of the INS building. Under the Justice Department's plan, the building would have accommodated 200 minimum security prisoners and prisoners awaiting trial. The International District community joined forces with the mayor's office and King County officials (who had seen the light), applied pressure against the plan, and the Justice Department backed off.

Years later, in 1993, the I.D. received word that the U. S. Department of Corrections was looking to build a new federal prison to house 500 prisoners just south of the District's boundaries at Eighth Avenue South and South Charles Street on property owned by the city engineering department. The feds wanted a prison close to the federal courthouse at Fifth Avenue South and Madison Street, only five minutes away by I-5. When the feds started negotiations with Seattle city officials to acquire the property, the International District mobilized quickly to voice its opposition to the prison. We were concerned that the proposed prison would have been only one block away from the proposed Village Square site. We didn't believe that a prison, elderly housing, retail stores, and a childcare center were a good mix.

The International District's two community newspapers, the *International Examiner* and the *Northwest Asian Weekly*, carried the story and published editorials in opposition to the prison. When federal corrections officials visited Seattle, representatives from several community groups voiced their loud collective opposition. During one community meeting at the Wing Luke Asian Museum, one federal official noted that the prison would create jobs for the community. "Oh yes," I retorted. "You would hire five-foot, two-inch tall, 120-pound Asian guards and Asian cooks to serve hum bows to the 500 prisoners." Seattle Mayor Norm Rice finally stepped in and declared that the property was not for sale. No sale, no prison. This was one of the quicker victories for the community. The campaign to defeat the prison only took five months.

Union Station — Derailing a Transportation Center

Union Station was a classic railroad station, a large majestic cavernous building. In its heyday, Union Station was a bustling transportation hub where hundreds of passengers boarded and got off trains from such railroad lines as the Union Pacific, the Northern Pacific, and Burlington Northern. Railroad traffic became so heavy that a second train station, the King Street Station, was built across the street from Union Station. After air travel replaced railroads as the preferred means of interstate travel, the trains cut back on passenger service. By the late 1960s, there was no longer a need for two railroad stations. Railroad traffic was eventually consolidated at King Street Station. Union Station became an empty shell.

During the 1970s, a couple of proposals floated around the community concerning the use of the vacant Union Station property at Fifth Avenue South and Jackson Street as an "intermodal transportation center." The "intermodal transportation center" was a fancy term for a transportation hub, in a centralized location, where buses and trains dropped off travelers for pick up by cars and taxis lined up for blocks. In 1975, plans by Port of Seattle officials to convert Union Station into a transportation center were dropped because the Port wasn't given the assurance by the federal government that 15 to 20 million dollars in federal funds would be available for the conversion.

In 1978, Inter*Im learned that Port of Seattle officials were again considering a proposal to convert Union Station into a transportation center. Inter*Im staff — Dan Rounds, Elaine (Ikoma) Ko, Shari Woo, and I — went to a Port Commission meeting where we had heard a vote was to be taken on funding a feasibility study. We had heard that the transportation center facility had already identified prospective tenants such as Greyhound, Continental Trailways, the Airporter (Airport Shuttle), Amtrak, and Metro.

At the Commission meeting, Chairman Paul Friedlander said, "This is a good idea because nothing ever happens in that part of the city anyway and no one would be impacted."

I jumped to my feet. "What do you mean, 'No one would be impacted?'" I yelled. "Why, just yesterday, we heard that if your plans go through, the owners of the Downtowner Apartments want to convert their building to a first class hotel to cater to travelers coming out of Union Station." I wasn't bluffing or exaggerating. The owners, Howard and Martin Seelig (not the Martin Selig who developed the 76-story Columbia Center in downtown Seattle) had met with me to push their proposal.

"Those low-income people don't spend money like the people who will be coming from out of town," Friedlander replied.

"You mean you would displace 200 low-income residents out of their homes to cater to out-of-town visitors." I was livid.

This short debate ended when Richard D. Ford, executive director of the Port of Seattle, stated, "This is only a study that will look into the feasibility of such a project."

"A $250,000 study looks like an investment to me," I shouted back as we stormed out. "We will fight this. You haven't heard the last of us." (I think this line came from an old Henry Fonda movie.)

For the next six months, Inter*Im developed a battle plan that was very well thought out, researched, and implemented. We wanted to show that increased vehicular traffic caused extreme difficulty for the elderly residents in the neighborhood. We developed charts that showed more than 200 Metro buses would travel daily through the I.D. We researched air and noise pollution levels and made the case that the cumulative effect of having so many buses was detrimental to the health of our elderly residents. We came up with figures that showed a net loss of parking would have a negative impact on I.D. businesses. The Port assigned Art Yoshioka to win the community over. Everywhere he went, I followed. He presented their charts showing the benefits, I presented our charts showing the impacts.

The Port contracted with a consultant group headed by former Mayor Wes Uhlman with his partner, Dan Dingfield, doing most of the research to prepare the proposal for the $250,000 planning grant. Dingfield called one day to set up a meeting with me before his trip to Washington, D.C. to meet with Department of Transportation officials. I told him the only time and place I'd meet him was at the Milwaukee Hotel during my 6 a.m. fire watch shift.

Dingfield showed up acting like he'd been in these kinds of hotels all his life, but I knew better. I made him walk with me on my rounds through the building. I noticed he walked in the middle of the hallways, careful not to touch the walls, and he talked real fast. One of the things he offered was a consultant contract for Inter*Im, which he insisted was financially beneficial for the agency. "Wow," I thought, "is this a bribe or what?" Well, it didn't matter because I told him the bottom line was still the same: we would not support the planning study.

A week later, I received a call from Mayor Charles Royer, who had succeeded Uhlman. As I walked into the mayor's office, Royer was on the phone. He waved me to a chair in front of a coffee table with a fifth of Jack Daniels next to an ice bucket and two glasses. He got off the phone. After pouring a couple of bourbons on the rocks, the mayor told me how much he wanted the planning grant. He wanted to know why we didn't support it. I gave him my well-practiced pitch about negative impacts, which didn't seem to impress him. The meeting ended and neither of us convinced the other to change his position. I believed I stayed until we finished the bottle.

We found out that as a condition of securing the Port's planning grant, each prospective tenant for the transportation center was required to contribute seed money. The city was also required to submit $25,000 as their share of the match. We knew city funds for the match had to come from its emergency account, requiring the city council's approval with at least five "yea" votes from the nine council members. That meant it also took only five "nay" votes to stop this project. We knew we had Dolores Sibonga's vote because she had been an Inter*Im board member before her election to the council. Three other council members, Paul Kraabel, Sam Smith, and John Miller, had always supported our work. We probably had two more votes, more than enough, to stop it. But we didn't need the votes. After six months of meetings, briefings, and city council hearings, we learned that Greyhound was pulling out of the controversial project. Victory was ours.

Eventually, a scaled down version of the transportation center was placed underground at the King Street Station, across the street from Union Station. The version that was built was really an extended bus terminal limited to Metro buses. In 1979, when Metro first proposed a south transfer terminal at Union Station as part of a new transit system, we raised concerns over increased traffic, pollution, and noise. Metro officials, to their credit, listened to our community's concerns.

Metro took its new transit system underground, a quasi-subway system, where the buses traveled to terminals under downtown streets, then reemerged outside the downtown areas to the surface streets. The Metro tunnel had a much less negative impact on the International District than the proposed intermodal transportation center because the buses entering the tunnel carried commuters who walked to their destinations. There was no increase in vehicular traffic, noise, or pollution.

In 1992, as the bus tunnel neared completion, International District representatives, led by the PDA and the International District Economic Association, negotiated with Metro staff members to use the bus tunnel lid for a community sponsored project. The idea of a farmers market was a popular idea. Filipino farmers were already selling their produce every Saturday off the back of pick-up trucks at the curbs next to Hing Hay Park at Maynard and King Street.

Metro gave its consent and the decision was made to open the International District Farmers Market. Contractors added water access and electric power to the covered portions of the lid along Fifth Avenue South. Several venders, such as Uwajimaya, were recruited to open produce stands and food booths. After struggling for two years, however, the market was closed. We could never get the Filipino farmers, who sold their produce at Hing Hay Park, to move to the lid. They kept making good profits by selling out their produce at the park every Saturday morning by noon.

A Garbage Burning Facility — Trash Talk

Sometimes, it seems that government agencies, whether city, county, or federal, look at the International District as a dumping ground. Need a downtown freeway? Tear out half of the International District; they won't mind, nobody lives there. Need a domed stadium for the sports fans? Stick it near the International District; it's accessible to downtown and the freeway. Need a prison for inmates? Build it near the International District; there are no families there. Need a central transportation center? Put it in the International District; it's where all the bus lines are.

These projects taught us to be vigilant. In the mid-1980s, Seattle city officials floated a proposal about using the vacant Washington Iron Works property, about four square blocks in area, just south of the International District, as a garbage burning facility. This facility would have burned 2,000 tons of garbage each day, releasing 10 tons of flying ash and 32 tons of garbage vapors into the air. Burning the garbage would have released tons of nitric oxide, sulfur oxide, hydrochloric acid, lead, mercury, and cadmium residue into the air we breathed. Potential risks to health would have included increased infant mortality, paralysis, neurological damage, weakening of the body's immune system, and destruction of white blood cells. After we learned of this proposal, we alerted the community, organized a protest to these plans, and told city officials we weren't going to allow their plans to go forward without a fight. Fortunately, the city's plans for a garbage burning facility went no further.

At left, my mom Virginia Santos with Sam, her firstborn son, 1933

This 1934 family photo of Virginia, Sammy, Sam (right), and I was the last one taken before my mom passed away

My great grandmother Caroline Gilbert (Grandma Gilbert) with my grandfather Cornelius Nicol (center back), Aunt Toni and Uncle Joe Adriatico, their daughter Adela, me, and Sam, 1939

Here I am with my first car, 1938

Shirley Obillo and I dance the *tinikling* while my cousin, Adela Adriatico, and Henry Gamido clap the bamboo poles, 1951

The Filipino Cavaliers basketball team: ball boy Michael Castillano. Kneeling from left: Albert Mendoza, Eddie Laigo, me, and Ray Cantil. Back row: Fred Cordova, Sal DelFierro, George Lagasca, Leo Mamon, Bob Murray, Jim Beltran, Bernie Cantil, Bill Mamon, and Domingo SanGabrial, 1950 — Wally Almanzor photo

Opposite page: Sockin' Sammy Santos, circa 1928, *Seattle Post-Intelligencer*

SAMMY SANTOS SCORES KAYO OVER PORTER IN THIRD ROUND

By JIMMY GREENE

Looks are oft times deceiving. For instance, in the second round of the Sammy Santos-Len Porter bout last night, it looked as though Porter was going to be able to make it a bad night for Sammy.

The colored boy with considerable advantage in reach, was holding Sammy off pretty well and Sammy was missing a heavy right by any distance from inches to miles.

But it was a different story in the third round when Sammy shortened up the right and caught Brother Porter square on the chops, dropping him for the nine count. Porter struggled to his feet only to stop another one with his jaw and this time he stayed down and out. They lugged Porter to his corner where he came to and to show that he was okay, he pranced around a bit after congratulating Santos. The prancing was too much and down he went again. He was quickly revived but there were no doubts in his mind that he had been hit and hit awfully hard.

Both boys showed plenty of skill and kept things about even in the opening round. They were throwing hard punches, many of which missed because the fellow at whom they were aimed ducked too quickly.

[illegible]r took the second by a [illegible] keeping Sammy off balance [illegible]is left, though toward the [illegible] the round Santos was work[illegible]de the colored boy's guard [illegible] home several stiff punch[illegible]. [illegible] end came with little [illegible] than one minute of fighting [illegible] the third.

[illegible] Colima, giving a good im[illegible] of a lunging football guard, [illegible] the decision from Lorenzo [illegible]on in the first half of the [illegible]le main event. Colima, who [illegible] as though he were muc[illegible] [illegible]nd, did some boxing in [illegible] [illegible] couple of rounds and there[illegible] [illegible]fter adopted a policy of lunge in [illegible]nd clinch.

Sisson, fighting flat footed, was [illegible]ontinually knocked off balance by [illegible]e lunges, and on several occas[illegible]ns went to the floor for no count. [illegible] no case were they clean knock[illegible] [illegible] Neither boxer showed any [illegible] much aggressiveness [illegible] at times their work was slovenly, causing caustic comments from the crowd. Twice the referee had to caution Colima for roughness.

David Wins Again

For about two minutes it looked as though Blas Romero would make good his boast that he could lick any Filipino in Imperial Valley. The Tijuana flash was credited with the statement earlier in the week and when he tangled with Young David he set out to make it good. Fast as chain lightning and packing plenty of wallop despite a seemingly frail body, Romero tore after the Filipino, smacking hard blows to the head which caused David's knees to bend.

David never once backed water but showed a willingness to slug it out with Romero. He caught the little Mexican over in a corner and cracked him down with a terrific hook, ending the bout one minute and 50 seconds after it started.

Tex Mills, the Texas sheriff, took the opener from Tiger Flowers. Mills should have knocked out the colored boy, having him in a bad way on several occasions but lacked the necessary skill to put him away. It was a good scrap for the opener.

Bobby Pacho, the idol of the valley, gets his first big test next week, taking on none other than Ignacio Fernandez, who fought for the world's featherweight championship only six months ago with Bat Battalino.

Bert Morse figures that Bobby has enough experience under his belt now to tackle the real tough ones and he certainly has picked a tough one in Fernandez.

The boxing fan who will m[illegible] that fight will never forgive [illegible]self. It ought to be a sell out.

Sammy Santos.

Sammy Santos, Filipino slugger, meets Johnny Casebeer in tonight's main event. The fights will be moved from the Auditorium to Will Maylon's new Model arena, 714½ Sprague avenue, upstairs over the Model cafe. It's the former Spokane Amateur Boxing club's quar-

My dad Sammy Santos and I, a private in the U.S. Marine Corps, on Christmas Day 1952 — photo courtesy of *Seattle Post-Intelligencer*

I joined the boxing team while serving in the Marine Corps and defeated Sgt. Evans for the Fifth Airforce Championship in Korea, 1954

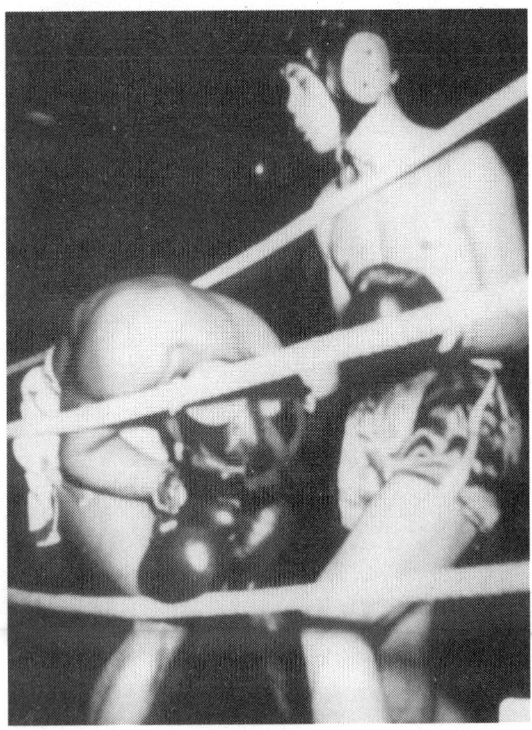

Above, the clan in 1964. First row: my brother Sam's children, Barry and Tracy, and my children Tom, Simone, Robin, and Danny. Second row: Sam, his son Tony, daughter Kim, my wife Anita, and I. Third row: my sister-in-law Mary holding her youngest son Brad, my cousin Pat Adriatico, Aunt Toni, and Uncle Valentine

Sammy with grandchildren Tom (center) and Simone, 1963

Above, community activists march to HUD in support of elderly low-income housing. From left: Angel Doniego, Sherrie Chinn, Susan Alfonzo, Reme Bacho, Norris Bacho, me, and Al Sugiyama, 1973 — Eugene Tagawa photo, courtesy of *Asian Family Affair*

A demonstration at King County Executive John Spellman's office over the county's lack of response to impacts from the Kingdome. From left: Dave Okimoto (standing), Jerry Shigaki, me (far right), Rhonda Gossett (front row), and others, 1973 — photo courtesy of Inter*Im

Tyree Scott, Todd Hawkins, and I are being arrested for trespassing during a demonstration for minority hiring at Seattle Central Community College, 1970 — photo courtesy of *The Seattle Times*

Below, my son Dan and I before our arrest for trespassing during an anti-apartheid demonstration at the South African consulate in Seattle, January 28, 1985 — Dean Wong photo

Above, International District Housing Alliance organizers meet with I.D. residents to report their success in stopping the proposed displacement of elderly Asian tenants from public housing. Standing from left: Edgar Silverio, Elaine (Ikoma) Ko, Sisi Asis, Rick Furukawa, Aurora Esteban, and Ken Mar. Seated at end of table: Shari Woo (left), the translator, and Al Masigat, circa 1979 — photo courtesy of *International Examiner*

Opposite page: (top photo) Anti-Marcos activists in Seattle occupy the Philippine consulate the day after President Ferdinand Marcos was overthrown. At left is a Philippine consulate spokesman, Joe Pascual, myself, Viquie Claravell, David Della, and Marlene Pedregosa, February 26, 1986 — Dean Wong photo

My first campaign for a seat in the Washington state Senate. Seated from left: Sonny Tangalin, Jeanette Tiffany, Mary Castillano, Angie Flores, Godfrey Agbalog, and Roy Flores. Standing: Dale Tiffany, me, and Tony Ogilvie, 1973 — Ted Bundy photo

right here on Philippine Airlines.
vote –

Above, a spring party welcoming Father Harvey McIntyre to his new parish at St. Edward's, circa late 1970s. From left: Pete Jamero, Father McIntyre, Teri Jamero, me, Walt Hubbard, and Diane Castillano — photo courtesy of Dale Tiffany

A barbecue for Congressman Mike Lowry's 1989 U.S. Senate campaign. From left: Evelyn Tangalin, Pete Jamero, Mike Lowry, Sonny Tangalin, Jeanette Tiffany, and Dale Tiffany — photo courtesy of Pete Jamero

International Examiner staff. First row (kneeling): Karen Chinn and Vicki Woo. Second row: Julie King, Kathryn Chinn, Sue Chin, Ron Chew, and Jesse Reyes. Third row: Melody Leo, Lorraine Sako, Michael Cervantes, Gary Iwamoto, Julia Laranang, Jeanette Aguilar, Debbie Murakami, Randy Okimoto, Georgene Kumasaka, Mark Mano, Gene Viernes, Tim Otani, and Anne Mori, December 1978 — photo courtesy of *International Examiner*

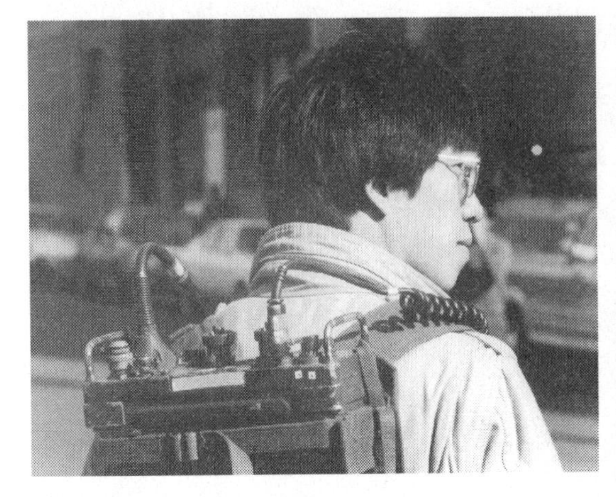

Clockwise from top left: Donnie Chin, director of the International District Emergency Center; Gene Viernes and Silme Domingo, slain Local 37 Union leaders — photos courtesy of *International Examiner*. World-renown oil painter, Seattle University art professor, and Bob Santos hero Val Laigo — Kamol Sudthayakorn photo

Above, a dinner honoring Asian American activists in Los Angeles: Jim Miyano (second from left), Al Mendoza, Tommy Chun, and I, 1975 — Royal Morales photo

Founders of the Minority Executive Directors Coalition of King County: Larry Gossett (second from left), Bernie Whitebear, Roberto Maestas, and myself, 1984

A Bush-Asia Annex capital fund raising event with Inter*Im board members Shigeko Uno and Tomio Moriguchi (right), 1979 — photo courtesy of Inter*Im

Planning the development of the International District Village Square, a comprehensive project involving elderly housing, assisted living units, social service office space, kitchen and dining areas, retail space, family housing, space for a city branch library, and a community center/hall. From left: George Patterson, Sue Taoka (center), and Wendy Watanabe, 1993 — Dean Wong photo

Above, one of my many walking tours of the International District with former Seattle Mayor Norm Rice (second from left) and Inter*Im Executive Director Ken Katahira, 1992 — Dean Wong photo

Longtime International District resident Joe Kitamura and I take a break from work in the Danny Woo International District Community Garden, 1993 — photo courtesy of Inter*Im

Above, the kitchen crew at the annual Mike Lowry Shrimp Feed. From left: Leland Allen, Nancy Santos, Cris Baruso (kneeling), Tim Burton, me, George Patterson, Sharon Tomiko Santos, Odette Polintan, Paolo Poydras (in back), Dan Santos, Denise Frank, and Ken Katahira, 1992 — photo courtesy of Jeff Berreca

Butchers Frank McGuire (center) and Scotty Galarosa (right) get ready to slice the *lechon* at the Inter*Im annual pig roast while I look on, 2000 — photo courtesy of Frank Kiuchi

Top photo: Friends Ben Laigo, Ed Laigo, Fred Maxie (second from right), and Gerry Laigo with me at my installation as Secretary's Representative to the Department of Housing and Urban Development, 1994. Bottom photo: A visit by HUD Secretary Henry Cisneros (in dark suit) to the Northwest Alaska Area Office, with Roberto Maestas (far right), Ricardo Sanchez, and myself, 1995 — photos courtesy of HUD

Sharon Tomiko and me, 2002. Below, my ever-growing family. First row: Maurizio Santos, Bobiono Santos Sims, and Marissa Busby. Second row: Macaria and Valencia Santos, Denise Roberson, and Thomas Santos. Third row: Nancy Santos, myself, Sharon Tomiko, Meagan and Melise Santos. Fourth row: Nancy V. Santos, Tiffany Roberson, Enrique, Niko, Marcianna, and Robin Santos. Fifth row: Dan, Chauncey, and Tom Santos, Brendan and Simone Busby, Shante and Nicole Roberson, and John Santos, 2002 — John Santos photos

CHAPTER FIVE

It's Just Politics

Three Campaigns Equal Zero

In 1970, Tony Baruso, a prominent leader in the Filipino community establishment, decided to run as a Democrat for state representative in the 37th legislative district of the Washington state legislature. Baruso worked at Boeing and was also involved in the leadership of Local 37, the Alaska Cannery Workers Union. Many younger Filipinos like Anthony Ogilvie, Andres "Sonny" Tangalin, Roy and Larry Flores, Dorothy and Fred Cordova, Pete Jamero, and myself, the so-called "Young Turks," flocked to his campaign. Baruso's campaign presented a chance to have Filipino American community representation at the state level. Door belling, fund raising, formulating political strategy, planning political events — partisan politics was a new exciting experience. Unfortunately, Baruso was little known outside of the Filipino community and lost. But my interest in politics was born.

In the spring of 1973, a staff aide in Governor Dan Evans' office in Olympia called to request I meet with state Republican party officials. The next day, I met with Michael Ross, a Black activist I had known from the UCWA demonstrations (and one of the few Black Republicans in Seattle), and Ross Davis from the state Republican party. They told me state Senator Bob Ridder, a Democrat, had resigned. There was going to be a special election in the 35th legislative district, the district I lived in, to fill his seat. They asked if I was interested in replacing him.

I always believed I could make a difference as an elected official. Everything I had accomplished generating the resources for social services, housing, and health care was a matter of combining persistence, successful lobbying, and a great local political network of activists.

There were strong assets I could bring to be a successful, effective office holder. I knew how to navigate the political system to get projects funded. I knew I was able to speak persuasively one-on-one or with a group promoting my issues. My role as an advocate for the International District had prepared me with the necessary experience to be a legislative representative. And I had that fantastic network of like-minded activists to advise me.

Many of those activists, by the way, have since gone on to forge successful careers in other arenas. Alan Sugiyama heads a very successful employment training agency and became a Seattle Public Schools board member. Peter Bacho became an award-winning author. Ruthann Kurose worked as a top aide to Congressman Mike Lowry. Doug Chin and Alan Kurimura worked for city agencies which funded our projects. Mayumi Tsutakawa wrote for *The Seattle Times.* Elaine (Ikoma) Ko headed the city's Office for Women's Rights. Sharon Maeda served as HUD's deputy assistant secretary for Public Affairs. Roy Flores and Bea Kiyohara served as community college administrators. Larry Gossett, Bernie Whitebear, and Roberto Maestas all headed successful social service agencies and were well-respected leaders in their minority communities. These were people I could count on.

A year earlier, I had expressed an interest in running as a Democrat for the seat held by John O'Brien in the state House of Representatives. O'Brien had been a good Democrat and served countless terms, but I believed he was out of touch with the minority communities. The state House office building was eventually named after him, an honor reserved for lifetime office holders. Every Democrat I knew wanted to talk me out of running against the venerable and likable O'Brien. The Democrats, it became clear, were not interested in supporting my bid.

So when the Republicans came calling, I said yes. It wasn't too difficult to be talked into running in the special election as a Republican. Governor Dan Evans, a Republican, stood out as a moderate leader who had earned a good reputation for including minorities on his staff. It was Governor Evans who appointed Asian Americans to his newly formed Governor's Asian American Advisory Council and had initiated similar advisory councils for Mexican Americans and Native Americans.

The 35th district was one of the strongest Democratic districts in the state. There didn't seem to be any concern by the Democrats that a Republican could ever win the seat. Located in southeast Seattle, the 35th legislative district included the Seward Park and Rainier Beach neighborhoods. At that time, the 35th was still predominantly White, although more minorities were beginning to live there.

The Republicans were really excited by the fact that a minority activist was willing to run in the largest ethnically diverse district in the state. Ralph Munro, who served later as Washington state's secretary of state for 20 years, was a top aide for Governor Evans. He sent out handwritten notes to other highly ranked Republican party officials to announce door belling sessions in our district. One weekend, a dozen staff and other elected officials from Olympia descended upon Rainier Valley. Among the dozen door bellers were state Senator Jack Metcalf, who later served as a congressman from the first congressional district, and state Attorney General Slade Gorton, who later served 30 years as a U.S. senator from Washington state. The delegation from Olympia plus two dozen volunteers from the community covered the entire district that weekend.

Ralph Munro proved to be the best campaigner I had ever seen, then and now. As volunteers walked into the campaign office, they were assigned a precinct and given a list and materials to deliver to homes of registered voters. Ralph came into the campaign office one Saturday and said, "Santos, I'm with you today." He picked up a pile of precinct addresses and a box of materials. "We'll be back an hour after sunset," he said. Hell, we didn't even eat lunch. He mentioned we should eat a late dinner, an hour after sunset.

The state Republican party was so enthusiastic about my chances of winning this race, they brought in Sen. Charles Percy of Illinois to promote our campaign. The only problem was that all the media who attended the press conference only had questions about the ongoing Watergate scandal in the other Washington and cared little for our local campaign.

More than a few of my friends called to voice their displeasure that I had even thought about running as a Republican. On top of the list was my Uncle Joe, a lifelong Democrat and unionist. Arlene Oki, a tireless advocate for civil rights, also expressed concern. My childhood buddy, Bob Maxie, verbally hit me up one side and down the other. But I still wanted to run.

The state Republican Central Committee assigned a young coordinator to kick off my campaign as my public affairs director. I had read previously that this guy had infiltrated the campaign staff of Governor Al Rosellini during his last campaign for re-election. He was a glib, well-dressed, polite young man with a lot of political savvy who was thinking of going to law school. He was going to make a name for himself in the world. Well, this guy went on to spend a lot of time in court and did make his name well-known to the world. His name was Ted Bundy. Bundy became infamous as one of the country's most notorious serial killers. He was linked to the murders of at least 22 young women, although the exact number of Bundy's victims may never be known. He never told. Ted Bundy was executed by the state of Florida on January 24, 1989.

There was only one time in my dealings with Ted Bundy that he acted out of the ordinary. When my campaign committee was planning to send out a letter announcing my candidacy, Bundy offered the use of the Washington Republican State Committee offices in the Horton Building for a committee mail out evening. After a long evening of letter drafting, printing, and stuffing, we were ready to leave for the main post office terminal. But first, Bundy moved from room to room collecting all the paper we used in a plastic garbage bag and cleaning each room to look like we had never been there. As it turned out, he did not have permission for us to use the office.

For most of the young campaign volunteers, this was their first political venture. There was no sophisticated polling and targeting in those days, so we did the unthinkable and door belled the whole district not once, but twice. I lost by only a few percentage points to Ruthe Ridder, Bob's wife, in a close election. It didn't help that these were the Watergate years of Richard Nixon. Running as a Republican was a serious case of bad timing.

I thought my chances were better the next year when the regular election cycle was held for the same seat and I campaigned this time as a Democrat. It didn't help. I lost again in the primary to Sen. Ruthe Ridder, now campaigning with a year of experience behind her. She ran unopposed in the general election and kept her senate seat. In hindsight, it probably wasn't a good idea to switch political parties so soon.

I lost the bug...temporarily. I didn't think about politics until 11 years later, when I decided to challenge Ruby Chow, a venerable Democrat, for her district seat on the King County Council. I felt I had a good chance of winning. I even resigned as the executive director of Inter*Im to devote full-time to the campaign, something I didn't do when I ran for the state legislature.

Soon after I announced, Ruby decided to step down. I was left to run against Democrats Cheryl Chow, Ruby's daughter; Ron Sims; and my old friend Michael Ross, the only Republican. I actually saw Michael running around with a Santos campaign T-shirt. Maybe he felt guilty about the Bundy thing — you go figure. Ron Sims went on to win the council seat and I have to admit, did a great job on the County Council. Cheryl went on to win a Seattle City Council seat a few years later, and I retired from elective politics with a perfect record, but not one to brag about.

I have to admit I ran my campaign managers ragged. Dale Tiffany, later director of the Seattle Department of Licensing, ran my second campaign. Dale was a long-time pal, married to Jeanette Castillano. Jan Kumasaka, a steady influence on the lives of many activists through the 1980s and 1990s, managed my last campaign. The final result was not her fault. However, she must have learned what not to do, because she ran a successful campaign and won election to the Seattle Public Schools board.

Be Like Mike — Working for Congressman Lowry

After my last campaign, which kept my unblemished record as a political candidate intact (three tries, three losses), Congressman Mike Lowry offered me a job in his local district office. Mike represented Washington state's Seventh Congressional District in the United States Congress. He was our local congressman and future Washington state governor. Mike had developed a reputation as a progressive, innovative leader who stood up for equal rights, workers, the elderly, and the poor. It was a great assignment working for one of the great congressmen of our time.

I was assigned to Asian American, Native American, Mexican American, and Central American issues. In 1986, Mike received a call from the Seattle Committee in Solidarity with the People of El Salvador (CISPES), an advocacy group with ties to human rights groups and religious organizations in El Salvador. CISPES wanted Mike to fly to El Salvador to negotiate the release of eight Salvadorian human rights officials, six men and two women, who had been arrested late at night from their homes and sent to prison for "consorting with left-wing insurgents." Mike was busy with budget negotiations, so he sent me in his place.

Since Mike was one of the ranking members on the Congressional Budget Committee, I had a certain amount of clout as a staff member. Our three-member delegation was led by Karen Parker, an attorney and expert on international and human rights law. She was asked by the United Nations International Federation of Human Rights Organizations to investigate a series of recent arrests by Salvadorian military. The other person was Kay Hubbard, a professor of international studies at the University of Washington who represented CISPES.

We flew to El Salvador. Soon, we were in a taxi, cruising at 60 mph down the highway from the airport to San Salvador, the capital. In the mid morning heat, we saw the campesinos swinging their machetes in the fields. After traveling about 10 miles, a taxi driver coming from the direction of San Salvador waved out the window and we slowed to a stop. He yelled something in Spanish. Karen Parker translated that there was hostile action off the highway less than a mile ahead of us. So we just sat there and waited while traffic backed up behind us.

After about four minutes, a helicopter gun ship swooped down from the hill to our left and flew over the highway into the valley. Shortly, two military vehicles loaded with troops, rifles trained outwards, drove by and waved us on. As we led the procession down the highway, we saw puffs of black smoke rising from the tree lined hills. I thought to myself, "This is a real war. Did I pay my life insurance premiums? Did both sides know why we were here?" As it turned out, this was the closest we came to any action for the rest of our trip.

We met with Edwin G. Corr, the U.S. ambassador to El Salvador. He justified American support of the Salvadorian government. It was his view that the "left wing" included not only the rebel army, but the wide range of human rights agencies that sympathized with the rebels. I mentioned to the ambassador that Congress, especially the budget committee, was watching the developments in that country and would not allow human rights abuses to continue.

During the week we were there, we met with the Salvadorian Army leadership. They told us they were fighting to keep the country out of communist hands and needed continued U.S. support to fund the military. We also met with human rights officials who blamed the Salvadorian government, the military, and its secret right wing death squads for atrocities resulting in thousands of missing Salvadorians. Finally, we visited the men's and women's prisons and spoke with the jailed human rights workers, all of whom said they were not part of any leftist group trying to overthrow the government.

After we returned to the United States, I reported our findings to Mike. Several weeks later, all the prisoners were released. We found out later that two of those released were reported missing and one had fled to Nicaragua with her family. The fate of the other former prisoners was not known at the time. The three of us — Karen, Kay, and I — feared that any opponent to the U.S. supported Salvadorian government, whether leftist or moderate, might be dealt with harshly and swiftly, ending up in the so-called category of "missing."

I made it a point to pick Mike up from Sea-Tac Airport upon his arrival on the red eye flight from Washington, D.C. and drive him back to the airport on his return trip. It was important for me to spend the drive time briefing him on the issues I thought he needed to know. It was also a chore no one else wanted because the red eye came and went so late at night.

In the late1970s, during his first term in Congress, Mike introduced the first Japanese American redress bill. During World War II, approximately 120,000 Japanese Americans and permanent resident aliens of Japanese ancestry were interned, relocated or evacuated from their homes in the United States because of their race — including my Japanese American classmates from Maryknoll. The idea of a redress bill started with a few progressive members of the Seattle Chapter of the Japanese American Citizens League. Henry Miyatake and Cherry Kinoshita, in particular, were involved from beginning to end. Ruthann Kurose was hired on Mike's original Congressional staff and was responsible for keeping the issue on course in the halls of Congress.

Mike's redress bill called for direct payments of $15,000 plus $15 per day to each Japanese American who had been sent to internment camps during World War II. His bill wasn't popular. Many Republicans and southern Democrats were against it. A compromise bill which called for a commission to study the World War II internment of Japanese Americans passed instead.

In 1981, the Commission on Wartime Relocation and Internment of Civilians held 20 days of hearings in cities like Seattle, Los Angeles, and San Francisco on the West Coast.

More than 750 witnesses testified, many of whom gave first hand accounts of the hardships which they endured as a result of their forced evacuation. Aiko Herzig-Yoshinaga conducted archival research, uncovering military classified documents. After reviewing the documents and testimony, the commission concluded that the evacuation and internment of Japanese Americans was not justified because of military necessity.

The Civil Liberties Act of 1988 was signed into law by then President Ronald Reagan. Under this law, the federal government authorized payments of $20,000 to each Japanese American who had been interned and formally apologized to the Japanese American community nearly 50 years after their internment for this grave injustice. As it turned out, the law which Congress passed was not very different from the one that Mike had proposed 10 years earlier.

After the redress legislation passed, I couldn't help, but think about my Japanese American classmates who left the Maryknoll school to be interned at Camp Harmony at the Puyallup fairgrounds. When the Seattle City Council held hearings on redress for Japanese Americans who had lost their city jobs because of the internment, I testified in support of the legislation, recalling my feelings when my Japanese American classmates had to leave.

The internment had different impacts on my classmates. I remember one afternoon in high school when Pauline Matsudaira, who had been sent to Minidoka with her family, and I were walking through the Seattle University campus. I pointed to the fence topped by barbed wire surrounding the Glacier Beverage Company near the school and mentioned that it looked like a concentration camp. Pauline glared at me and said it wasn't very funny. I felt really embarrassed. I then understood that the camp experience was something I shouldn't mention to her. Years later, I asked Pauline what she remembered most about the internment. She replied that she spent almost every day helping her mother with the laundry, using the old washboards to scrub the clothes for her very large family. Her brother Mich had a completely different reaction to the internment experience. He was several years younger than Pauline and talked about being with his buddies as they roamed the camp looking for fun things to do.

When President Reagan announced that he was coming to Seattle to raise funds for the Republican Party at a $15,000-a-plate lunch, Mike decided to counter with a soup line fund raiser for food banks in the area. The event was held at Carpenters Hall in downtown Seattle. I was in charge of cooking the soup. I called Mike Castillano, Sr., a manager at Ivar's restaurant. He had Ivar's donate all the clam chowder we needed, but insisted that it be done anonymously. When the news media covered the story, a TV crew came into the kitchen to interview the cooking crew. When the reporter asked who cooked the delicious clam chowder, everyone pointed to me. I was given the credit for cooking the chowder that people said tasted better than Ivar's. Several hundred people showed up and the soup line became a popular annual fund-raising event for the food banks.

Mike Lowry's annual political fund raiser was his famous Shrimp Feed. The idea for the Shrimp Feed came from a volunteer campaign worker who coordinated fund-raising events and had success in an earlier campaign in Louisiana. Fifteen different herbs and spices were mixed in a huge pot, water was brought to a boil, and the large farm grown prawns added and cooked until done. French bread, corn on the cob, and boiled potatoes rounded out the meal. When Mike campaigned for the U.S. Senate seat in 1988, 1,200 supporters attended the event at Kay Bullitt's estate in Seattle's Capitol Hill neighborhood.

When Mike campaigned, he was a stickler for detail. For example, Mike insisted that his yard signs be placed on key arterials throughout his Seventh Congressional district. But we couldn't get the signs up fast enough as Mike criss-crossed his district to attend events. Campaign staff resorted to placing his signs on streets that led from campaign headquarters to streets where events were being held. As Mike was driven from one event to another, the signs were up on every street we passed. He then commented that he was happy the yard sign crew was doing their job.

When Mike wanted to relax, he often came down to the International District and looked me up at the Four Seas or Bush Garden. We often talked about issues and ways he could be more effective in the community. There were some conversations that were more animated than others, depending on how passionate Mike felt about his position. But after the usual lecture, we talked about Whitebear, Gossett, or Maestas, and the conversation usually ended on a light note.

On one of the last times I drove Mike to catch his red eye flight to the other Washington, he was unusually grumpy, directing me to change lanes, glancing at his watch every few minutes and reminding me that his flight was leaving within the hour. Even though I got him there with plenty of time to spare, he hustled off to his gate with just a wave of his hand. The next morning, I woke up to the news that he had passed out at Chicago's O'Hare Airport and had been rushed to a hospital. He was diagnosed with a bleeding ulcer. To this day I, wonder if it was, in fact, my driving that gave him that ulcer.

In 1988, Mike left Congress after he lost to incumbent Sen. Slade Gorton. But four years later, he was elected as governor of Washington state and served for one term. While governor, Mike was always concerned about his public image. One afternoon, Mike called me. He was on his way to an event at the Westin Hotel in downtown Seattle, but had a few hours to relax before his speaking engagement. We met at the Bush Garden. After we exchanged pleasantries, he asked, "How am I doing in the communities?" I gave him high marks, but.

"What do you mean, but?" Mike continued.

"Some of the community leaders are concerned that the farm workers were exempted from the health initiative."

At that moment, he stood up and angrily announced, "Dammit Santos, I'm the best governor this state has ever had."

"Gee, Mike, I only knew four of them (Evans, Rosellini, Spellman, and Mike)." I was trying to be funny, but Mike was not amused. Not only did his face turn beet-red, he was actually speechless for about 10 seconds. Then he laughed. Mike and I still remain close friends today.

CHAPTER SIX

Justice for Cannery Workers

Canneries, Corruption, and Conspiracy to Commit

After the success of UCWA in opening up the construction trades for minorities, a group of us wanted to address the decades of segregation and discrimination by the Alaska seafood industry against Filipino cannery workers. This group included Nemesio and Silme Domingo, Michael Woo, attorney Abraham "Rami" Arditi, Tyree Scott, and myself. We met regularly in Tyree's office in Capitol Hill. As I began to realize that I wasn't able to devote much time on this issue, I excused myself from the planning group, but I did continue to support the effort.

The Alaska Cannery Workers Association (ACWA) was born out of these discussions. A plan was developed to file a class action lawsuit against the seafood industry on behalf of Filipino and other minority cannery workers. Michael and Silme, under the guise of graduate students doing academic research for the University of Washington's School of Fisheries, traveled to several canneries in Alaska and documented the unequal treatment of Filipino and other minority workers. It was not difficult to document the segregated housing nor the difference in mess halls. Whites were served a steady diet of steaks, pork chops, roasts, and a variety of desserts. Filipinos were served fish heads and rice. Then there were the differences in the types of jobs and the pay. Only the White workers were allowed to maintain the machinery and heavy equipment, where, not coincidentally, the best paying jobs were.

On November 28, 1973, a class action lawsuit was filed on behalf of Alaska Cannery Workers Association members in the federal District Court in Seattle. The lawsuit went after the biggest company in the industry, the New England Fish Company (NEFCO). Attorneys

Rami Arditi and Michael Fox from the Northwest Labor Employment Law Office (LELO) represented ACWA. At the same time, class action lawsuits were also filed against NEFCO-Fidalgo Packing Company, Wards Cove Packing Company, Columbia Ward's Fisheries, and Bumble Bee Seafoods. Eventually, more than 700 minority cannery workers signed on as plaintiffs. Never before had a seasonal migratory labor force been represented in a class action employment discrimination lawsuit.

In 1977, Domingo vs. NEFCO went to trial. The cannery workers won the case. NEFCO appealed. The cannery workers won the appeal. When the lawsuit against NEFCO-Fidalgo Packing Company went to trial, the cannery workers won that case, too. Financial settlements were negotiated with NEFCO and NEFCO-Fidalgo. However, NEFCO's insurance companies refused to cover its legal costs because the insurance coverage did not apply to "intentional discrimination." Faced with a multimillion-dollar judgment and a multimillion-dollar legal bill (NEFCO was represented by Bogle and Gates, one of the highest-priced downtown Seattle law firms), the company filed for bankruptcy.

The young ACWA members were involved in a life and death struggle. Most had been blacklisted from Alaska cannery work, with the complicity of their own union (ILWU), for challenging cannery management. Gene Viernes, for example, had been blacklisted for his role in leading a hunger strike at Wards Cove in 1972. Silme and Nemesio Domingo had been blacklisted for filing grievances and complaints with the Equal Employment Opportunities Commission over unfair working conditions and for organizing activities. They pushed for reforms not only against the seafood cannery industry, but they went after their own union, Local 37 of the International Longshoremen's and Warehousemen's Union, as well. In response, Local 37 tried to kick them out of the union.

I knew that pushing for union reform was very dangerous and mentioned my fears to some of the ACWA leaders. I remembered people like Gene Navarro, the old dispatcher, who once held the most powerful position in the union. Navarro had a temper and I never knew anyone who won an argument with him. All the dispatchers who followed him also inherited his formula of intimidation. He never followed the seniority system. If you were skilled at gambling and he liked your action, you were dispatched. As a young kid in the cannery in Ugashik, I saw coworkers gamble and lose their whole season's pay before the first fish came through the sliming tables. Gambling was the second biggest business in the canneries. ACWA members Silme, Gene, and David Della led the reform movement to wrestle away the leadership positions from the old guard with the goal of establishing a fair dispatching system.

Silme, Gene, and David were also active in the movement to fight the corrupt dictatorship of Ferdinand Marcos, president of the Philippines, especially after he declared martial law in September of 1972. Some members of ACWA, Silme and David, in particular, were founding members of the local Union of Democratic Pilipinos (KDP). KDP was a member of the Anti-Martial Law Alliance, a larger group that brought together many factions such as the KDP, radical socialist groups, and unions. The alliance organized broad-based opposition to the U.S. backed Marcos regime and gained national and international support. The alliance held frequent demonstrations outside the local Philippine embassy. The police were often called and KDP members were arrested for trespassing.

I participated in many of the demonstrations in front of the Philippines Consulate on Third Avenue to protest martial law in the Philippines. One afternoon, while walking the picket line outside the consulate, I bore the brunt of a garbage can full of water dumped from the third floor balcony of the Central building that housed the offices of the Philippine Travel agency. I raced up the stairs to the third floor, only to be met by a Seattle police officer, there to provide security, who would not let me into the consulate office to complain about the drenching. Of course, I did look a little menacing, dripping from head to toe with 35 gallons of water soaked into my wool suit.

The opposition to Marcos created problems locally within the Filipino community. Many of Local 37's leaders and for that matter, the Filipino Community of Seattle, the largest Filipino community organization, were from the same Philippine province as President Marcos. For much of the Filipino "old guard," Ferdinand and Imelda Marcos were like family, and no matter how much of a tyrant Marcos was, he was still their main man.

When Local 37 held their elections, Tony Baruso, from that "old guard," was re-elected president. Baruso was a former president of the Filipino Community of Seattle and even though he spent most mornings in the union hall, he kept his full-time job at Boeing. I got to know Baruso quite well when he ran his unsuccessful campaign for the state House of

Representatives. A family man, he joined the Democratic Party and was active in his precinct. After he lost his only attempt for public office, he focused his energy on being a leader in Filipino community politics. He served many years on the community's council, executive committee, and as president for a couple terms.

Baruso had worked his way up to Local 37's executive committee and served several years as union dispatcher before he was finally elected as president. The president of Local 37 was a very prominent and powerful position in the Filipino community. Although Baruso won, the reform candidates took the next three top positions. David Della was elected vice president, Silme was elected secretary-treasurer, and Gene was elected to the powerful dispatcher position.

Gene was sent by the International Longshoremen's and Warehousemen's Union (ILWU) to an international meeting in the Philippines to document repressive working conditions. A short time later, Gene and Silme gave a report at the ILWU convention in Hawaii about working conditions under martial law in the Philippines. Military intelligence agents from the Philippines, equivalent to our CIA, shadowed Gene in the Philippines and both Gene and Silme in Hawaii.

Upon arriving back home in Seattle, the newly elected officers of Local 37 faced the challenge of dispatching laborers to the fish canneries in Alaska. Things were not going too well. A fight loomed between the reform leadership and the Tulisans, a large organized gang of young Filipino immigrant males. The gang had traditionally sent their members up to Alaska as dealers of the gambling games set up in each cannery. To get dispatched, it was the customary practice of the Tulisan gang to slip a couple of bucks on the sly to the dispatcher, who ignored fair dispatching rules and looked the other way. But when Gene became the new dispatcher, it wasn't to be that way. If you built up years of seniority, you were dispatched — very simple. But the Tulisan wanted its people up north, regardless of Gene's system, so they could work the lucrative gambling tables. Since the Tulisans were immigrants, they had little seniority over some of the old-timers who had gone north year after year to Alaska.

It was not unusual to hear threats from union members not dispatched to the canneries. For the new leaders in the reform movement, who were simultaneously coordinating a successful anti-martial law movement and stopping the traditional bribery system, the threat of violence became real, very real. The Tulisan gang was a bunch of thugs. There were stories floating around that Tulisan members had scooped up the pots at illegal games, daring the players to call the cops. During the afternoon, the gang hung out near their storefront "office" at the corner of Maynard and King Street. At night, they worked in gambling clubs throughout the I.D. Often, late at night, I ran into them at the China Gate, where they were always very polite and occasionally bought me a drink. After all, people regarded me as "Uncle Bob, the Mayor of Chinatown."

In 1981, just before the cannery season, Tony Dictado, the leader of Tulisan, presented Gene with a list of gang members he wanted dispatched to the canneries. When Gene reminded Dictado that the union membership had agreed to follow the seniority system, Dictado warned Gene that his people be dispatched or he'd "pay the price."

On June 1, 1981, just after 4 p.m., a black Trans Am driven by Tony Dictado stopped in the alley next to the Local 37 Union office and dropped off Ben Guloy and Jimmy Ramil. A fourth person, Teodoro Dominguez, also known as "Boy Pilay," was believed to have been a lookout. A few minutes later, Gene Viernes lay dead and Silme Domingo, dying, was rushed to the trauma unit at Harborview Hospital. Both had been shot numerous times. But before Silme lapsed into unconsciousness, he identified the shooters. Silme died the next day.

In the little town of Wapato in the farm country of the Yakima Valley, the Filipino community was stunned by news that its young, restless former wrestling champion was murdered by a gang, a ruthless gang that stopped at nothing to get back at the dispatcher because he had cost them their bread and butter — gambling revenue. He had lost his life defending the workers. They went after Gene and gunned him down. Silme, who tried to protect his close friend, was also a target. As it turned out, these good young men were killed for sinister reasons that went beyond a gang vendetta that involved the political machinations of a diabolical head of state.

The criminal trials resulted in life sentences without the possibility of parole for the three Tulisan gang members. They were spared the death penalty. Charges were never brought against Boy Pilay, but he was later murdered in retaliation for an earlier, unrelated killing. For Tony Dictado, Jimmy Ramil, and Ben Guloy, the killings were a reaction to union reforms that ended their monopoly of the gambling tables. But the orders came from overseas. Gene and Silme were targeted because they were spearheading a movement which ultimately succeeded in bringing down the corrupt Marcos regime.

At the criminal trials of Ben Guloy and Jimmy Ramil, Tony Dictado testified that the two shooters were with him at a gambling club in the International District at the time of the killings. Later, during his own trial, Dictado testified that he had lied earlier, that Guloy and Ramil had not been with him. He denied that he ordered or took part in the killings, said he knew who ordered them, but was afraid to identify that person and lied because of threats against his family. However, Dictado's lawyer, John Henry Browne, and the prosecutor, Joanne Maida, identified the man who issued the orders. They pointed the finger at Tony Baruso, president of Local 37, the same Tony Baruso I had supported so many years before when he ran for the state legislature. Baruso's gun was used to kill Silme and Gene.

Tony Baruso was a witness at the murder trials. When called to the stand, he pleaded the "Fifth" more than a hundred times when asked about his involvement in the murders. And yet, he wasn't arrested. Not enough evidence, we were told. The community was outraged. Justice had been denied. However, Tony Baruso was recalled and removed as president of Local 37 by its membership. Terri Mast, Silme's wife and mother of their two daughters, Kalayaan and Ligaya, later was elected as president/business agent for Local 37, continuing Silme's work with the union reform movement. She was the first female president of Local 37, a union which had been and continued to have a predominantly male membership.

Gus the Gecko

After Silme and Gene were murdered, the King County Prosecutor's Office decided to serve papers on Boy Pilay, suspected of being the lookout in the plot to murder the two. Michael Withey, one of the attorneys with the Committee for Justice, called me to keep an eye out for Pilay, who had been rumored to have returned to Seattle from Maryland and was known to hang out at the Tulisan hangout at 615 King Street. Withey asked me to call the Prosecutor's Office if he was spotted.

Dan Rounds and I, along with our office pet, Gus, spent parts of every day monitoring activity at the store front. Actually, Gus was a gecko, which I purchased to help control the roach population that settled in the International District after the Ice Age. Gus lived in the office plants and would wander the walls looking for nourishment. Many afternoons, Gus could be spotted perched on the windowsill sunning himself while spying on the Tulisan headquarters. Unfortunately, we could never get Gus to share his views and tell us what he saw.

Revenge Is Sweet — The Civil Trial

From the outrage over the murders of Silme and Gene, a movement began: the Committee for Justice for Domingo and Viernes. Under the leadership of Cindy Domingo, Silme's sister; Terri Mast; and others, the Committee for Justice endured a 10-year struggle to make all those responsible accountable for the murders of Gene and Silme. Ironically, it was Tony Baruso who contacted me to be a part of the committee. He told me that the committee was being formed to "find those sons of bitches who murdered our young union leaders."

On September 14, 1982, the families of Silme Domingo and Gene Viernes filed a wrongful death civil suit against Ferdinand and Imelda Marcos, the Philippine government, Tony Baruso, and several United States government agencies — such as the FBI, the CIA, and the U.S. State Department. When the lawsuit was filed, the Philippine embassy in Washington, D.C. issued a prepared statement, calling the suit "frivolous and politically inspired, designed to embarrass the state visit of President Marcos to the United States." The lawsuit had been filed on the eve of a state visit from Marcos to Washington, D.C. to meet with President Ronald Reagan.

Marcos was originally dismissed from the lawsuit because, as the head of state, he had immunity. But when he was overthrown, he lost that immunity and was reinstated as a defendant. There were many delays due to procedural challenges, legal rulings, and a lengthy battle to obtain classified United States and Philippine documents. Marcos died, but not before he gave a taped deposition. Finally, the case went to trial in late 1989, almost seven years from the date it was filed.

During opening arguments, Jeff Robinson, the plaintiffs' attorney, said the responsibility for the murders rested on the lap of Ferdinand Marcos. Robinson said there was a broad plan to monitor, harass, and intimidate anti-Marcos activists in the United States and that Viernes and Domingo were targeted because of their well-known opposition to the Marcos regime. He said Marcos was especially upset because one month before the murders, Viernes and Domingo had sponsored a resolution critical of the Marcos government at the national ILWU convention in Honolulu. This, he said, was Marcos' motivation for the killings.

The lawyers for the families of Gene and Silme did a fantastic job of showing a link between the murders and the Marcos regime. Former Philippines intelligence agents and leading U.S. anti-Marcos activists testified about the existence of a spy network employed by Marcos in the United States. Surveillance reports obtained from the Philippine government documented the role played by Philippine embassies in gathering information about the Anti-Martial Law Alliance.

The link to the murders was Constantine "Tony" Baruso, president of Local 37. Phone records, checks stubs, and bank records showed the Mabuhay Corporation, a dummy corporation used to fund Marcos' intelligence operations in the United States, paid Baruso $15,000 for a "special security project" on May 17, 1981, about two weeks before the murders. Baruso had gone to San Francisco to meet with Leonilo Malabed, president of the Mabuhay Corporation.

Witnesses testified that Tony Dictado met with Baruso at the Local 37 office on May 30, 1981. Robert San Pablo testified that Dictado and Jimmy Ramil told him they were going to kill Gene on May 31, 1981, the day before the murder. San Pablo further testified he was told by Dictado that Baruso was going to pay Dictado $5,000 for the hit. Bank records further established that Baruso deposited more than $10,000 in his account over a period of several months after the murders. And the murder weapon, a 45-caliber semi-automatic submachine gun, belonged to Tony Baruso.

The defense attorneys tried to distance Tony Baruso from President Marcos while our legal team tried to prove that Tony Baruso was a personal friend of Ferdinand Marcos. This was important because it would show Baruso had a direct link to Marcos who wanted to silence Silme and Gene. I testified during the trial that I heard Baruso brag about his relationship with Marcos, recalling a conversation where Baruso pointed to a photo on his office wall which showed Marcos shaking hands with him. Baruso's attorney tried to get the jury to believe the photo of Baruso with Marcos was a posed photo and not personal at all. When I was cross-examined by Baruso's attorney, he asked if I had a photo of Marcos in my office. I answered that I would never hang a photo of a dictator like Marcos on my wall. I added, however, that I did have a photo of President Daniel Ortega of Nicaragua on my wall. The defense almost asked for a mistrial.

Cindy Domingo chaired the Committee for Justice. While assisting the legal team of Michael Withey, Jim Douglas, and Jeff Robinson, she was constantly in danger from the agents sent to Seattle by the Philippine CIA to intimidate and monitor the investigation and civil trial. Strangers we had never seen before appeared at Committee for Justice meetings. Since it was our belief that Marcos ordered the murders of Silme and Gene, we couldn't be sure the killings would stop. Fortunately, nothing happened. Cindy later became King County Councilman Larry Gossett's top aide and continued her struggle for workers' rights with LELO, the labor rights advocacy organization which had represented the cannery workers in their class action lawsuits.

I was one of several people called on by the Committee for Justice to read statements at the regular press conferences held to update local media on the civil trial. At the press conferences, Cindy or Elaine (Ikoma) Ko usually gave the current background — where the case was, using charts and graphs depicting the flow of money from Marcos to Baruso and everybody in between. It seemed like almost each press conference ended with John Staments, a member of the media, asking, "Where's the smoking gun?"

Prior to the civil trial, Baruso had been tried and convicted of embezzling funds from Local 37. He had been sentenced to three years in jail. When Baruso took the stand for the civil trial, he once again took the "Fifth" when asked about union dispatching reforms, KDP activities in the union, intelligence operations in the United States, and his gun, the murder weapon. He denied bragging about his "close personal" relationship with Marcos to me and others who so testified. When asked to explain why we had testified about his friendship with Marcos, Baruso said we lied. When asked about the trip to San Francisco, he said he had gone to a meeting of his fraternal order which, it turned out, occurred two years before he claimed it did. Baruso was vague, contradictory, and acted like he had something to hide.

The wrongful death civil trial took 18 days. After deliberating for five hours, the jury returned a $15,000,000 dollar verdict against Imelda Marcos and the estate of Ferdinand

Marcos. Judge Barbara Rothstein later ruled that Tony Baruso and Leonilo Malabed (who both waived their rights to a jury trial) were also legally responsible for their roles in the murders. The actual amount paid to the plaintiffs was negotiated, and the verdict was not appealed.

Based on the evidence presented at the civil trial in 1989, Tony Baruso was eventually arrested and went on trial two years later in 1991. Coincidentally, Baruso's defense attorney was the same Anthony Savage who had prosecuted me in that incident with the fork lift driver so many years before. The trial lasted two weeks. It took the jury two days to convict Tony Baruso of the murders. The verdict came almost 10 years from the date that Silme and Gene were murdered. Baruso was sentenced to life without parole at the state penitentiary in Walla Walla, Washington. It was quite a fall from grace for a man who I once considered a respected leader in the Filipino community.

Wards Cove — Justice Denied

After Gene and Silme died, their class action lawsuit against the canneries continued. The Wards Cove case dragged on for years. The owners filed motion after motion to delay the trial. They even asked the court to dismiss the case because one of the named plaintiffs, Gene, had died. The case finally went to trial in 1984. The political climate had changed. Reagan was in the White House and many of his federal judge appointees reflected his conservative views. The cannery workers lost at trial, but they appealed and proved their case to the Ninth Circuit Court of Appeals. Wards Cove appealed to the Supreme Court, which consisted mainly of Reagan and Bush appointees. The high court ruled against the workers in 1989.

The Wards Cove decision was criticized by many civil rights groups and helped spur Congressional passage of the Civil Rights Act of 1991 to provide protection against workplace discrimination. Unfortunately, the political compromise to pass the law, brokered by Alaska's cannery-backed senators Frank Murkowski and Ted Stevens, specifically excluded the Filipino cannery workers. Although Congressman Jim McDermott introduced legislation to amend the Civil Rights Act to include the Filipino cannery workers, his bill received little support. Neither the Republican majority nor the Democratic Party leadership in Congress had any interest in protecting Filipino cannery workers.

Regardless, the Wards Cove case and the other cannery lawsuits gave me personal satisfaction that the discrimination we felt as young Filipino cannery workers in the early 1950s was finally going to be addressed. The shame of being a lowly fish house slimer gave way to pride as those younger than me fought to end discrimination in the seafood industry. Many of our dads, uncles, and friends took for granted the intolerable conditions we lived under until young activists like Silme, Gene, David, and the others took a stand. But even as this case got buried under the political manipulations of the cannery-backed politicians, we were still extremely grateful for those who stuck with it for so long.

In the years following the class action lawsuits, union activity in the seafood industry reduced dramatically to about 1,000 union members left working in 10 canneries. One of the major reasons for declining union membership was the acquisition of many American seafood companies by foreign corporations from Japan, Taiwan, and Russia. These foreign corporations purchased large transport ships or freighters and converted them to floating canneries which remained on the seas, sometimes beyond the protection of our laws.

Students, former migrant farm workers, and refugees from Southeast Asia and Eastern Europe were recruited to work on the cannery ships. These recruits were non-union members who lived and worked aboard these floating canneries under harsh conditions. Regardless of these deplorable working conditions, the short cannery season drew workers who worked and saved their income until the end of the cannery season and traveled home with a tidy sum. Working the canneries was still the best paying jobs in the seasonal industries.

CHAPTER SEVEN

From the Wah Mee to Village Square

Lunar Madness — The Wah Mee Shootings

By 1983, jogging had become a daily habit for me. I often took an early morning jog along the waterfront when I lived at the Freedman Building in the International District. It was a great way to clear my head to prepare for the day. I was participating in a fun run at Seward Park to raise money for Asian Counseling and Referral Service when I heard the news about the murders at the Wah Mee Club. That Sunday just happened to coincide with the Lunar New Year.

During the Lunar New Year festivities, many Chinese families congregated in the International District to attend celebrations at their family association headquarters and at restaurants. For many, the Lunar New Year was their only chance to play a few hands of pai gow and other games. One of the old clubs with a colorful history of gambling was the Wah Mee Club, an after hours joint popular with older Chinese community members.

Three Chinese youths, Benjamin Ng, Willie Mak, and Tony Ng, knocked on the door of the club. They were known to the doorman who let them in. The three pulled out guns and while one forced the 12 men and one woman face down on the carpet, the other two hog-tied them with twine they had brought with them. At some point, two of them shot each person in the back of the head. All but one died instantly.

It wasn't a total shock to me that this kind of robbery would happen. Asian old timers talked about young hoods grabbing money off the gambling tables and getting away. The owners couldn't call the police to complain because gambling was illegal. What was so mind-blowing was the brutality of the murders. I couldn't help but imagine how helpless the victims felt as they were hog-tied, then executed one by one with a shot to the back of the head. Fortunately, the doorman survived and was able to identify the killers.

One of the victims was Dewey Mar, a great friend of mine. Dewey ran the Chinese movies at the Kokusai Theater. His three sons, Richard, Kenny, and Tommy, were activists from the Kingdome days and daughter Becky was always a supporter. Dewey was a staunch Seattle Sonics fan who attended many home games. His favorite player was Jack Sikma.

It was reported by the media that after the Wah Mee murders, business in the International District had dropped by as much as 30 percent. That figure was also quoted to me by one of the Moriguchi brothers, who mentioned that Uwajimaya felt the drop in business soon after the shootings.

I didn't realize the impact was that severe until I talked with Jerry Kemp, a local television news reporter, who told me that before the Wah Mee murders, he regularly brought his family to several restaurants in the International District. But after he covered the trial for his station and heard the testimony by several waiters that they carried pistols while waiting tables, he decided he'd take his family out to dinner elsewhere. The International District was negatively affected by the publicity because Seattleites envisioned the community with gangs controlling the streets. It took years for the International District to rebound from the murders at the Wah Mee Club.

Benjamin Ng and Willie Mak were each convicted of 12 counts of murder. Tony Ng was sentenced to life in prison on robbery charges. Benjamin Ng was sentenced to life in prison without parole. Mak was sentenced to death. But in 1991, U.S. District Judge William Dwyer — the same man who, as an attorney, had represented Larry Gossett years before — overturned Mak's death penalty on procedural grounds and ordered a new resentencing hearing. Eleven years later, Mak is still awaiting his new resentencing hearing. All are still in prison. The Wah Mee Club never reopened.

But Life Goes On....

Despite the negative publicity from the Wah Mee shootings, the International District eventually recovered. More housing was planned and built. For many years, there had been a hesitancy among Chinese family associations to apply for public resources to renovate their property. They believed that public funds had strings attached and they wouldn't have complete control over occupancy.

At Inter*Im, we formed a good team to work with the owners of buildings in the Chinatown core. I made the initial contact, and Dan Rounds and Ken Katahira provided the numbers that persuaded the owners to renovate their buildings. I would talk about the need to bring more low-income housing into the District. The owners, however, were not impressed. But after Dan and Ken presented them the numbers that showed they could make a profit, the owners became converts to the cause of housing preservation.

For example, Dan, and later, Ken worked with architect Joey Ing to design the renovation of the Rex Apartments owned by Ray Chinn and his family. The successful renovation of the Rex Apartments helped Ken persuade the Oak Tin Association to renovate its building on Seventh Avenue South, with the assistance of Inter*Im. The Oak Tin building had served as the association's headquarters since 1921. Established in 1900, the Gee How Oak Tin Family Association is the largest Chinese family association in Washington state. Like most Chinese family associations, the Oak Tin Association was formed to foster a spirit of mutual help, promoting the happiness and welfare of its members.

Ken also successfully negotiated, on Inter*Im's behalf, the acquisition of the N.P. Hotel from Jack Buttnick, who also owned several buildings in Pioneer Square. The N.P. Hotel underwent a total renovation and when completed, provided studios as well as one- and two-bedroom apartments for working people. After the renovation was completed, Inter*Im once again pulled up stakes and moved its office, returning to its original site at the N.P. Hotel after an absence of 30 years. The renovation of the N.P. Hotel had special meaning for me. Walking through the old hallways brought back memories of my dad and the times we spent there when I was a kid.

Redeveloping Chinatowns — The National Perspective

One of the most important alliances in which the International District Improvement Association (Inter*Im) and the Seattle Chinatown-International District Preservation and Development Authority (SCIDPDA) became involved was an ad hoc collection of similar Asian American development agencies in Chinatowns and other Asian American communities from throughout the nation. The International District wasn't alone in its goal to preserve and develop our historic ethnic neighborhoods.

In 1992, Gordon Chin, executive director of the Chinatown Resource Center in San Francisco's Chinatown, submitted a successful proposal to the Ford Foundation to fund a meeting of successful developers from San Francisco, Los Angeles, Seattle, Oakland, Chicago, Boston, Philadelphia, and New York. Chin is one of the most prominent and successful developers in the nation with a number of projects built in Chinatown and the surrounding areas in the City by the Bay.

The two-day meeting was held in Oakland with all the Chinatown agencies sharing their information about their past and future development plans and the resources used. After listening to all the presentations from the various Asian communities across the nation, it was clear to me that the International District, unlike the other Asian communities, was the most cohesive community because business owners, property owners, residents, and activists made a point of working together for the common good. The Seattle contingent impressed our colleagues. I presented "Uncle Bob's Neighborhood" and Ken Katahira introduced our formula for successful rehabilitation. It didn't hurt my reputation with the activists from the other communities that I could recite the local hangouts that I partied at when visiting their cities.

This alliance led to the formation, in 1999, of the National Coalition of Asian Pacific Community Development (CAPACD), which dedicates itself to the housing and community development needs of the Asian Pacific population. The formation of CAPACD will coordinate the work of non-profit organizations serving these rapidly expanding communities. Most of the member organizations in CAPACD generate a combination of public and private resources to build their projects, using HUD as a big player in development funds.

The International District is not the only Asian ethnic neighborhood that has come under pressure from internal and external development. Philadelphia's Chinatown was threatened with the planned development of a football stadium, but pressure from the surrounding communities forced city officials to build it in another location. In Los Angeles, the Little Tokyo Service Center, Community Development Corporation, has plans to develop a one-square-block community recreation and athletic center. This plan faces opposition from Little Tokyo's business community who want to expand its retail core.

To Park or Not to Park

In 1990, the state Department of Transportation notified Inter*Im that it was canceling the parking lot lease to widen Interstate 5. A wide range of business people, property owners, residents, and I.D. workers who would be affected by this action protested. The parking lot lease and the revenue it generated were important to Inter*Im's successful operation and future. It was also important for Inter*Im to continue operating the parking lot to keep parking prices affordable for community residents and social service workers.

Ken Katahira and Tony Lee from Inter*Im, Glenn Chinn from Merchants Parking Association, and I met with state transportation staff to discuss the cancellation of the lease. At the time, I was the executive director of the Public Development Authority. We entered the conference room and were met by 12 staff members from several state agencies, including staff from transportation, engineering, and the Attorney General's office. The engineers said the lot was needed for a storage and staging area during the intense construction phase. They also said that the lease had to be canceled and opened up for bid. We were upset not only because this was bad news, but also because of the arrogance shown to us by these government bureaucrats.

I called attorney Jerry Hillis, who said his firm would assist *pro bono.* A week later, in the same conference room with the same staff from the state, Ken, Tony, Glenn, and I walked in, but this time we were followed by our legal team of attorneys — Jerry Hillis, Rick Peterson, and Tom Ehrlichman — armed with files and notebooks of legal documents. Bringing our legal team into the mix was a calculated move to show these bureaucrats we weren't going down without a legal fight. This time, we were in a festive mood. Needless to say, the state didn't want any delays in its construction schedule. Inter*Im got the lot back and parking continued during construction except in the sections closed where the actual construction took place.

International District Village Square — The Real Deal

One of our most important accomplishments in the International District was the development of the International District Village Square (IDVS). In 1974, while director of Inter*Im, I received a letter from Alan Kurimura, legislative aide to Seattle City Council member George Benson, alerting us that the property at Eighth Avenue South and South Dearborn Street had been sold to Metro. Alan's letter indicated that after 20 years, the Metro property would be surplused and that the International District community should make preparations to acquire the property when it became available to the public. The Eighth and Dearborn site was a one and two-thirds acre parcel of land Metro used for maintenance, repair, and parking of its buses. For years, Inter*Im, then later, the PDA, expressed interest in acquiring the property.

Fourteen years passed. I had gone to work for Congressman Mike Lowry. In 1988, Mike decided to run for the United States Senate against the incumbent, Slade Gorton. When Mike lost, I was out of a job. I applied for two job openings, one with the city of Seattle's new Office of Neighborhoods and the other for the open executive director position at the PDA. I was interviewed by the PDA, but it took a while for the PDA to make a decision. In the meantime, I was hired by the city and worked in the Office of Neighborhoods as a community outreach worker for eight months.

Finally, in 1989, the PDA offered me the position of executive director. I had no experience managing property, but inherited a hardworking and knowledgeable staff. My number one responsibility was the acquisition of the property at Eighth and Dearborn. Even while I worked for Mike Lowry when he was a congressman and later as an unsuccessful U.S. Senate candidate, I kept up with the goings-on in the International District, especially negotiations between the PDA and Metro over the large piece of property at Eighth and Dearborn. I really wanted to get back to the excitement and action of community development. I wanted the opportunity to build my dream project on the Eighth and Dearborn property.

My dream for the property included a two-phase development. The first phase involved the building of low-income elderly housing, including "assisted living" units; a commercial kitchen and dining area for the elderly and the community; and office space for the International District Community Health Center, Asian Counseling and Referral Service, and the Denise Louie Early Childhood Education Center. The second phase involved the building of low-income family housing, a community center/hall, and space for a branch library. We promoted this project as a state-of-the-art, multi-lingual, multi-cultural, intergenerational facility with the capacity to provide a wide range of services throughout the region.

When I was hired, Tomio Moriguchi was concerned that I didn't have the necessary contacts with influential developers. He was partially right. I knew some, but hadn't worked closely with them. In order to prove to Tomio that I did have contacts in the development field, I formed an ad hoc committee to provide professional input to me in the acquisition and development of the Eighth and Dearborn project. This committee had some of the most seasoned developers in the city such as Paul Schell, a developer and later mayor of Seattle; Virginia Anderson, director of the Seattle Center; Walt Hubbard (my old mentor) and Tom Bangasser of Midtown Commons; Phil Sherburne, executive director of the Pac-Med Medical Center; Alan Cornell of Baugh Construction; and Kit Freudenburg, director of the Wing Luke Asian Museum and PDA board member. We only met a few times, but these seasoned pros confirmed that we were on the right track with our development plan. Finally, we learned that Metro no longer needed the property.

In 1990, when the time to surplus the property grew near, federal officials from the Urban Mass Transit Administration (UMTA), a division within the U.S. Department of Transportation, notified Metro officials the property had to be put up for bid on the open market. Several Metro council members favored the transfer of the land to the I.D. community. When Metro officials mentioned that the International District community was in line for the land, UMTA officials insisted that the sale occur immediately.

I contacted the offices of senators Slade Gorton and Brock Adams and met with their senior staff members to lobby for the acquisition of the site. I met individually with each senator's legislative aide — Rita Jean Butterworth of Sen. Gorton's office and Jim Gunsolus of Sen. Adams' office — to brief their bosses, requesting that they delay any action on the sale of the property for one year. Gorton was a member of the Senate Transportation Committee and Adams had been a former secretary of transportation. Staff from both offices worked in cooperation and delayed any action on the property for six months.

After learning we had the support of our two U.S. senators, I met immediately with Terry Ebersole, UMTA's regional administrator, to ask why his department insisted on an immediate sale of the Eighth and Dearborn site. Ebersole explained that the property was sitting dormant and needed to be taken off the books. I replied that if getting this liability off the books was the only problem UMTA had, which Ebersole said it was, I had a solution. Knowing the property was appraised at $2,000,000 and that UMTA had lent Metro two-thirds of the purchase price, we needed to raise $1,400,000 to pay off the government debt. I then contacted Sue Taoka. Sue, who had worked for me at Inter*Im and replaced me as Inter*Im's executive director, was a special assistant to Mayor Norm Rice. I asked her to get the mayor's support for a major land transfer.

I presented Ebersole with a very simple proposal: First, UMTA would transfer its reversionary rights to HUD; second, HUD would then transfer those same rights to the city of Seattle as a community development block grant (CDBG); and third, the city would then allocate the property, in the form of a $1,400,000 block grant, to the PDA. To my amazement, officials from UMTA, HUD, and the Seattle city officials all agreed with the transfer plan. This turned out to be a $1,400,000 gift to the International District community.

However, Metro officials did not feel obligated to follow the transfer plan and instead asked the PDA for $600,000, the balance of the payment for their share of the property. We were upset at Metro because we felt that if the federal government, in cooperation with the city of Seattle, was willing to contribute their share of the reversionary rights to the community, then Metro should as well.

We decided it was necessary to lobby each Metro council member to "sell" the agreed upon transfer plan. Every member of the Metro council received a visit from me and Ken Katahira, executive director of Inter*Im, or Sue Taoka, who helped us lobby from her position with the mayor's office. The only problem in lobbying 38 Metro Council members was time. I often requested time with one council member, then ran from office to office, setting up times on the calendars of the other council members for meetings.

An incident occurred, which, if made public, would have ended our chances of acquiring the property. In August of 1990, Cherie Montanez of the PDA's accounting staff reported to our comptroller, Dan Wagner, that she had witnessed Mark Jones, the PDA's assistant director, endorsing a check that had been mailed to a tenant of the Bush-Asia Center. After Dan reported this incident to me, I authorized an internal audit of accounting records from the previous 18 months. The audit showed that more than $60,000 had been embezzled from the Bush-Asia Hotel account.

As the assistant director of the PDA, Mark was in charge of hotel operations. He was responsible for making the cash deposits. To hide his embezzlement, Mark had destroyed the daily receipt reports of cash received at the front desk. What he didn't know was that the clerks had kept a log, a second record, which kept track of cash receipts.

After I reported the theft to the Seattle Police Department, a detective advised me that embezzlements similar to this were hard to prove because of a lack of witnesses. I asked the detective to give me a few days to work out a solution before he arrested Mark. I alerted Rod Kawakami, our attorney, of the problem. I told him I would confront Mark and try to come up with a resolution. Mark agreed to meet me for a beer at the Bush Garden. When Mark sat down at the table, I looked him in the eye and said, "What the hell did you do to me? Why did you take the money?"

"Oh! You found out?" he answered. "How much did I end up taking?"

"Sixty thousand. I've talked to the police department to have you busted."

He leaned forward and said in a low voice, "Bob, I don't want to go to jail cuz you know what they do to White guys there."

"Mark, you need to pay back all the money you took." I could tell he was desperate.

"I'll do anything. I'll even sign over my house."

"Then follow me to Rod Kawakami's office," I said, getting up, "and see what he thinks."

Within an hour, Mark signed over his house, his new Honda motorcycle, his new computer, and half the money in his bank account for a grand total of $60,000. He worked out a plea agreement and eventually moved to another state.

Keep in mind that this incident had occurred during the course of delicate negotiations with the Metro council to get the Eighth and Dearborn site. We hoped that criminal charges against Mark would not surface until after the state auditor's report came out. We had to keep Mark's embezzlement out of the media. But a lot of people knew about the embezzlement. In a community as tight knit as the I.D., it's hard to keep secrets. Bob Shimabukuro, then editor of the *International Examiner*, knew about the embezzlement. But he knew that printing the embezzlement story would hurt our negotiations. Even though he had a "juicy scoop," he sat on the story until we could talk about it. Thanks, Bob. Fortunately, as things turned out, we acquired the Eighth and Dearborn property before the story hit the papers.

Seattle City Councilwoman Dolores Sibonga and King County Councilman Ron Sims, who later became King County executive, were our leading advocates on the Metro council. We also needed and received strong support from Metro Council members from the Eastside (the suburbs east of Seattle). A Metro Council committee was formed to make recommendations to the larger body. Dolores and Ron co-chaired the committee that also included Redmond Mayor Doreen Marchione, Bellevue City Council member Jean Carpenter, and Seattle Mayor Norm Rice. The committee got the legislation passed through the various council committees.

There was a slight hang-up in the Metro council's finance subcommittee. Should the property be donated at no cost? And if there was contamination, who would pay for the cleanup? As Metro removed its buses and closed down the facility, five underground storage tanks (one fresh motor oil tank, two unleaded gasoline tanks, and two diesel tanks) were decommissioned and removed in 1990. When the tanks were removed, it was discovered that the site soil had been contaminated with oil and gas.

The Sibonga/Sims committee decided that the price of the property should be commensurate with the cleanup cost. In comparison to similar remedial projects undertaken by Metro, $150,000 seemed like an appropriate sale price. The PDA jumped at this offer. A resolution was passed in committee to sell the property to the PDA for $150,000. The final cleanup bill was in excess of $2,000,000, and when some members of the Metro council wanted to renegotiate the price, Ron Sims reminded them of all the negative impacts which Metro imposed on the I.D. during the 20 years the site operated as a bus maintenance facility. Ron was emphatic. He said, "A deal is a deal." Metro sold the property, appraised at $2,000,000, to the PDA for $150,000.

It took a couple of years before title to the property changed hands. The PDA didn't want to take title to the property until it was decontaminated. The cleanup took almost three years before we were convinced that it was safe to start construction. While the cleanup took place, we took the time to fully develop our plans for the Village Square project. Sue Taoka was hired as the project director. Wendy Watanabe joined the staff to coordinate arrangements for space, floor plans, and tenant improvements with all the prospective agency tenants. Anne Clark was promoted from the PDA's receptionist to the new position of fund-raising manager. The Village Square project team was set. In March of 1995, legal title to the Eighth and Dearborn site was formally transferred to the PDA.

On August 29, 1995, we had a formal ground breaking ceremony at the Eighth and Dearborn site. The PDA brought three religious monks from the Southeast Asian community (one Cambodian, one Laotian, and one Vietnamese) to symbolically "purify" the land and drive away the evil spirits. Our time to celebrate was short-lived because the PDA needed to raise $20,000,000 to build the state-of-the-art facility. Donations came in all forms, small, medium, large, and extra large. The Boeing Company and the Paul Allen Foundation each gave more than $250,000. Other local companies and foundations followed closely behind with generous grants and donations. Family memorial funds and private donations came in extremely generous amounts.

The construction of the International District Village Square took about three years. It officially opened in April 1998. Legacy House, in the main building, housed 75 low-income elderly residents, with lunch and dinner provided by a professional culinary staff. There were more than 40 different languages and dialects spoken by the professional staff of our social service agency tenants — Asian Counseling and Referral Service, the Denise Louie Education Center, and the International Community Health Services. Artists from the Asian Pacific Islander community were commissioned to provide works which are found throughout the facilities, in the outdoor courtyard, and on the building's walls leading to the dining area on the main floor.

By 2000, the second phase of the I.D. Village Square was underway. A community center, library, and several units of low-income housing for families were planned for the property on the west side of Eighth Avenue South. Funds for building the community center and library came from the successful passage of two city funding propositions in recent elections.

The construction and expansion of the IDVS came at a time of extreme pressure from outside development in and near the I.D. The IDVS project anchored the southeast portion of the District. Village Square was important because it was visible proof that despite the encroachment from outside development, the I.D. was still our neighborhood and that we were here to stay. Village Square was our crowning achievement.

The Dreamers and Schemers — Key Board Members, Staff, and Community Supporters

It is important to stress that the effort to save the International District was a *community* effort. While I have been one of the more visible advocates for the I.D., this story wouldn't be complete without acknowledging the "dreamers and schemers" with whom I had the pleasure of working. Most, if not all, of the programs we started came from ideas formulated by one or more of these innovators. I just helped implement them.

In my role as the executive director of Inter*Im and later as the executive director of the PDA, I had tremendously committed board members. I call them the "dreamers" because they had a vision of the International District as a thriving community. The following board members deserve mention here:

Shigeko Uno, long-time manager of Rainier Heat and Power Co., administered the Chappell Trust. She coordinated the sale of the properties owned by the trust and was instrumental in a behind-the-scene role during the sale of the Bush Hotel to the PDA. Shigeko was an original board member of Inter*Im when she insisted I be hired as its executive director. She worked in the District almost all of her life, first at her father's dairy, then as a proprietor of an ice cream shop. Shigeko always volunteered her time at fund-raising dinners, mail outs, and any event when we needed bodies. She was also very supportive through the years I worked in the community. She also held her liquor well — Scotch, with a water back.

Ben Woo, architect, was the bridge between the old Ruby Chow-led Chong Wa establishment and the vocal militant activists on issues dealing with the International District. He was also, like Shigeko and myself, a child of the I.D. He brought credibility to the negotiation table and didn't mind marching with the activists as long as his views were respected. Ben chaired boards for both Inter*Im and the PDA during the critical years. In meetings where tempers flared, Ben was the calm voice of reason, even when I didn't agree with him, which wasn't often. He was the one to whom I often turned for advice when dealing with sensitive issues. Aside from saving the International District, Ben's other passion was mushrooms. He is one of the Northwest's leading experts, with several published articles no less.

Tomio Moriguchi will forever be associated with Uwajimaya, his family business. Tomio was always honest in his assessment that economic development was the key to preserving and revitalizing the International District. At the same time, he always supported our housing efforts. While government and financial leaders may have considered us as "rabble-rousers," they couldn't pin that tag on Tomio. They listened to him. So did we. Tomio also wanted Inter*Im and the PDA to think regionally when transportation issues were planned. He was always aware that the International District was in the center of the transportation hub.

Barry Mar was another of Inter*Im's early board members. He was also a property owner, the first property owner on King Street who applied for public funds to renovate his building, the Atlas Hotel. Barry was a practical, no nonsense kind of guy. While on the Inter*Im staff, he conducted the original needs assessment to support the need for housing and social services in the International District.

Vera Chan Ing grew up in Chinatown. As a board member, she brought a lot of ideas, energy, and spirit to the meetings. One of her many strengths was her political connections. Like me, she ran for elective office, and like me, she lost. She was later appointed to the state liquor board.

Tom Kubota, architect and a long-time Inter*Im board member, brought professionalism to the board meetings and served on almost every major development project.

Jesse Tam first became involved with the PDA board as a bank manager for Rainier Bank. He was also very active with the International District Rotary Club. His financial expertise and credibility were very important in our campaign to build the I.D. Village Square. He stayed involved even after he left the District to run his own bank, the Northwest International Bank.

Along with the "dreamers," we also had the "schemers," the staff and community volunteers who wrote the proposals, organized the residents, testified at hearings, and gleefully plotted our next moves. As the executive director, I got a lot of the credit for the work performed by the following individuals:

Elaine (Ikoma) Ko was a dedicated community organizer and generated many programs that benefited the elderly residents of the International District. It was Elaine who started the

Housing Alliance, an organization geared specifically for residents. Along with Shari Woo, Andy Mizuki, and Rick Furukawa, Elaine did a tremendous job of mobilizing the residents for participation in demonstrations and public hearings. She was a tireless worker and an articulate, attractive advocate. Elaine was also a very good writer who helped me with my speeches and public presentations. She went on to head the city's Office for Women's Rights.

Donna Yee, who served on both the Inter*Im board and staff, helped develop the early Model Cities strategies for identifying funding priorities in the International District. It was Donna who did the grunt work to get Inter*Im off the ground. It's safe to say that without Donna, there would be no Inter*Im. She later became an expert on Asian elderly issues with the National Asian Pacific Center On Aging.

Dan Rounds, a tall, bearded, gentle soul, was our technical nuts-and-bolts guy. He wasn't much of a public speaker, but he was bright, creative, and wrote great grants. He's the guy who put the proposals together with all the right facts and figures. It was my role to say to Dan, "Make the figures work." And Dan did just that. In fact, he put together the most innovative proposal for the Danny Woo Community Garden.

Bruce Miyahara first made his mark as a public health activist. It was his vision, along with Jon Nakagawara, Al Muramoto, and Ken Mayeda, to start an Asian community health clinic, which became the International District Community Health Center. Bruce was on our staff, getting the funding together, before the clinic got off the ground. I will forever have a picture in my mind of Bruce, stroking his mustache during lengthy boring meetings. Bruce's reputation led to an appointment by Governor Mike Lowry to head the Washington State Health Department.

The first time I met Sue Taoka was at a White House Conference on Aging in the early 1970s. Then she was a pigtailed country girl from Colorado who looked completely lost in the lobby of the conference hotel. Jim Miyano, from Los Angeles, and I picked Sue up by her elbows and said, "You're coming with us." That was the beginning of a great friendship. When Sue decided to go to law school, she ended up at the University of Puget Sound in Tacoma. I quickly hired her for the Inter*Im staff. With her analytical mind, Sue had the innate ability to identify the pros and cons of any project we wanted to undertake. And when I left Inter*Im to run for the County Council, I felt very comfortable knowing that Inter*Im was in Sue's capable hands. Later, when I left the PDA to go to HUD, I was again pleased to leave the reins to Sue. Whatever I started, Sue was there to finish. She deserves a lot of the credit for turning the International District Village Square from a dream to a reality.

Sharon Lee has the reputation for being one of the most productive housing advocates for low-income housing in the country. "Never say never." Sharon came from Boston. She had been hired by the city of Seattle in 1983 to work on housing-related issues. But when her job with the city didn't work out, we brought her on staff. She quickly got a foothold and was called to do bigger and better things. She later became executive director of the Low-income Housing Institute. She also encouraged me to negotiate the peaceful exit by the anarchists who occupied a downtown building in the days following the 1999 World Trade Organization conference in Seattle.

Jeff Hattori was one of the younger activists. He was one of the young jocks who hung out at the Four Seas and posed relevant questions to me about the community. He followed through on this interest by volunteering at community agencies. I hired him to coordinate the first survey for the development of the International District Village Square. Jeff later became the administrator for the Keiro Nursing Home.

Rod Kawakami, although not technically on staff, served as Inter*Im's attorney during our battles with the Port of Seattle and the Milwaukee Hotel. Rod, who has a private practice in the I.D., was one of the original Asian attorneys who provided *pro bono* legal assistance to the community. He never turned down a request to assist in other important legal battles. Rod was the lead attorney for an Asian American legal team which successfully overturned Gordon Hirabayashi's World War II conviction for defying the internment of Japanese Americans. It was a landmark case. The judges found that federal archival documents proved the internment was based on racial prejudice.

There were other talented folks who worked on my staff at Inter*Im. These included Ron Chew, later executive director of the Wing Luke Asian Museum, who Inter*Im had funded under a Comprehensive Employment Training Act (CETA) grant to be the editor of the *International Examiner*; Vic Kubo, graphic artist, who designed and illustrated many of Inter*Im's promotional materials; Michio Teshima, a graduate student I hired to document the health hazards from a proposed energy recovery steam plant just south of the International District and who later served as director of the Housing Alliance; Diony Dionisio, who used his expertise in the renovation of the Bush-Asia Center and the N.P. Hotel; and Tom Ko, our accountant, who kept the books. There were others:

Doug Chin, as chair of Inter*Im's Social Welfare Task Force, researched funding sources and wrote many of the early proposals that led the delivery of social services to the community. As a staff person of the city's Department of Community Development, Doug was instrumental in identifying city resources for both the PDA and Inter*Im. Doug talked like he was from the ghetto, but wrote like he was a learned scholar, which he was. As a writer, he was also a historian who researched and documented the history of our community. As an activist, Doug monitored the hiring practices of government agencies, taking to task those who didn't meet affirmative action goals. Doug was a great strategic thinker.

Frank Irigon probably served, at one time or another, on the boards of almost every social service agency in the I.D. Frankie was like a pit bull, an outspoken advocate for equality in employment, education, and housing. At demonstrations, he was the one with the bullhorn, leading the chants. He was also a very funny guy with a great sense of humor.

Theresa Fujiwara first crossed my path as one of my CARITAS tutors. She later went to the UW School of Social Work. Along with Dave Okimoto, Tony Ishisaka, and Y.K. Kuniyuki, Theresa was instrumental in establishing Asian Counseling and Referral Service, which started out sharing space at Inter*Im. While we concentrated on providing more affordable housing, Theresa concentrated on mental health counseling and social services. Under her leadership, ACRS grew to become one of the largest social service agencies in the region.

Alan Kurimura was an "insider." Working as a legislative aide for former city Council member George Benson and later as the city's International Special Review District Board manager, Alan was always on the alert to possible resources for the I.D. He was the first person to identify the Eighth and Dearborn property as a potential development project.

Joe Edmonds was the first commercial developer I knew socially. At first, Joe was a potential "enemy" because he had plans to build an upscale hotel at Fifth Avenue South and South Jackson. But he quickly became an I.D. supporter. As the PDA got involved in development projects, I used Joe as a sounding board for his professional advice.

George Patterson from New York was a nationally recognized expert in housing development issues. He was a guy with credibility who helped us not only with grants from the Local Initiatives Support Group, a Ford Foundation program, but he also provided invaluable feedback in developing our original funding strategy for the International District Village Square project.

Every community needs a good mechanic. Pat Abe, the main man at Seventh Avenue Service, was one of the most important people in the community because he kept our cars in good shape to get to and from home. More than once Pat has mentioned, "Gee Bob, how in the hell did you do that?" Pat got to you no matter where you were and took care of the problem. He also contributed to the community causes.

As I look back, I realize there are a lot of other people in the community who were there when we needed them — Diane Narasaki, Elaine Shoji Ishihara, Gail Tanaka, Eliane Dao, Jan Kubota, Dorothy Wong, Craig Shimabukuro, Irene Woo, Emma Catague, Patricia Lee, Benson Wong, Diane Sugimura, Ruth Chinn, James Mason, Paul Mar, Ted Choi, the list goes on and on. So I apologize if I left off any names.

Finally, there were the residents who carried the signs for demonstrations, testified at public hearings, cleaned up Hing Hay Park, cooked at the pig roast, and reminded us of what we were fighting for. Al Masigat and Leo Lorenzo were both articulate spokesmen for the residents. Joe Kitamura was a daily visitor to our offices in the International District. Joe had spent his life as a laborer who worked on the railroad and other backbreaking jobs. He could spot a phony a mile away. Felipe Vides was always there to help at the pig roast. Lino Garcia, Tue Yuen Chan, Sammy Reyes, Kwak Leung Tse, and Dawn Canton worked many years for Inter*Im maintaining Hing Hay Park and Kobe Terrace Park.

Greasing the Wheel — The Political Process

To get the resources to protect, preserve, and develop the community as a viable commercial, retail and residential neighborhood, we had to learn "the political process." I had to build credibility with the influential "liberal political establishment." And the Seattle political scene was just that. Each mayor I worked with, Wesley J. Uhlman, Charles M. Royer, and Norman B. Rice, started their political careers as Democrats or in support of Democratic Party principles. The Seattle City Council was also a major player in the process. Many of the city council members were lifelong card-carrying Democrats who believed that government had a role in improving the lives of its neediest citizens. The challenge was getting the Mayor's Office and the City Council and their staff to know us and our plans.

Not that I always wanted to, mind you, but I needed to attend every reception where the mayor or city council members showed up. I also made sure I was introduced during the opening acknowledgments at banquets and dinners. It was important that influential people kept hearing my name. When I went to City Council hearings, I made sure I was called up to testify. I had noticed that in community gatherings or town hall meetings, certain people were always called on, by name. Then I noticed these people wore nametags with their names written large enough for the mayor to read. I printed "BOB" on my nametag and started getting called on by name, too. Everyone at these gatherings and meetings thought the mayor knew me personally.

Eventually, I established good working relationships with each of the mayors. Mayor Wes Uhlman prioritized the International District for low-income elderly housing. He also hired staff persons of color. Mayor Charles Royer was also an advocate of the International District. He supported funding for elderly nutrition programs, health care programs, social service programs, and the community garden. He appointed Arlene Oki, a long-time Asian community activist, as a high level assistant and appointed other Asians as key department heads. Mayor Norm Rice supported almost every program we put in front of him. He was key in lobbying other mayors on the Metro council for their support of the International District Village Square.

It was also very important for us to respect the legislative staff, both support staff and legislative aides. The support staff were important because they scheduled you to meet with their boss. The legislative aides were important because we knew they were asked for their opinions on our issues. In many cases, legislative aides later became aides to someone in a higher office or were themselves elected to office. It didn't hurt that many of the politicians had Asian Americans on staff, individuals like Rita Brogan, Junko Whitaker, Vera Ing, Alan Kurimura, Philip Fujii, Bob Flor, Alan Osaki, Anne Takekawa, and Peter Moy.

Access to the political process was key. The African American community gave us Mayor Norm Rice and King County Executive Ron Sims, both of whom had great working relationships with me. On the Seattle City Council, the African American community gave us Sam Smith, who was first elected in the late 1960s and served until the late 1980s. Richard McIver has continued the tradition of working cooperatively with the activists in the International District. And of course, there was King County Councilman Larry Gossett, a tremendous friend of the International District.

Having Asian Americans in elective office was a bonus. Back in the early 1970s, there were very few Asian Americans in political office. But as the Asian American community became a political force, we were able to get in the political game. Gary Locke was elected to the state legislature and Dolores Sibonga, a former Inter*Im board president, was elected to the City Council at a crucial time when we needed their support to preserve the I.D. Gary was very helpful as a state representative in providing funds for the Wing Luke Asian Museum and the Theater Off Jackson in the PDA's Bush-Asia Annex. When Gary was elected as the King County executive and later as governor, he was always supportive of the I.D. Village Square. Dolores and Ron Sims, as a King County councilman, spearheaded the early effort for local government support of the I.D. Village Square. This access continued with the later elections of Martha Choe and Cheryl Chow to the City Council.

Velma Veloria and Kip Tokuda continued that pattern in the state legislature. Velma first became active in the Anti-Martial Law Alliance and the Committee for Justice for Domingo and Viernes when she moved to Seattle. She won election to the state House of Representatives from the 11th legislative district, which included the International District. She played an important role in the successful passage of the funding bill to mitigate the impacts of the Seahawks football stadium on the surrounding neighborhoods. Kip, state representative from the 37th legislative district, earned a reputation as a strong advocate for communities of color and for children's issues during his career in the state House.

In the Asian American political community, one name deserves special mention. Ruth Woo has never run for office herself, but has played an invaluable role for many prospective and successful candidates. She worked for successful candidates from Governor Dan Evans to Governor Gary Locke and scores in between.

CHAPTER EIGHT

Life Outside the I.D.

The Move to HUD — Bob the Bureaucrat

SOON AFTER HENRY CISNEROS was appointed secretary for the federal Department of Housing and Urban Development, he spent several months putting together his management team, including assistant secretaries for each department. After each assistant secretary was appointed, they in turn put together their department management teams including deputy assistant secretaries. After Jean Nolan, assistant secretary for the Department of Public Affairs, was appointed, job announcements circulated for the deputy assistant secretary of Public Affairs position. Sharon Maeda, an activist from the old Kingdome and HUD demonstrations, by then a media consultant, applied for the position. Sharon used me as one of her references. When Jean Nolan's office called me on a reference check, I gave Sharon high marks as a public affairs professional. She got the job and moved from Seattle to Washington, D.C.

In 1994, the secretary's representative position in HUD's Northwest/Alaska Region remained vacant after the Clinton administration came to power. When Secretary Cisneros decided to appoint his Northwest/Alaska Representative for HUD, his office called the Seattle Chinatown-International District Preservation and Development Association requesting seven resumes of people with experience in housing and economic development in the Northwest. The PDA staff rounded up six resumes and sent mine along as the seventh. When Secretary Cisneros asked Sharon Maeda if she knew any of the candidates, she told him she knew me. Sharon told him about some of our projects in the International District, including the planned development of the International District

Village Square. The very next week, I received a call from Cisneros' office for an interview.

When I showed up for the interview at HUD headquarters, Cisneros offered me the job without asking if I knew anything about HUD programs. I had to decide whether I wanted to leave the comfort zone of the I.D. to work in the great bureaucracy of the federal government. I remembered the old demonstration days when we marched on HUD's regional office. How would I deal with a conference room full of angry protesters? After I visited HUD headquarters and saw the large comfortable airy office (my PDA office had no windows), the conference room with matching red chairs, the executive restroom, and heard about the salary, it didn't take long for me to make a decision. Talk about irony, now I would become a government bureaucrat.

I knew HUD was a bureaucracy with more than 400 staff members in the four states (Alaska, Idaho, Oregon, and Washington) covered under the secretary's representative's office. These were career staffers responsible for the prompt processing of FHA loans; ensuring that cities, counties, and non-profit organizations received block grants in a timely manner, and managing the hundred programs that made up the HUD portfolio. These were professionals who knew their jobs very well. They didn't need an extra bureaucrat to look over their shoulder. My job was to put a "face" on government by attending ground breakings, ribbon cuttings, apartment openings, installation ceremonies, retirement parties, and community events, wherever and whenever I could get to them....which was often.

One of the reasons I was appointed to the secretary's representative position was to fulfill affirmative action goals set by Henry Cisneros, HUD secretary. The 10 regional directors were a model mix of gender and race. For my part, I was more than the token Asian American. I had the experience of more than three decades of work in a multi-cultural and multiracial community. I was also well-connected to a large network of low-income housing and homeless advocates; not only could I assist with HUD resources, but I could also count on for their assistance whenever I needed it.

I used my network of community activists to get a handle on burning issues in the areas of housing and homelessness affecting neighborhoods and urban centers. In my first year at HUD, Seattle city officials gave notice to a homeless group camped on the west side of north Beacon Hill to leave "the jungle," an area overgrown with brush and weeds. The homeless had lived in "the jungle" in the spring and summer months for several years. But a brush fire in "the jungle" attracted the attention of the Seattle fire department and soon after, the Seattle-King County Health Department. There were reports that between 50 and 100 people lived in "the jungle" at any given time, without the usual amenities like bathrooms and showers. The Health Department had no choice, but to shut "the jungle" down.

Two days before the Seattle police department planned a sweep of "the jungle," I gathered my staff at HUD into a meeting to find out the kinds of programs we had available to help these homeless people. We had to be prepared to respond if we were called in for assistance. Two days after the sweep, Sharon Lee of the Low-income Housing Institute (LIHI) called me and said that six people, forced out of "the jungle" by the sweep, were sitting in LIHI's office with nowhere to go. Could we help? I told Sharon to bring the six people to our office the next day.

With the top staff at HUD in attendance, the homeless and their advocates explained their individual plights and asked for our assistance with shelter. Our housing staff offered the use of a duplex and a three-bedroom home, reacquired by our office on default. We transferred the titles for these two homes to LIHI under a modest lease. Two days later, we handed over the keys to the six homeless people willing to do minor repairs to the two homes in lieu of rent payments.

The next winter, in 1995, I negotiated the use of the receiving area in the lower level of the Old Federal Building with the General Services Administration (GSA) as a homeless shelter for 20 homeless peoples in cooperation with SHARE, a homeless advocacy agency. My local HUD office had set a precedent by establishing the nation's first and only homeless shelter in a federal office building. I believed that if we had public facilities with heat, light, restrooms, and showers paid for and maintained by public resources, we should use them.

The plight of migrant workers was another very important issue for our office. For too long, migrant farm worker families had been relegated to live the harvest seasons without shelter, in parking lots, on vacant farmland, on the riverbanks, or irrigation ditches in farming communities. There were no specific HUD programs that addressed the migrant farm worker problem outside of California and Texas. Every year during the harvest season, I read about the plight of the homeless farm workers and their families, forced to live off the land in the shadow of mansions owned by wealthy farm owners they helped make rich. I wanted to help and took my case for farm worker housing to Saul Ramirez, the deputy secretary of HUD. He okayed my request to find HUD money for migrant families. Working with his highest ranking assistant, Ricardo Perez, and our local funding wizard, Jack Peters, I found enough HUD resources through community development block grant funds to build clean, safe, affordable housing in Mattawa, Washington for a number of families who had lived on a riverbank.

When HUD Secretary Henry Cisneros moved on to work at Univision, the Spanish-speaking cable channel, President Clinton had Seattle Mayor Norm Rice on the top of his list as Cisneros' replacement. But Norm didn't mount an aggressive campaign to win the appointment. A last minute interest shown by Andrew Cuomo forced Clinton to delay the appointment, which turned out to benefit Cuomo.

Andrew Cuomo is the son of Mario Cuomo, the former governor of New York. He is married to Kerry Kennedy, the daughter of Ethel and the late Robert Kennedy. Andrew had originally planned to resign from the position of assistant secretary for Community Planning and Development at HUD to take a high profile job in New York. As soon as Cuomo's interests in the HUD secretary position became known, a very aggressive campaign was thrown into gear and the way was cleared for his elevation to the high profile position.

Mayor Rice had been the front runner, but was busy defending the city's controversial attempts in assisting the Nordstrom Company, then planning to develop its flagship store in the old vacated downtown Frederick and Nelson department store. The city applied for a $25,000,000 guaranteed loan HUD grant to help Nordstrom renovate the old Frederick and Nelson space on the theory that, under HUD guidelines, the vacated department store posed the threat of "blight" in the surrounding area. The proposed loan infuriated low-income housing activists.

The Seattle Displacement Coalition, led by the fiery and uncompromising John Fox, opposed the HUD low-interest loan because it benefited the wealthy and powerful Nordstrom family. The Displacement Coalition felt that this loan should have gone to small business ventures that could revitalize inner city neighborhoods. To stop the loan, the Displacement Coalition lodged a formal complaint with HUD headquarters. The Coalition charged that the Seattle city officials, in justifying using the term "blight" and the effects that "blight" would have on the surrounding area, submitted crime statistics that were not current.

Cuomo knew that a delay in the naming of a replacement to head HUD would help his chances for the post. He requested that HUD's inspector general investigate the charges by the Displacement Coalition. With the drawn out investigation, Mayor Rice was replaced by Cuomo as the top candidate for HUD secretary. Cuomo slid into the post and held it until the Clinton administration left in early 2001.

I had witnessed a political move by a master. Cuomo, in his powerful position at HUD, bestowed millions of dollars of grant money on New York cities and counties. For example, he allocated $170,000,000 to provide economic development assistance to communities along the Erie Canal. Bill DeBlasio, my counterpart in New York was hired by Andrew and after a short stay, resigned to run Hillary Clinton's campaign in her successful run for the U.S. Senate. Less than two months after leaving HUD, Andrew announced his candidacy for governor of New York for the 2002 election.

I relished my opportunity representing the federal Department of Housing and Urban Development in the Northwest Alaska Region. I was able to create some innovative programs that were of great benefit to people in our communities. But I could not stand the politics of Andrew Cuomo, the self-anointed leader of the new Camelot era who never knew or cared about how we, his representatives, worked our butts off to make communities in our regions a better place to live and raise families. He took credit for every successful program at HUD — past and present. He wanted to leave a lasting legacy that he was the "greatest secretary that HUD ever had." Humility had no place on the 10th floor of the HUD building in Washington, D.C.

As a dedicated civil rights activist, there was one situation which occurred that still troubles me to this day. During one of Secretary Cuomo's infrequent conference calls with his top staff — the assistant secretaries and the 10 secretary's representatives from offices around the nation — he told us that Idaho Senator Larry Craig complained to him about the executive director of the Idaho Housing Council, a non-profit agency that HUD funded to monitor civil rights compliance. The Council found that 26 Idaho contractors failed to provide accessibility in the construction of new facilities needed for people with disabilities in the Boise,

Idaho area. These contractors were investigated, charged, and fined for their negligence in discriminating against the disabled.

At the time, Sen. Craig was a ranking member of the Senate Appropriations Committee which oversaw HUD funding. The senator had also been a former official of the Idaho Building and Construction Industry before his election to the powerful position in the U.S. Senate. After Sen. Craig's angry complaints to Secretary Cuomo that the Idaho Housing Council had "overreacted" toward Idaho's construction industry, the Council lost its funding to continue its civil rights compliance program without a whimper of protest by the secretary. I guess the Idaho Housing Council had done its job of upholding civil rights too well. Yet, in almost every speech delivered by Secretary Cuomo, he mentioned that no one would be discriminated against during his watch as the top national housing official in the United States. Yes, I represented Andrew Cuomo in the Northwest Alaska region, and yes, he will run for governor of New York and eventually, president of the United States. God help the Republic.

During the World Trade Organization (WTO) unrest that descended upon Seattle late in 1999, I was unexpectedly called upon to mediate a dispute. World leaders and trade representatives had come to Seattle to discuss international commerce issues and to explore ways to improve the free flow of trade. Opponents believed that WTO policies prioritized corporate profits at the expense of human rights in third world countries and encouraged an environment for corporations seeking cheaper labor in compromised labor conditions.

In addition to the 50,000 trade unionists, environmentalists, and human rights supporters who came to Seattle to peacefully rally and march, another 2,000 demonstrators from the Direct Action Network, the Ruckus Society, and anarchist groups from throughout the nation were poised to disrupt the entire WTO convention. And disrupt they did, causing several million dollars of damage in the ensuing days that followed. The anarchists broke windows, defaced private property, and created an environment for looting and rioting. The police were outnumbered.

Several young anarchists came to Seattle on Sunday, November 28, two days before the official opening of the WTO conference and proceeded to occupy a vacant building at Ninth Avenue and Virginia Street in downtown Seattle, a few blocks from the Washington State

Convention and Trade Center, where the WTO conference was being held. The building was used as a "squat" or home for out-of-town anarchists during the week of the conference. When the WTO conference ended, the anarchists refused to leave the building until they received assurances from the owner that the vacant building would be converted to low-income housing or a homeless shelter.

I was called in by Sharon Lee of LIHI to mediate a peaceful settlement between the owners, the protesters, the police, and the mayor's office. Wah Lui, the owner of the building, was extremely upset because the police did not respond when he complained that the anarchists were trespassing in his building. When Sharon Lee and I met with him, he didn't want to talk about the future of the building. He was really mad at everybody, including us, for pestering him. At the end of an hour-long meeting, he softened enough to say that he was willing to discuss his building's future use with SHARE, the homeless advocacy group, as long as they were not connected to the anarchists.

After the meeting with Wah Lui ended, I was sent in alone to brief the "squatters" about Wai's willingness to discuss the future of the occupied building with SHARE, emphasizing that there was yet no written agreement and no commitment. I was escorted to the roof where the masked youths monitored the police movements. The police had mobilized in the parking lot below, preparing to storm the building shortly. "Jeff H.," the anarchist who let me in the building, introduced me to the gathering by saying, "This is Bob Santos with the federal government, but he's okay. He does a mean Frank Sinatra at the Bush Garden karaoke bar." This melted the ice. The protesters trusted my promises to them. Discussions with the owner to build low rent housing would continue, but only if they walked out with me peacefully, which they did.

One of the highlights of my career at HUD occurred when the tenants of a newly renovated apartment structure for homeless people at the former Sandpoint Naval Air Station renamed the building "Santos Place" in my honor. The Low-income Housing Institute converted what had been several buildings of military housing at the old naval station into 94 units of transitional housing for the homeless.

Sharon Lee, director of the Low-income Housing Institute (LIHI), called me and said Building 224 was to be named after me. I explained to Sharon that because LIHI received

HUD funds to renovate the building, it wasn't ethical to name the building after a HUD official. I checked with HUD's legal counsel about the name change. He agreed that it was not ethical to name the building "Santos Place." I relayed our attorney's opinion to Sharon Lee, thanked her, and told her I couldn't accept the honor. A week later, Sharon Lee called to inform me the building's resident council voted to name the building "Santos Place" and "to hell with what HUD said." And so in early May 2000, I respectfully attended the naming ceremonies at Santos Place.

CHAPTER NINE

Hanging Out with Uncle Bob

Uncle Bob's Hangouts

When I started working in the International District, I learned that hanging out in the bars and lounges was an important part of lobbying for our causes. After working hours, I made the rounds of the restaurant lounges, strictly for business purposes, mind you, and met with local leaders and business people. I don't mean to glorify barflies or drinking, but socializing in the bars and lounges was an important part of getting to know other people in the community.

In the mid-1960s, after meetings in the Central Area regarding civil rights issues, Walt Hubbard and I met for a few drinks at Art Louie's, on the second floor of the Milwaukee Hotel. Charlie Ko was the bartender at the time. Down the street, the Gim Ling, owned by Tek Wong, was a popular spot with the "Young Turks" — the Filipino activists which included Tony Ogilvie (who later preferred to be called A. Baretto Ogilvie), Sonny Tangalin, Pete Jamero, and our "honorary" Filipino, Father Harvey McIntyre. Harvey, a priest, carried a blue Hawaiian shirt in the trunk of his car. When he met us for drinks, he tossed his collar into the trunk and out came the shirt, which he put on to blend in with the crowd.

On any given evening, I might sit and have a drink at the Gim Ling restaurant with Bob Chinn, founder of United Savings and Loan Bank, who always had an opinion, or Eddie Yip who always had a loud opinion (but Eddie always made a point of making me feel comfortable). Danny and Wilma Woo owned the popular New Chinatown. Up at the Four Seas restaurant, owned by Abe Lum and Wilbur Chin, there was always Ken Louie, Chinatown's master fortune cookie maker, with an opinion on every issue and, of course, he was always right, too. There were Robert Wong and Elaine Young, co-owners of the Linyen restaurant. Paul Woo hung out at Art Louie's, which changed hands and was renamed the Silver Dragon restaurant, managed by Wayne Yee. Dan Mar, Jimmy Leong, and Lippy Mar spent after work hours there and were always easy to talk with. Roy and Joan Seko ran the Bush Garden restaurant, which drew the Japanese American crowd. Irwin and Bruce Yoshimura had a host of regulars in their popular lounge at the Mikado restaurant. It was important that I visit the bars and cocktail lounges because I didn't expect these owners or business people to attend our community meetings.

It became a tradition after any Inter*Im board meeting for some board member to suggest having a few drinks at either the Four Seas, Quong Tuck, or Bush Garden. Even when we had heated arguments during board meetings, socializing in the bars afterward was a signal that our differences weren't personal. This great tradition continued after PDA board meetings, too. I always appreciated it when someone besides me suggested going to the lounge. Maybe that's why I always loved Shigeko Uno, who never turned down an opportunity to have one for the road.

But it wasn't all fun and games. We actually conducted business in those lounges and bars. Soon after the memorial service for Denise Louie in 1977, I had a conversation with Bob Chinn, president of United Savings and Loan, in the lounge of the China Gate. At the time, I was sitting with Bob in the lounge when Mickey Louie, Denise Louie's father, who worked the front desk at China Gate, thanked me for the words I had said at her memorial service. Bob asked me what he could do and I told him I'd get back to him. I then got the idea of asking money from the International District's three banks, including Bob's bank, for start-up costs for the Denise Louie Early Childhood Education Center. Shortly thereafter, I arranged for a meeting with the managers of the three International District banks.

And it was during a conversation with Danny Woo at the Quong Tuck lounge that I was able to negotiate the $1 lease for the Danny Woo Community Garden property. The important thing about relaxing with Chinese community leaders like Bob Chinn, Alan Louie, Eddie Yip, Robert Wong, Sonny Lew, and Danny and Wilma Woo was that I didn't try to pressure them to support our "liberal" causes. They found I wasn't a "wild-eyed" radical and what we were doing truly benefited the whole community. They didn't understand why we demonstrated and held rallies, but if we brought them business, we must have been okay.

The Four Seas had been "the place to be" for young activists. The Alaska Cannery Workers Association's office was right across the street. Silme Domingo, David Della and others relaxed there after long meetings on the fight against martial law in the Philippines, the reform movement in Local 37, or the Kingdome struggles. The "Seas" was also the watering hole for owners and managers from the companies in the industrial area, south of Dearborn Street. Thursday night was the traditional gathering spot for the recreational basketball and baseball players after their hard fought games. The "Seas" was one of my hangouts until too many teenagers without adult identification told the bartender they knew me when they were carded. It became embarrassing when some of these teenagers told the bartender they were "friends of Uncle Bob" and I really didn't know them, especially when I was in the bar at the same time.

After leaving the "Seas" as a hangout, we moved our business to Danny and Wilma Woo's new place, Quong Tuck. The Quong Tuck was a family-run business (their kids Curtis, Teresa, and Clinton helped out) which served American food — hamburgers, fries, sandwiches. This place was like a private club for the I.D. activists who wanted a relaxing place away from "the struggle." The "QT" was our little secret. It wasn't a place for tourists and it wasn't a place for people to be seen. It was like "Cheers," where everybody knew your name. There were never ending cribbage, pinochle, and rummy games. There were meetings about NWAAT scripts and skits. Although we were political, we tried not to make our conversation too obvious. Out-of-towners who needed to find friends in the community just showed up from the airport and connections were made. Wilma Woo, the owner/bartender, always had messages for those who ended their workday there.

Because I lived in the community, I visited with an endless list of interesting people, most of whom were good at heart, but a few you didn't want to be seen with. At the Silver Dragon, an after-work group of business leaders in the community were regulars, but late at night when the bands played, one could really get in trouble. One musician in particular often turned up stoned and didn't mind if people joined in.

When Tek Wong sold the Gim Ling to Alan Louie, Alan changed the name to China Gate and hired hostesses who hustled customers for drinks. The hostesses ordered very expensive drinks for the customers while they drank very expensive sodas paid by the customers to sit with them. They sat with the customers, they danced with the customers. Some customers expected a good time and didn't mind paying for it. Others who didn't think they ordered as much as the bill stated didn't come back. I quit hanging out at the China Gate after a shootout left two dead and one seriously wounded in a gang incident believed to be started by the Tulisans. The Hanil restaurant in the Bush-Asia Center was another cocktail lounge that hired sexy hostesses who brought in male customers.

The place that still drew the regulars, those who had been customers for as many as three and even four decades, was the Bush Garden. Roy and Joan Seko sold the business after 40 years, but still spent much of their time there with old childhood friends who still came to the cocktail lounge. The newer customers like me had only been regulars since the early 1980s when karaoke became popular. The Bush Garden became the destination point for all the would-be singers in town. Owners of Northwest restaurants came in to check out this new form of entertainment, and the novelty grew steadily into a fad. Friday and Saturday nights were usually packed with regulars, mixed in with a new wave of talented and not so talented singers. It became the gathering spot after the many fund-raising and celebration dinners held throughout the city by Asian American organizations. The lounge is still a popular place to meet after community meetings.

Marriage on the Rocks

My marriage to Anita didn't survive. We divorced in 1981. There were several reasons that led to the breakup of our marriage, most of which were my priorities outside the family. In many cases, community issues took precedent over family responsibilities. There were the endless community meetings, board meetings, legislative hearings, and Seattle City Council sessions. There were also the receptions and fund-raising dinners, which became a drain on the family household budget. There were also perhaps some insensitive decisions that benefited members of the community at the expense of my family. For example, Silme once asked me to put up our house as collateral for bail on behalf of a young Alaskero member of Local 37, who had been charged with assault of another union member in an I.D. cocktail lounge. I agreed and managed to convince Anita that it wasn't such a big thing to put the house up. But truth be told, we were one Greyhound bus ride away from being homeless if Silme's friend had skipped bail.

There was a second marriage in my life that occurred on the rebound after my divorce from Anita. It lasted only a short time. Nina Sullivan worked in the lounges of the Linyen, Four Seas, and the Quong Tuck restaurants, places where I was a regular. I saw her often, first on a casual basis, then the next thing I knew, we were married. Impulsive? Perhaps. A mistake? Most definitely. We really weren't right for each other. There were a lot of differences between us which became difficult to overcome. But we remained friends after we split. Nina was a beautiful, bright, lighthearted woman who lived a full life in a short lifetime. She died on New Year's Eve, 1998.

SANTOS, A NAME YOU CAN TRUST — SHARON TOMIKO SANTOS

I first met Sharon Tomiko Miyake in 1989, when we were both working on Mike Lowry's campaign for the U.S. Senate. I was on Mike's congressional staff and Sharon Tomiko coordinated the campaign's phone bank committee. Being the gallant person that I am, I invited Sharon Tomiko for an after-work refreshment at the Bush Garden, and it became the place for us to meet after tough, and not so tough, campaign days. On evenings when I went through my list of potential dinner dates only to come up empty, I called my pal Sharon Tomiko, and more often than not, she agreed to go. We had much in common and thoroughly loved each other's humor and company. Finally, we decided to share our lives together and were married on September 12, 1992.

I was welcomed with open arms into Sharon's family. Joyce and Ken Miyake, my in-laws, were both active in the community for many years. Joyce, a retired special education teacher, was an active union member with the teachers union, and Ken was a retired minister formerly with Blaine Memorial Methodist Church. The in-laws included Sharon's brother and his family: Matt, Shari, Daniel, and Christopher Miyake; and Sharon's sister and her family: Miriam, John, and Alex Johnson.

Sharon Tomiko got heavily involved in national and international women's issues and was selected as a voting delegate to the 1995 International Women's Conference in Beijing, China. Knowing Sharon Tomiko was very opinionated, I warned her to be very careful and not do anything embarrassing to her hosts in China, a country not known for progressive views on women's issues. I didn't want to read that my wife was being detained for revolutionary activities.

The second day Sharon was in China, I turned to the "CBS Morning News Hour" to hear two women being interviewed about the exciting conference and how well the host country was handling things. After the second interview, there was Sharon Tomiko, being interviewed by the CBS crew in Beijing. She complained, for all the world to hear, about the unequal treatment she had received from Chinese security guards. They had allowed the Chinese male dignitaries the freedom to go in and out of the meeting hall without being questioned, but had not allowed her to return to the meeting hall to pick up her elderly travel companion. I thought I'd never see her again. As things turned out, the women from the conference were given more freedom to enter and exit conference events after she complained.

In 1999, Sharon Tomiko was elected to the Washington state House of Representatives by campaigning harder than anyone I've ever seen. She loved every minute of it. Sharon Tomiko was smart, politically savvy, did her homework, and enjoyed the give and take in the trenches. In 2000, in just her second term, she was elected by her peers in the House Democratic Caucus as the House Democratic Whip, which elevated her to a top leadership position in the Democratic Party.

Her biggest fan in Olympia is Representative Bill Grant, the House Democratic Caucus Chairman who represents one of the largest state districts in Walla Walla, Washington. Representative Grant is a farmer who annually harvests over 2,000 acres of wheat. At dinner on the evening of Sharon's election to the House Democratic leadership, Bill said, "Sharon represents the most ethnically diverse district in the state while I represent an almost totally White rural district, but we both understand each other's constituency base because we've taken the time to communicate the particular issues facing the people we represent. Sharon is one of our brightest members. She spends the time to educate us on issues she is passionate about without dragging us through the guilt process. She is really a positive force in Olympia and I really love working with her."

One of the reasons Sharon is so successful in Olympia is that she can absorb much of the information that people throw at her as they lobby for her support. She is also willing to devote hours and hours researching issues. Sharon gets along with her colleagues — she is outgoing, does not pass up an opportunity to attend receptions and dinners, and can hang with the best of them. She knows her limits and almost never gets into an argument unless it's with me.

Another quality she has, although it's one I don't know anyone would want to have, is her insistence on reading labels. She reads the labels on prescription and non-prescription drugs, food items, clothing, and just about everything else. She berated my doctor once when he prescribed medication that included iron. She reminded him that tests showed my blood had a high content of iron, so why was he prescribing this medication? Of course, the prescription was changed.

On a sad note, Joyce Miyake passed suddenly on the last day of Sharon's second session in Olympia. In the mid-1970s, Joyce served as chair of the Minority Affairs Commission of the Washington Education Association. Joyce, in her role as chair, presented a resolution to the WEA to name January 15 for the late Martin Luther King, Jr. This was a very controversial issue at the time and it was presented years before the national holiday was declared in Congress. Joyce was also influential in getting the WEA to send a telegram to the White House encouraging President Ronald Reagan to sign the Japanese American redress bill.

I can just imagine how uncomfortable Joyce made some board members of WEA when she questioned decision makers on matters that meant much to her. When Joyce became involved in an issue, she was very tenacious, not letting go unless she was satisfied with the response. She had no hesitancy putting those she questioned in the hot seat. I believe that tenacity is one quality that was handed down from mom to daughter.

We Are Family — My Family

With most of my life goals achieved, I've tried to make up for the years when everything I did outside of family seemed of equal importance. All my children and grandchildren live and work in King County, so I look forward to gathering a few of the grandkids on a Saturday "knocking around" the International District for *dim sum*; or a trinket shopping spree on the waterfront, in the Pike Place Market, or downtown. We have had the usual holiday dinners and summertime picnics where everybody fusses over the youngest newborn.

Dan, the oldest of the six siblings, had his own construction business, but works out of the carpenters' union for that regular paycheck. He and his wife Vicki are parents of Chauncey, Briana, Enrique, Valencia, and Maurizio. Simone Busby has a lot to handle at home with Tiffany, Denise, Marissa, and Brendan. Two of Simone's kids, Shante and Nicole, have left the nest to start life on their own. Robin Santos has three children, Marcianna, Macaria, and Bobiono. You might read about all three someday in the local sports pages. Tom is at Alaska Airlines and spends-off hours coaching basketball at the high school level. He and wife Nancy have two boys, Niko and Thomas, who are also active in sports. They are politically conscious as well, and enjoyed marching with their cousin Macaria in their first Martin Luther King, Jr. march in 2000. John owns his own graphics business and he, his wife Meagan, and daughter Melise bounce all around the city together. Then there's Nancy, the youngest. Nancy only has her dog Bishop to worry about. She and Robin opened up their own printing business, United Reprographics, in 1999, along with Robin's partner Brian Sims and his brother Allen.

The End of an Era, The Beginning of a New Era

The Battle Rages On — What the I.D. Is Now

THE INTERNATIONAL DISTRICT HAS changed since the early 1970s when I first took over the helm at Inter*Im. There are now more than 70 restaurants. Uwajimaya has expanded. More than one million square feet of new office space and several hundred thousand square feet of new retail space have been added by new construction. There has been a more diversified business section, but the residential base has stayed intact despite the construction of more than one million square feet of new office space and several hundred thousand square feet of new retail space.

Over to the west, the 45,000-seat Safeco Field (Mariner baseball stadium) and a new 70,000-seat Seahawk football stadium have become the International District's newest neighbors. In order to take advantage of this inflow, the McDonalds Corporation negotiated for space in the I.D. to cater exclusively to the 5,000 new workers in this fragile community. Once again, the activists of the District rose to meet the challenge of unwanted development. McDonalds eventually backed away.

But as we entered the 21st century, threats to our community's stability not only came from outside developers, but also from within. There is a certain segment of the Chinese community who continue to argue that our neighborhood should be called "Chinatown," not the "International District." This group has taken the position that Chinatown is for the Chinese, although the rest of us, Japanese, Filipino, Southeast Asian, among others, are welcome in *their* neighborhood.

This group organized over the closure of one block of Lane Street after the Seattle city officials approved a request from Uwajimaya's owners for the street closure to expand their store. With the street closure, Uwajimaya developed a store twice its former size to 50,000 square feet with another 23,000 square feet for additional retail space and 176 market-rate apartments on the upper floors. Uwajimaya is one of the few companies in the International District which invested millions of dollars promoting the International District. They have grown and prospered. Uwajimaya is also the only local company that poured its profits back into the community, both with this expansion and with generous donations to local social service organizations.

The closure of Lane Street is between Fifth Avenue South and Sixth Avenue South. In that one block, there are no historical buildings, no major businesses, no restaurants, and no housing. It is not a major thoroughfare. The group protesting the street closure took the matter to court, but lost every legal challenge they made. While they say it's a matter of street access, in reality, the issue is really one of who has the power in the International District.

In all of my years working in the International District, this particular group has been more of an obstacle in our efforts to bring more housing and revitalize the community. There could be a more troubling development than the closure of Lane Street; that could be the closure of King Street. This street is in the core of the historic Chinatown. There are seven vacant deteriorating buildings, owned by some of the same people protesting the closure of Lane Street, that pose a danger to people walking on the sidewalks in front of these buildings. To address this danger, either the buildings get the needed repairs or King Street needs to be closed.

The Doomed Stadium

Looking at the old issues of the *International Examiner*, I came across a memorable photo of a guy holding a sign that read, "DON'T LET THE DOME DOOM CHINATOWN!" I could really stress the obvious and say who doomed who, but I won't. The reality is that on the site of the once busy Kingdome, construction of a new $500 million Seahawk stadium took place. Along with the new $500 million Safeco Field, these two stadiums will actually have less total events in their facilities than that of the multi-purpose Kingdome and therefore, will have less negative impacts — such as fan disruption — on the International District.

However, it will be hard to predict what all the hundreds of millions of dollars worth of construction, not only of the athletic inspired spectator stadiums, but the other office and commercial buildings, will have on the International District. Mitigation of the Kingdome on the International District actually came down to the preservation and respect for a culturally proud Asian ethnic neighborhood. Will the $10,000,000 mitigation fund that will be shared by the International District for the Seahawk stadium be enough to save it from extinction? It seems to me that most of the mitigation fund will go towards making it easier for fans to commute in and out of the impacted communities, to and from the sports events. We fought for programs to ease the impacts of the Kingdome on the community and we were successful. Did we really want to see the massive structure turned to dust?

When the Kingdome was built, there were people in the International District who felt that it would be good for business. But most of the event goers paid little attention about what was happening in the neighborhood. Even when the International District street fair was held, Kingdome customers scurried through the District before and after events without even bothering to find out what was going on. I see no changes with the development of Safeco Field and the new Seahawk stadium. As I continue to face west towards the encroachment of the new wave of development, I feel we are being slowly inched aside, and it doesn't feel good. Gee, maybe the Dome wasn't that bad after all. Certainly, the end of the Kingdome signifies the end of one era and the beginning of another.

The International District will always hold a special place in my heart. I have great, vivid memories of my childhood days in my dad's hotel room at the N.P. Hotel. Most of my adult life has been spent in the International District, doing the people's work and meeting unforgettable, dedicated activists who believed in community service. Despite all of the tremendous threats to the survival of the International District, there is a resilience within the community to overcome the obstacles put in our path toward the goal of community revitalization. I'm convinced that our hard fought struggles prove that the International District can and will survive. Its survival is my lasting legacy and a tribute to the hard work of those who were with me for the ride.

Bibliography

Berner, Richard C., "Seattle Transformed, Seattle in the 20th Century, *From World War II to the Cold War, Vol. 3*, Charles Press, Seattle, Wash., c. 1999, pps. 192-193

Chew, Ron, "District Organizations Oppose County Plan," *International Examiner*, July 1979, p. 3; "Hearing Examiner Rules in Favor of County Work Release Program," *International Examiner*, August 1979, p. 5; "County Releases Draft Environmental Impact Statement," *International Examiner*, September 1979, p. 1; "King County Proposes Alternative Work Release Site," *International Examiner*, November 1979, p. 9

Chew, Ron, "Domingo and Viernes were Murdered to Silence Marcos Critics, Says Lawsuit," *International Examiner*, October 1982, p. 5; "Marcos Asks for Immunity from Civil Suit," *International Examiner*, January 19, 1983, pps. 1-3; "Judge Hears Arguments on Domingo-Viernes Civil Suit," *International Examiner*, May 4, 1983, p. 1

Chew, Ron, "Willie Mak Goes on Trial, "*International Examiner*, September 7, 1983, pps. 1-2; "Jury Convicts Willie Mak," *International Examiner*, October 19, 1983, pps. 1, 11

Chew, Ron, "Will Union Station Become New City Hall Campus," *International Examiner*, April 1, 1987, pps. 1, 2

Chew, Ron and Honda, Sharon, "Court Closes Milwaukee Hotel," *International Examiner*, September 1977, p. 1

Chin, Doug and Bacho, Peter, "A History of an Urban Ethnic Community: Asian Americans and the Development of Seattle's International District," published in the *International Examiner*, October 17, 1984, November 21, 1984, and December 19, 1984

Chin, Sue, "We Don't Want a Jail in Our Backyard," *International Examiner*, September 15-October 15, 1980, p. 1

Churchill, Thomas, "Triumph Over Marcos," Open Hand Pub., Seattle, Wash., c. 1995

Crowley, Walt, "National Trust Guide, Seattle: America's Guide for Architecture and History Treasures," John Wiley and Sons, Inc., New York, c. 1998, pps. 51-62

Crowley, Walt, *Rites of Passage: A Memoir of the Sixties in Seattle,* University of Washington Press, Seattle, Wash., c. 1995, pps. 11-13, 29, 43, 114-115, 118, 157

DeBarros, Paul, *Jackson Street After Dark: The Roots of Jazz in Seattle,* Sasquatch Books, Seattle, Wash., c. 1993

Domingo, Silme, "Asian Workers File Suit," *Asian Family Affair*, December 1973, pps. 6-7

Dorpat, Paul and McCoy, Genevieve, *Building Washington: A History of Washington State's Public Works,* Tartu Publications, Seattle, Wash., c. 1998, pps. 94-97

Fujii, Ann, "Baruso Trial Verdict," District Notes, *International Examiner*, March 20, 1991, p. 4

Gee How Oak Tin Association 90th Anniversary and Building Re-Inauguration Journal, 1900-1990, pages 37-39

Hanford, C.H., "Seattle and Environs," Vol. 3, Pioneer Historical Publishing Company, Chicago, c. 1924, pps. 164-167

Hatch, Walter, "Wheels of Justice Grind Slowly in Landmark Case," *Seattle Sun,* May 16, 1979, pps. 8, 12

Interim Community Development Association, "King Street Historic District," Nomination Form, National Register of Historic Places Inventory, United States Department of the Interior, (draft, undated)

"International Center New Name of Chinatown," *The Seattle Times*, July 24, 1951, p. D6

International District, Neighborhood Profile, "International District: A Walking Tour," *Seattle Post-Intelligencer*, July 19, 1997, p. D6

Ito, Kazuo, *Issei, A History of Japanese Immigrants in North America,* translated by Shinichiro Nakamura and Jean S. Gerard, Japanese Community Service, Japan Publications, 1973

Iwamoto, Gary, "Judge Reverses Earlier Decision: Community Volunteers Keep Milwaukee Hotel Open," *International Examiner*, October 1977, p. 1

Kiyomizu, Ellen, "Kokusai: 60 Years of Asian Films," *International Examiner*, October 12-November 15, 1980, p. 8

Lee, Bill, *Chinese Playground: A Memoir,* Rhapsody Press, San Francisco, c. 1999, pps. 143-173

Memorandum, Review of Seacom Financial Data, from John Schlosser to Larry Gossett, CAMP, and other Cable Coalition Members and Sean Bleck, Evergreen Legal Services, dated November 24, 1987

Multidisciplinary Associates, Wright, Anthony D., Adalfae, Michael H., Haden, Judy, "A Planning Report for Seattle's International District," prepared for the Seattle Model City Program, 1974, pps. 1-2

"Personal Justice Denied," A Report of the Commission on Wartime Relocation and Internment of Civilians, Summary and Recommendations, Washington, D.C., 1982, p. 28

Records of Civic Unity Committee, "*International Center News,*" Jackson Street Community Council, March 1, 1952, Box 14, File 9, Special Collections, Allen Library, University of Washington

Records of Powell Barnett, "Jackson Street Community Council," Special Collections, Allen Library, University of Washington

Records of Elmer Ogawa, "Jackson Street Community Council," Box 7, Files 8-17, Box 89, Files 1-11, Special Collections, Allen Library, University of Washington

Records of Victorio Velasco, "Jackson Street Community Council," Box 10, Files 25-33, Box 11, Files 1-29, Special Collections, Allen Library, University of Washington

Santos, Bob, "Our Very Good Friends Silme and Gene," *International Examiner*, June 16, 1981, p. 12

Sugiyama, Alan, "Rise of the Movement," *Asian Family Affair*, April 1975, pps. 4-6

Sunde, Scott, "Willie Mak, FBI Wrangle Over Files," *Seattle Post-Intelligencer*, February 3, 1999, pps. B1-2; "Willie Mak Cleared for Sentencing," *Seattle Post-Intelligencer*, May 5, 1999, p. B1

Takami, David, *Divided Destiny: A History of Japanese Americans in Seattle*, Wing Luke Asian Museum and the University of Washington, Seattle, Wash., c. 1998

Takami, David, "Domingo v. Marcos Trial Begins: Plaintiff Attorneys Argue that Marcos Responsible for Union Murders," *International Examiner*, December 6, 1989, pps. 1, 10-11

Takami, David, *Executive Order 9066: 50 Years Before and 50 Years After, A History of Japanese Americans in the Seattle Area,* Wing Luke Asian Museum, Seattle, Wash., c. 1991

Taylor, Quintard, "The Forging of a Black Community: Seattle's Central District, From 1870 through the Civil Rights Era," University of Washington Press, Seattle, Wash., c. 1994, p. 174, chp. 6, nt. 38

Viernes, Gene, "NEFCO Goes Under," *International Examiner*, May 15-June 15, 1980, p. 12

Zia, Helen, *Asian American Dreams — The Emergence of an American People,* Farrar, Straus, and Giroux. New York, c. 2000, pps. 146-152, 154-164

Acknowledgments

I CANNOT SAY ENOUGH ABOUT the contribution that Gary Iwamoto made to get this book out. Gary was my editor, spellchecker, and researcher, and did all the formatting on a laptop as I shared my stories. He also had the patience to listen to these memories and the courage to say, "Gee Bob, that story sucks." Gary was present at the first meeting in 1986 to talk about doing a book on my life experiences.

Ron Chew was also involved from the beginning and because of his experience in the publishing field, took on the role as coordinator of the team. Vic Kubo created the front cover design and his artistic style shows why he is an international superstar in the arts field. John Santos designed the back cover, John D. Pai took on the responsibility of photo design, and Debbie Louie coordinated the layout.

Special thanks go to Diane Wong, who took the time to review an early draft of the book and helped us set the tone for a very personal life story, and to Peter Jamero for editing the final draft. And for her unwavering support all through the entire process, I am especially grateful to my wife, Sharon Tomiko, who taught me that "save" is good.

I also want to acknowledge the following for their assistance and input throughout the past two years of production: Anita Agbalog, Donnie Chin, Doug Chin, Dorothy Cordova, David Della, Cindy Domingo, Theresa Fujiwara, Chong-Suk Han, Jonathan Hewes, Ed Hidano, Alice Ito, Bea Kiyohara, Alan Lau, Richard Mar, Robin Santos, Dolores Sibonga, Brian Sims, Kathy Sugiyama, Bob Summerise, Eugene Tagawa, David Takami, Sue Taoka, Mayumi Tsutakawa, United Reprographics, Wing Luke Asian Museum, and Shari Woo.

Index

A

Abe, Pat, 168
Adams, Brock, 158
Adriatico, Adela, 125
Adriatico, Joe, 18, 20, 21, 25-26, 36, 41, 133
Adriatico, Joe Paul, 25
Adriatico, Macario, 25
Adriatico, Patrick, 25
Adriatico, Toni (*see also* Nicol, Antonia), 20, 25-26, 41
AFL-CIO Agricultural Workers Organizing Committee, 69-70
Agbalog, Anita, 42, 44-45, 69, 106, 182-183
Agbalog, Godfrey, 45, 70
Agbalog, Mildred, 70
Air Force One, 42
Airporter (Airport Shuttle), 127
Alaska Cannery Workers Association (ACWA), 57, 86, 97, 103, 123, 141-143, 181
Ambrose, Wayne, 37
American Basketball Association, 44
American Hotel, 22
American Jewish Committee, 47
Amtrak, 127
Anderson, Virginia, 158
Anti-Defamation League of B'nai B'rith, 47
Anti-Martial Law Alliance, 143, 148, 170
Arditi, Abraham "Rami", 141, 142
Arias, Edna, 123
Art Louie's, 179, 180
Asian American Student Coalition, University of Washington, 72
Asian Americans for Political Action, 73
Asian Coalition for Equality (ACE), 47, 49, 71
Asian Counseling and Referral Service (ACRS), 50, 57, 94, 95-96, 106, 115, 152, 157, 162, 167
Asian Drop-In Center, 72
Asian Family Affair (AFA), 72
Asian Multi-Media Center, 70, 108
Asians For Unity Emergency Squad, 100
Asis, Cissy, 123
Asis, Norma, 82
Asis, Stan, 118
Atlanta Hawks, 44
Atlas Apartments, 86
Atlas Hotel, 82, 91, 164
Atlas Theater, 15, 19, 24, 28
Atrium, 38

B

Bacho, Norris, 110

Bacho, Peter, 79, 81, 82, 132
Bacho, Vic, 70
Bailey Gatzert Elementary School, 74
Baker, Bearcat, 16
Balcena, Bobby, 41
Bangasser, Tom, 158
Bartelle, Richard, 86
Baruso, Constantin "Tony", 131, 143-144, 146-150
Basin Street Club, 28
Bataan Recreation Club, 23
Batayola, Maria, 118
Baugh Construction, 158
Bayagawan, Lonnie, 90
Beacon Hill, 60, 66, 77, 172
Beacon Hill Elementary School, 60-61, 62
Bellarmine Prep High School, 25
Bellemont, Harold, 61
Beltran, Ed, 38
Beltran, Jim, 19, 32, 34, 38
Beltran, Mary, 28
Belushi, John, 22
Benny, Jack, 21
Benson, George, 157, 167
Berle, Milton, 36
Biddle, Toyo, 73
Bing, Woo Quan, 102
Bishop, Alex, 74, 77
Bishop Drugs, 77
Black and Tan Club, 29
Black Panther Party, 48, 63
Black Student Union, University of Washington, 63
Black Studies Program, University of Washington, 63
Blackfeet Indians of Montana, 48-49
Blaine Memorial Methodist Church, 183
Bloom, David, 61
Bocanegra, Juan, 60
Boeing Company, 21, 26, 41, 42, 43, 44, 56, 131, 143, 162
Bogle and Gates, 142
Bolero, Lois, 32
Bolo, Mission, 16, 21-23
Bon Rob Drug Store, 32
Borgeson, Dale, 123
Bower, Diana, 88-90, 91
Bowman's Joint, 29
Bown, Patty, 27-28
Bowsfield, Ted, 88
Boy Pilay, 145-146
Braganza, Belen, 6
Braganza, Pashong, 36
Bratton, Bob, 88
Bristol Bay, Alaska, 30
Broadway High School, 17
Broadway Playfield, 34
Brogan, Rita, 169
Brubeck, Dave, 43
Bullitt, Kay, 139
Bumble Bee Seafoods, 142
Bundy, Ted, 134
Burlington Northern Railroad, 103, 126
Bush-Asia Annex, 117-118, 170
Bush-Asia Center, 114, 116, 159, 166, 182
Bush Garden, 38, 57, 139, 140, 160, 177, 180, 182, 183
Bush, George H., 62
Bush Hotel, 20, 28, 94, 96, 113-115, 117, 160, 163
Butterworth, Rita Jean, 158
Buttnick, Jack, 154

C

CBS Morning News Hour, 184
Cabildo, Sabino, 72, 79
Cabuena, Pantel, 86
Caesar's, 38
Calawing, Manuel, 118
Calder, Joe, 16
Camp Harmony, 138
Cannery Workers' and Farm Laborers' Union, Local 18257, 31
Cannery Workers Union, Local 7, 29, 30, 31
Cantil, Bernie, 34
Cantil, Ray, 34
Canton Alley, 100, 101
Canton, Dawn, 81-82, 86, 168
Capistrano, Cappy, 105
CARITAS (Community Action, Remedial Instruction, Tutorial, and Assistance Service), 47-50, 70, 78, 167
Carpenter, Jean, 161
Carter, Sylvester, 52
Carter, Wildcat, 16
Castillano, Bibiana, 37
Castillano, Frances, 37
Castillano, Jeanette, 37, 68, 135
Castillano, Marya, 37, 68
Castillano, Mike, Jr., 37
Castillano, Mike, Sr, 37, 139
Castillio, Ann, 25
Catague, Emma, 168
Catholic Archdiocese of Seattle, 47, 48
Catholic Interracial Council (CIC), 46, 47, 48, 70
Central Area, 18, 25, 26, 34, 54, 63, 64, 66, 77, 88, 179
Central Area Civil Rights Committee, 47, 48
Central Area Community Council, 76
Central Area Motivation Program (CAMP), 48, 57, 63-64, 66
Central District Youth Club, 46
Central Intelligence Agency, Philippines, 149
Central Intelligence Agency, U.S. (CIA), 62, 144, 147
Central Seattle Community Council, 76
Chan, Charlie, 108
Chan, John, 20
Chan, Mary, 20
Chan, Maxine, 93, 123
Chan, Tue Yuen, 168
Chan, Vera, 20, 164
Chapman, Bruce, 79
Chappell Trust, 113, 163
Chappell, William, 113
Charles, Ray, 29
Chavez, Cesar, 69, 70
Chew, Ron, 13, 97-98, 117-118, 123, 166
Chiba Drug Store, 20
Chick's Ice Creamery, 20
Chihara Jewelers, 20
Chikahisa, Paul, 73
Chin, Connie, 101
Chin, Don, 74, 77, 101
Chin, Donnie, 92, 98, 100-101, 120, 123
Chin, Doug, 72, 97, 98, 132, 167
Chin, Gordon, 155
Chin, Hong, 77
Chin, Myra, 101
Chin, Susie, 92, 94, 108, 123
Chin, Wilbur, 179
China Gate, 28, 57, 145, 180, 181-182

Chinatown, 11, 15, 16, 17, 19-22, 25, 28, 31, 42, 43, 74-75, 77, 104, 112, 114, 145, 154, 164, 179, 187, 188
Chinatown Chamber of Commerce, 77, 111
Chinatown, Los Angeles, 85
Chinatown, San Francisco, 79, 85, 108, 154-155
Chinese Baptist Church, 109
Chinese Gardens, 28
Chinese Information & Service Center, 115
Chinn, Bob, 179, 180
Chinn, Glenn, 100, 156
Chinn, Ray, 154
Chinn, Ruth, 168
Choi, Ted, 112, 168
Chong Wa Benevolent Association, 110, 111-113, 163
Chow, Cheryl, 135, 170
Chow, Ruby, 111, 112, 125, 134, 163
Cincinnati Reds, 41
Cisneros, Henry, 171-172, 174
Civil Liberties Act of 1988, 138
Civil Rights Act of 1991, 150
Clark, Anne Xuan, 162
Clinton, Bill, 174
Clinton, Gordon, 46, 75
Clinton, Hillary, 36, 175
Club Maynard, 29
Coalition Against Discrimination (CAD), 47, 49
Cohen, Orville, 86
Collins, Chuck, 88
Collins Playfield, 34
Columbia Center, 127
Columbia Ward's Fisheries, 142
Colville Confederated Tribe, 56
Committee for Corrective Action in the International District, 87, 88
Committee for Justice for Domingo and Viernes (CJDV), 146, 147-149, 170
Comprehensive Employment Training Act (CETA), 92, 97, 166
Concerned Asians for the International District, 87
Concerned Filipino Residents of the International District, 79
Congo Club, 28
Conlan, Mike, 77-78
Connoly Center, Seattle University, 35
Connors Furniture Store, 33
Continental Trailways, 127
Contras, 61-62
Cordova, Dorothy, 38, 48, 67, 68, 69, 70, 73, 131
Cordova, Fred, 34, 38, 67, 68, 69, 70, 74, 131
Cornell, Alan, 158
Corr, Edwin G., 136
Couples, Fred, 44
Craig, Larry, 175-176
Crosby, Bing, 24
Crosby, Dixie, 24
Cuomo, Andrew, 174-175, 176
Cuomo, Kerry Kennedy, 174
Cuomo, Mario, 174

D

Daba, Pio, 74
Damondon, Rose Rallos, 39
Danny Woo International District Community Garden, 102, 104, 106, 115, 165, 169, 180
Dao, Eliane, 168
Davis, Ross, 131

Daybreak Star Center, 38, 56, 57, 58, 59
DeBlasio, Bill, 175
de Chamorro, Violeta, 62
DeCuir, Tandra, 50
Dela Cruz, Joe, 35
Delano, California, 49, 69, 70
Del Fierro, Sal, 34
Delfin's Barbershop, 22
Della, David, 143, 144, 151, 181
Della, Mark, 123
Delma, Cookie, 36
Democratic House Caucus, Washington State, 184
Democratic Party, Washington State, 144, 151, 168, 184
Demonstration Project for Asian Americans (DPAA), 38, 48, 73
Dempsey, Jack, 18
Dempsey, Little, 16, 21
Denise Louie Early Childhood Education Center, 110, 157, 162, 180
Devin, William A., 75
Dictado, Tony, 145-146, 148
Dingfield, Barbara, 83
Dingfield, Dan, 128
Dionisio, Diony, 166
Dip, Goon, 120
Direct Action Network, 176
Discovery Park, 58
Dixon, Aaron, 63
Dixon, Elmer, 63
Domingo, Cindy, 147, 149
Domingo, Kalayaan, 146
Domingo, Ligaya, 146
Domingo, Nemesio, Jr., 68, 69, 72, 81, 97, 141, 142
Domingo, Silme, 12, 57, 68, 72, 86, 103, 123, 141, 142, 143, 144, 145, 146, 147, 148, 149, 150, 151, 181, 182-183
Dominguez, Teodoro "Boy Pilay", 145-146
Don Ting, 15, 20
Dong, Howard, 112
Douglas, Jim, 149
Downtowner Apartments, 127
Dreamland Hotel, 113
Druxman Gym, 18, 19
Dukes II, 15
Dunston, Ernie, 44
Duyungan, Virgil, 31
Dwyer, William, 63, 153

E

Eastern Hotel, 20, 82, 93
Ebony Club, 28, 29
Ebersole, Terry, 158-159
Edmonds, Joe, 167
Educational Opportunity Program, University of Washington, 71
Edwardo's, 38
Ehrlichman, Tom, 156
El Centro de la Raza, 48, 55, 57, 61, 62, 63, 64, 65, 66
El Salvador, 135-137
Elias, Dorry, 65
Elks Club, 28, 29, 47
Elks Club, Everett, 71
Ellsworth, Cheryl, 66
Eng, John, 71
Environmental Works, 115
Esperanza, Sammy, 68

Evans, Daniel, 73, 131, 132, 133, 140, 170
Evergreen Apartments, 96
Evergreen Legal Services, 79, 94
Executive Order 9066, 26

F

Family Leadership Fund, 65
Federal Bureau of Investigation (FBI), 42, 123, 124, 147
Fibber McGee and Molly, 21
Figueros, Sam, 12
Filipino American Coalition for Equality, 47
Filipino Cavaliers, 34
Filipino Community Council, 68-69
Filipino Community of Seattle, 110, 143
Filipino Far West Convention, 68
Filipino Farm Labor Union, 69
Filipino Improvement Club, 20, 22
Filipino Youth Activities (FYA), 67-68, 70
Finnish Hall, 32
Firlands Sanitarium, 17
First Avenue Service Center (FASC), 92-93
Fleming, George, 117
Fleming, Lois, 71
Flor, Bob, 68, 169
Flor, Louise, 36
Flor, Vince, 36
Flores, Becky, 153
Flores, Larry, 131
Flores, Roy, 68, 73, 83, 131, 132
Fonda, Henry, 128
Fonda, Jane, 56
Ford, Richard D., 127
Foreman, George, 18
Fort Lawton, 49, 56
Four Seas, 57, 139, 166, 179, 180, 181, 183
Fox, John, 174
Fox, Michael, 142
Foz, John, 115
Franklin High School, 32, 41, 42, 45, 63
Franklin, John, 92
Fraser, Clara, 60
Frederick and Nelson, 174
Freedman Building, 22, 118, 152
Freudenberg, Kit, 158
Friedlander, Paul, 127
Fujii, Frank (Shobo), 34, 72
Fujii Hotel, 20
Fujii, Philip, 169
Fujii, Sharon, 73, 96
Fujiwara, Theresa, 50, 66, 96, 167
Furukawa, Rick, 86, 123, 164

G

G.O. Guy Drugs, 37
Galarosa, Annie, 119
Gallegos, Roberto, 60
Gamido, Angie, 39
Gamido, Henry, 39
Gandhi, Mahatma, 54
Garcia, Joe, 65
Garcia, Lino, 168
Gardner, Booth, 117
Garfield High School, 32, 35
Garfield Playfield, 34
Garland, Judy, 15
Garvin, Sylvester, 43
Gasperetti's, 80

Gaudia, Joe, 33
Gibson, Barney, 50
Gilbert, Adaline, 17
Gilbert, Caroline, 18, 19, 25, 35
Gim Ling, 28, 179, 181
Goldberg, Carol, 61
Goldberg, Sam, 61
Golden Dragon, 108
Golden Pheasant, 20
Goon, Steve, 123
Gordon, Flash, 19
Gordon, Karen, 114
Gorton, Slade, 133, 140, 157, 158
Gossett, Larry, 48, 51, 55, 57, 59, 63-64, 65, 66, 67, 82, 118, 132, 139, 149, 153, 170
Goudeau, Mary, 41
Grant, Bill, 184
Great Seattle Fire, 104
Green Lake Aqua Theater, 43
Greyhound Bus Lines, 127, 129, 183
Guiang, Mariano, 16
Guloy, Ben, 145-146
Gunsolus, Jim, 158
Gyokko-Ken, 20

H

H., Jeff, 177
Hanil, 115, 182
Harbor Club, 38
Hattori, Frank, 74
Hattori, Jeff, 166
Hawaii Convention Center, 88
Hawkins, Todd, 52-53
Hayasaka, Lois, 69
Hayasaka, Phil, 32, 46, 54, 71, 84
Head Start Program, 57, 108
Herzig-Yoshinaga, Aiko, 138
Hidano, Ed, 89, 99
Higo's Ten Cent Store, 19-20, 22
Higo's Variety Store, 20
Hill Top Tavern, 29,
Hillis, Jerry, 156
Hing Hay Park, 28, 81, 90, 91, 130, 168
Hirabayashi, Gordon, 166
Holiday Community Show-Off, NWAAT, 118
Holland, Michael, 54
Hom, George, 96
Hong Kong (restaurant), 20, 38
Hostak, Al, 18
Hsieh, Kathy, 118
Hubbard, Kay, 136-137
Hubbard, Walt, 46, 47, 70, 158, 179
Hurley, Jack, 18
Hutchinson, Fred, 41
Hutton, Bobby, 63

I

Idaho Housing Council, 175-176
Ignacio, Jo Pepita, 112
Ikeda, Ike, 65
Imamura, Larry, 97
Imanishi, Janis, 109
Immaculate Conception Church, 38, 48, 54
Immaculate Conception High School, 25, 27, 32
Immigration and Naturalization Service (INS), 124-125, 126
Imperial House, 86
Ing, Joey, 91, 154

Ing, Vera, 20, 91, 164, 169
Inouye, Daniel, 59
Inouye, Eric, 78
Inslee, Jay, 59
Inter*Im (International District Improvement Association), 10, 11, 13, 57, 58, 64, 66, 67, 74, 76-81, 82, 84, 85-86, 88, 89, 90-94, 95, 96, 97-100, 102-105, 108-109, 110, 111-112, 114, 115, 116, 120, 121-123, 127-129, 135, 154, 156, 157, 159, 163, 164, 165, 166, 167, 168, 170, 180, 187
Inter*Im Food Buying Club, 93, 114
Inter*Im Meal Voucher Program, 114
International Apartments, 86
International Center, 75
International Community Health Services (ICHS), 90, 162
International District Community Garden, 57, 89
International District Community Health Center, 87, 90, 95, 157, 165
International District Economic Association (IDEA), 111, 112, 129
International District Elderly Congregate Meal Program, 114
International District Emergency Center (IDEC), 92, 100-101, 121, 123
International District Farmers Market, 130
International District Housing Alliance (IDHA), 85, 86, 112, 121, 123
International District Improvement Association (Inter*Im), 10, 11, 13, 57, 58, 64, 66, 67, 74, 76-81, 82, 84, 85-86, 88, 89, 90-94, 95, 96, 97-100, 102-105, 108-109, 110, 111-112, 114, 115, 116, 120, 121-123, 127-129, 135, 154, 156, 157, 159, 163, 164, 165, 166, 167, 168, 170, 180, 187
International District Rotary Club, 164
International District Village Square (IDVS), 10, 156-162, 164, 165, 166, 168, 169, 170
International District Youth Council (IDYC), 85, 92
International Drop-In Center (IDIC), 12, 82, 86, 111, 114
International Examiner, 12, 97-98, 123, 126, 160, 166, 188
International House, 86
International Longshoremen and Warehousemen's Union, Local 37, 31, 131, 142, 143-145, 146, 148, 149, 181, 182
International Realty, 74, 94
International Settlement, 75
International Special Review District Board, 90, 167
International Terrace, 86, 105
International Women's Conference, 183
Irigon, Frank, 72, 82, 107, 167
Ishihara, Elaine Shoji, 168
Ishimitsu, Kaz, 91
Ishisaka, Tony, 95, 96, 106, 107, 167
Israel, Abe, 16
Itliong, Larry, 69-70
Ito, Alice, 66
Ivar's Acres of Clams, 37, 139
Iwamoto, Gary, 12, 13, 97, 118, 119, 123

J

Jackson Apartments, 116
Jackson Cafe, 21-22
Jackson, Henry, 56, 71, 114
Jackson Street Community Council (JSCC), 74-76

Jackson Street District, 75
Jackson Street Regrade, 120
Jamero, Pete, 68, 73, 91, 96, 106, 131, 179
Jamero, Terri, 68
James Apartments, 17
Jamilosa, Fidel, 25-26
Japanese American Citizens League, 29, 110, 137
Japanese Foundation Center for Global Partnership, 65-66
Jefferson golf course, 44
Joe Boys, 108, 109
Johnson, Alex, 183
Johnson, Bill, 66-67
Johnson, Charles V., 78
Johnson, Gerry, 104-105
Johnson, John, 183
Johnson, Lyndon, 77
Johnson, Miriam, 183
Jones, Mark, 159-160
Jones, Patricia, 61
Jones, Quincy, 27
Jones, Richard, 50
Josue, Lenora, 36
Josue, Serio, 36
Jung, Doralinn, 93, 107, 123

K

KDP, Union of Democratic Pilipinos, 143, 149
Kabuki, 16
Kamikawa, Louise, 73, 96
Kapisanan, 72
Katagiri, Mineo, 196
Katahira, Ken, 154, 155, 156, 159
Kawabe House, 82
Kawakami, Rod, 94, 121, 160, 166
Kawasaki, Ann, 87
Kay, Jacquie, 78
Kazama, Don, 71, 73, 96
Kazama, Sally, 71
Keiro Nursing Home, 166
Kemp, Jerry, 153
Kennedy, Ethel, 174
Kennedy, Robert, 174
Keyport, Washington, 40
King County Council, 64, 65, 134
King County Courthouse, 93
King County Jail, 21, 52, 64, 125
King County Office for Civil Rights, 47
King, Martin Luther, Jr., 54, 185, 186
King Street Station, 126-127, 129
KING-TV, 61
Kingdome, 50, 72, 78-81, 82, 87, 88, 90, 91, 93, 98, 110, 119, 153, 171, 181, 188, 189
Kinoshita, Cherry, 137
Kirkman, Boone, 18
Kis, Joan, 71
Kitamura, Joe, 168
Kiyohara, Bea, 117, 118, 119-120, 132
Knight, Gladys and the Pips, 119
Knights of Columbus, 44, 46
Knoblauch, Judy, 50
Ko, Charlie, 179
Ko, Elaine (Ikoma), 72, 86, 97, 127, 132, 149, 164-165
Ko, Tom, 166
Kobe, Japan, 66, 106
Kobe Municipal Arboretum, 106
Kobe Terrace Park, 90, 104, 106, 168

Kokusai Theater, 19, 153
Kozu, Michael, 100
Kraabel, Paul, 110, 117, 129
Krisologo, Bob, 96
Kubo, Vic, 166
Kubota, Jan, 168
Kubota, Tak, 74, 112
Kubota, Tom, 164
Kumasaka, Jan, 135
Kunitsugu, Kango, 85
Kuniyuki, Y.K., 96, 167
Kurimura, Alan, 132, 156-157, 167, 169
Kurose, Aki, 71
Kurose, Ruthann, 72, 132, 137
Kyoto, Japan, 66

L

La Voz, 61
Label, Abie, 77, 86
Lagasca, Amy, 35
Lagasca, Carol, 39
Lagasca, George, 34, 35, 38
Lagasca, Joe, 35
Laigo, Ben, 37, 38, 43
Laigo, Bibiana, 37
Laigo, Dorothy, 37, 38
Laigo, Ed, 37, 43
Laigo, Jerry, 34, 36, 87, 90, 91
Laigo, Val, 37
Laigo, Valeriano, 36-37
Lane Street, 187-188
Lau, Alan, 98
Lebree, Leo, 105
Lee, Aw Wing, 16
Lee, May, 72
Lee, Patricia, 168
Lee, Perry, 121
Lee, Sharon, 166, 173, 177-178
Lee, Tony, 94, 121, 156
Legacy House, 162
Leong, Jimmy, 180
Lew, Sonny, 180
Lewis, Tiger Al, 15
Lewis, Yale, 111
Liberty Playfield, 34-35
Lindbergh, William, 54
Linyen Cafe, 15, 180, 183
Little Tokyo (Los Angeles) Community Development Agency, 85, 155
Local Initiative Support Group, 167
Lock, Steve, 122
Locke, Gary, 59, 87, 117, 170
Locke, Rick, 92
Longacres Race Track, 57, 89, 104
Lorenzo, Leo, 12, 168
Louie, Alan, 180, 181
Louie, Denise, 103, 108-109, 110
Louie, Ken, 179-180
Louie, Mickey, 180
Low-Income Housing Institute (LIHI), 166, 173, 177-178
Lowry, Mike, 59, 132, 135-136, 137, 138-140, 157, 165, 183
Lui, Wah, 177
Luke, Dr. Henry, 74
Lum, Abe, 179
Luna, Doug, 107

M

Mabuhay Corporation, 148
Maderas, Andrew, 101, 123
Maeda, Sharon, 132, 171-172
Maestas, Roberto, 48, 51, 55, 57, 59, 60-63, 64, 65-66, 82, 118, 132, 139
Magic Carpet Zone, 90, 99
Magnuson, Warren, 56, 105, 114
Main Event Club, 29
Majors, Marshall, 82-83
Mak, Willie, 152-153
Malabed, Leonilo, 148, 150
Mamon, Bill, 15, 34, 36, 39
Mamon, Gloria, 39
Mamon, Helen, 15, 36
Mamon, Leo, 34, 36
Managua, Nicaragua, 61-62
Maneki, 21
Manila Cafe, 23, 42
Manilatown, 15, 20
Manilatown, San Francisco, 85
Mar, Al, 34
Mar, Barry, 86, 91, 164
Mar, Becky, 153
Mar, Dan, 180
Mar, Dewey, 153
Mar, Dicky, 65, 123, 153
Mar, Jimmy, 74
Mar, Kenny, 153
Mar, Lippy, 180
Mar, Paul, 168
Mar, Richard, 65, 123, 153
Mar, Roy, 112
Mar, Tommy, 153
Marchione, Doreen, 161
Marciano, Rocky, 18
Marcos, Ferdinand, 68, 143, 146, 147, 148, 149, 150
Marcos, Imelda, 143, 147, 150
Marion Club, 25, 48
Martinez, Alma, 61
Martinez, Sam, 61
Maryknoll Church, 26, 32, 48, 73
Maryknoll School, 25, 26, 27, 37, 48, 73, 137, 138
Masaoka, Ben, 105
Masigat, Al, 12, 86, 168
Mason, James, 168
Mast, Terri, 146, 147
Masuda, Min, 71, 73, 96
Matsuda, Larry, 71
Matsudaira, Martin "Mich", 39, 73, 138
Matsudaira, Pauline, 26, 28, 138
Matsuoka, James, 74
Matsuoka, Vi, 39
Matthews, Harry "Kid", 18
Mayeda, Dr. Ken, 90, 165
Maxie, Bob, 38, 42, 133
McDermott, Jim, 117, 150-151
McDonalds Corporation, 187
McIntyre, Father Harvey, 48, 49, 54, 179
McIver, Richard, 169-170
McKinney, Rev. Samuel, 56
McNeil Island, federal penitentiary, 125
Mendoza, Albert, 37
Merchants Parking Association, 100, 156
Metcalf, Jack, 133
Metcalf, Joni, 44
Metro, 88, 90, 127, 128, 129, 130, 157, 158, 159, 161

Metro Council, 158, 159, 160, 161, 169
Midtown Commons, 158
Mike's Tavern, 23
Miller, Floyd, 47, 53
Miller, John, 104, 129
Milwaukee Hotel, 83, 108, 120-124, 128, 166, 179
Mimbu, William, 74
Ministry of Foreign Affairs, Japan, 65
Minority Executive Directors Coalition of King County (MEDC), 65
Miss Minidoka, 118, 119
Miyahara, Bruce, 90, 92, 165
Miyake, Christopher, 183
Miyake, Daniel, 183
Miyake, Joyce, 183, 185
Miyake, Ken, 183
Miyake, Matt, 183
Miyake, Shari, 183
Miyano, Jim, 73, 165
Miyatake, Henry, 137
Mizuki, Andy, 86, 123, 164
Mochizuki, Ken, 97, 118
Model Cities Program, 77-78, 88-89, 94, 96, 165
Monarch Pool Hall, 29
Monillas, King, 91
Montanez, Cherie, 159
Moose Club, 47
Morales, Royal, 73
Morgan, Tod, 17
Moriguchi, Fujimatsu, 77
Moriguchi, Tomio, 77, 78, 111, 112, 153, 158, 163-164
Morrison Hotel, 93
Mt. Zion Baptist Church, 51, 55-56
Moy, Peter, 169
Munro, Ralph, 133
Murakami, Ayako, 20
Murakami, Masako, 20
Murakami, Sanzo, 19
Muramoto, Al, 72, 90, 165
Muramoto, Keith, 72
Murkowski, Frank, 150
Murray, Bob, 34
Murray, Patty, 59

N

N.P. (Northern Pacific) Hotel, 13, 15, 20-23, 25, 77, 82, 85, 92, 94, 154, 166, 189
Narasaki, Diane, 168
National Basketball Association, 44
National Labor Relations Board, 63
National Pacific Asian Center On Aging, 73, 165
Navarro, Gene, 29, 142
Navy Officer's Club, Pier 91, 37
NEFCO-Fidalgo Packing Company, 142
Neighborhood Technology Coalition, 115
New Central Hotel, 115-116
New Chinatown Supper Club, 102, 179
New England Fish Company, 141
New Orleans Jazz Club, 28
New Otani Hotel (Los Angeles), 85
Ng, Benjamin, 152-153
Ng, Tony, 152-153
Nicaragua, 61-62, 137, 149
Nicol, Antonia "Toni" (*see also* Adriatico, Toni), 17
Nicol, Cornelias, 17
Nicol, Lawrence, 17

Nicol, Virginia, 17
Nihonmachi (Japantown), 15
Nihonmachi, San Francisco, 79, 85
Nippon Kan (Japanese Hall), 15-16, 118
Nolan, Jean, 171
Nordstrom, 174
Northern Pacific Railroad, 20, 126
Northwest Asian American Theatre (NWAAT), 117, 118, 119, 120, 181
Northwest International Bank, 164
Northwest Labor Employment Law Office (LELO), 55, 142, 149
Northwest Progress, 38

O

Oak Tin Family Association, 154
O'Brien, John, 132
Ocean Shores, Washington, 45
O'Dea High School, 25, 32, 35, 36, 37
Office and Professional Employees International, Local 8, 63
Officemporium, 97
Ogilvie, Alan, 50
Ogilive, Anthony, 68, 69, 71, 131, 179
O'Hare Airport (Chicago), 140
Ohno Landscaping Company, 103
Ohno, Natch, 103
Ohno, Yosh, 103
Oki, Arlene, 133, 169
Okimoto, Dave, 65, 167
Okimoto, Joe, 71
One-Armed Jack, 29
Oriental Student Union, Seattle Central Community College, 71-72
Ortega, Daniel, 62, 149
Ortega, Frank, 35
Ortega, Stella, 60, 61
Osaki, Alan, 169
Osias, Frank, 32
Osoteo, Victor, 35
Otani, Hod, 34
Otani, Ray, 34
Otani, Shig, 34
Otani, Tim, 123

P

Pacific Coast League, 41
Pac-Med Medical Center, 158
Panama Hotel, 20, 82
Pantazama, Nicaragua, 62
Paramount Cafe, 21
Park, Nelson, 92
Parker, Karen, 136-137
Parreno, Sister Heide, 90
Patterson, Floyd, 18
Patterson, George, 167-168
Paul Allen Foundation, 162
People's Lodge, 58-59, 60
Percy, Charles, 133
Perez, Ricardo, 174
Perry, Harold, 70
Peters, Jack, 174
Peterson, Rick, 156
Philippine embassy, 143, 147
Philippines, Republic of the, 16, 17, 23, 25, 37, 68, 143, 144, 147, 148, 181
Phillips, Pellar, 44
Pike Place Market, 185

Pike Place Market Preservation and Development Authority, 111
Pinoy Hill, 32
Pinson, Vada, 41
Pioneer Square Health Station, 76
Port Blakely, Washington, 17
Port of Seattle, 127, 128, 166
Project Equality, 48
Providence Hospital, 26
Publix Hotel, 113
Puget Sound Hotel, 20

Q

Quezon, Manuel, 25
Quinault Indian Nation, 35
Quintero, Angie, 68
Quong Tuck Bar and Grill, 57, 58, 89, 102, 119, 180, 181, 183
Quong Tuck Company, 102

R

Rademacher, Pete, 18
Radical Women, Seattle, 60
Rainier Bank, 109, 164
Rainier Brewery, 41
Rainier Club, 47
Rainier Heat and Power Company, 77, 113, 114, 163
Rainier Playfield, 41, 45
Rainier Valley, 77, 106, 133
Rallos, Shirley, 39
Ramada Inn Corporation, 113
Ramil, Jimmy, 145-146, 148
Ramirez, Saul, 174
Ramon, Frank, 53
Reagan, Ronald, 61, 138, 147, 150, 185
Republican Party, Washington state, 131-134, 138
Revolutionary Communist Party, 79
Rex Apartments, 154
Reyes, Buddy, 35
Reyes, Lawney, 59
Reyes, Luana, 59
Reyes, Sammy, 168
Rib Pit, 43
Rice Bowl Cafe, 23
Rice, Norm, 109, 126, 159, 161, 169, 174-175
Ridder, Bob, 131
Ridder, Ruthe, 134
Rizal Cafe, 17
Roberson, Brendan, 186
Roberson, Denise, 186
Roberson, Marissa, 186
Roberson, Nicole, 186
Roberson, Shante, 186
Roberson, Simone, 186
Roberson, Tiffany, 186
Robinett, Clark, 68
Robinson, Jeff, 147-148, 149
Rocking Chair Club, 29
Rogers, Buck, 19
Roosevelt, Franklin D., 26
Rosellini, Albert, 75, 134, 140
Ross, Debbie, 55
Ross, Michael, 52, 131, 135
Ross, Teddy, 43-44
Rothstein, Barbara, 150
Rounds, Dan, 95, 104, 105, 107-108, 123, 127, 146-147, 154, 165
Royer, Charles, 114, 128-129, 168, 169

Ruckus Society, 176
Rundberg, Darlyn, 102-103
Russell's Meat Market, 20

S

Safeco Field, 187, 188, 189
Safeway, 49, 69
Sagamiya's, 20
St. Charles Hotel, 40-41
St. Edward's Seminary, 36
St. James Cathedral, 46
St. Mary's Church, 54
St. Patrick's Grade School, 25
St. Peter Claver Center, 48-50, 51, 53, 54, 60, 70-71, 81, 108
Sakahara, Toru, 74
Sakamoto, Jimmy, 16
Sako, Lorraine, 103
Sammish Tribe, 61
Samuel B. McKinney Manor, 55
San Pablo, Robert, 148
Sanchez, Ricardo, 61
Sandinistas, 61-62
Sandpoint Naval Station, 177
Santos, Briana, 186
Santos, Chauncey, 186
Santos, Danny, 44, 45, 186
Santos, David, 40
Santos, Enrique, 186
Santos, John, 44, 45, 186
Santos, Macaria, 186
Santos, Macario "Sammy", 16-19, 20, 21-25, 26, 40, 41, 42, 85, 154
Santos, Marcianna, 186
Santos, Maurizio, 186
Santos, Meagan, 186
Santos, Melise, 186
Santos, Nancy, 44, 45, 186
Santos, Nancy (Tom's wife), 186
Santos, Niko, 186
Santos, Nori, 40
Santos Place, 177-178
Santos, Ramona, 40
Santos, Robin, 44, 45, 186
Santos, Rudy, 22, 43
Santos, Sammy, Jr., 17, 18-19, 24, 25, 34, 38, 41
Santos, Samuel, 61
Santos, Sharon Tomiko, 59, 183-185
Santos, Simone, 44, 45
Santos, Thomas, 186
Santos, Tom, 44, 45, 186
Santos, Tommy, 16
Santos, Valencia, 186
Santos, Vicki, 186
Santos, Viva, 40
Sata, Shiz, 90
Satiacum, Bob, 56
Saturday Night Live, 22
Savage, Anthony, 43, 150
Schell, Paul, 50, 59, 158
Schlosser, John, 67
Schorr, Jon, 116
Scott, Tyree, 48, 51-56, 122, 141
SeaCom Communications, 66-67
Seafair, 37, 57, 68
Seafirst National Bank, 97, 109-110
Seahawk Stadium, 170, 187, 188, 189
Seale, Bobby, 63
Seattle Buddhist Church, 34
Seattle Center, 46, 78, 158

Seattle Central Community College (SCCC), 51-52, 71-72
Seattle Chinatown-I.D. Preservation and Development Authority (PDA), 112-113, 114-117, 124, 129, 154, 157-162, 163, 164, 165, 167, 171, 172, 180
Seattle City Board of Parks Commissioners, 104
Seattle City Building Department, 88
Seattle City Council, 11, 12, 46, 56, 64, 65, 66, 70, 75, 80, 81, 85, 87, 88, 91, 93, 99, 110, 117, 119, 125, 135, 138, 168, 169, 170, 182
Seattle City Department of Community Development, 83, 88, 110, 114, 167
Seattle City Department of Human Resources, 88
Seattle City Department of Licensing, 135
Seattle City Division on Aging Nutrition Program, 114
Seattle City Engineering Department, 88
Seattle City Light, 60
Seattle City Office for Women's Rights, 132, 165
Seattle City Office of Neighborhoods, 157
Seattle City Parks and Recreation Department, 32, 88
Seattle Committee in Solidarity with the People of El Salvador (CISPES), 135-136
Seattle Community P-Patch Program, 102, 104
Seattle Displacement Coalition, 174-175
Seattle Fire Department, 122, 173
Seattle Firefighters Union, 101
Seattle Housing Authority, 86
Seattle Human Rights Commission, 47, 52, 53, 54
Seattle Human Services Coalition, 65
Seattle Indian Services Commission, 111
Seattle-King County Health Department, 173
Seattle Little League, 41
Seattle-Managua Sister-City Association, 61
Seattle Mariners, 187, 188
Seattle Opportunities Industrialization Center (SOIC), 66
Seattle Park League, 34
Seattle Police Department, 124, 160, 173
Seattle Post-Intelligencer, 38, 57
Seattle Rainiers, 21, 26, 41
Seattle Seahawks, 98, 170, 187, 188, 189
Seattle School Board, 62, 132, 135
Seattle School District, 60-61
Seattle Sonics, 153
Seattle-Tacoma (Sea-Tac) Airport, 51, 53, 137
Seattle Times, The, 53, 66, 132
Seattle University, 35, 37-38, 44, 70, 138
Seattle World's Fair, 34, 43
Security Pacific, 86
Seelig, Howard, 127
Seelig, Martin, 127
Seko, Joan, 180, 182
Seko, Roy, 180, 182
Selig, Martin, 127
Seventh Avenue Service, 168
Seward Park, 31-32, 133, 152
Shadow, The, 21
SHARE, 173, 177
Sherburne, Phil, 158
Shigaki, Jerry, 96
Shimabukuro, Bob, 98, 160
Shimabukuro, Craig, 168
Shoji, Sam, 96
Shopping News, 32-33
Sibonga, Dolores, 54, 66, 117, 129, 161, 170

Sibonga/Sims Committee, 161
Sick, Emil, 41
Sick's Stadium, 41
Sikma, Jack, 153
Silver Dragon, 57, 180, 181
Simmons, Bob, 61
Simon, Aurelio, 31
Simon, Sy, 39
Sims, Allen, 186
Sims, Bobiono, 186
Sims, Brian, 186
Sims, Ron, 59, 117, 135, 161, 169, 170
Sinatra, Frank, 177
Smith, Sam, 129, 169
Snell, Doc, 16
Solis, Ramon, 61
Somoza, Anastasio, 62
Soo, Ray, 34
South Seattle Community College, 38
Spellman, John, 80-81, 87, 88, 90-91, 125, 140
Sports Illustrated, 18
Stadium Impact Resolutions, 80, 87, 88
Staments, John, 149
Steele, Freddie, 18
Stevens, Ted, 150
Sugimura, Diane, 168
Sugiyama, Alan, 72, 132
Sugiyama, Dick, 72
Sullivan, McDonald, 112-113
Sullivan, Nina, 183
Summerise, Bob, 29
Summit Communications, 67
Sun May Novelty Store, 101
Suto, Wendy, 109

T

Tacoma, Washington, 18, 25, 77, 165
Tagawa, Mike, 72
Tai Tung, 15
Takagi, Glenn, 104
Takayama, Jack, 105-106
Takekawa, Anne, 169
Talmadge, Phil, 117
Tam, Jesse, 164
Tanaka, Gail, 168
Tangalin, Andres "Sonny", 68, 69, 71, 131, 179
Tao, Wesley, 77
Taoka, Sue, 159, 161, 165
Tazuma 10 Cent Store, 29
Terada, Betty, 99
Teshima, Michio, 166
Texaco Hour, 36
Theater Off Jackson, 118, 170
Tiffany, Dale, 135
Tiger Al Lewis' Tavern, 15
Toda & Chin (T & C) Building, 94, 96
Tokuda, Kip, 118
Tokuda, Tama, 170
Tokyo, Japan, 66
Tomita, Susan, 72, 96
Tse, Kwak Leung, 168
Tsutakawa, Mayumi, 97, 98, 132
Tuai, Liem, 81
Tulisans, 144, 145, 146, 147

U

Ubangi Club, 28
Ugashik, Alaska, 29-31, 142
Uhlman, Wes, 53, 80, 111, 112, 128, 168, 169
Uncle Bob's Neighborhood, 119-120, 155
Union Apartments, 86
Union of Democratic Pilipinos, KDP, 143, 149
Union Pacific Railroad, 126
Union 76 Gas Station, 19
Union Station, 126-129
United Construction Workers Association (UCWA), 48, 51, 54, 63, 71, 131, 141
United Farm Workers (UFW), 49, 69, 70
United Indians of All Tribes, 35, 48, 56, 57, 59, 64
United Nations Association, Seattle Chapter, 61
United Nations International Federation of Human Rights Organizations, 136
United Savings and Loan Association, 94, 109, 179, 180
U.S. Commission on Wartime Relocation and Internment of Civilians, 137-138
U.S. Court of Appeals, Ninth Circuit, 150
U.S. Department of Corrections, 126
U.S. Department of Health, Education, and Welfare, 68
U.S. Department of Housing and Urban Development (HUD), 11, 81-83, 84, 86, 105, 115, 132, 155, 159 165, 171-178
U.S. Department of Housing and Urban Development, Neighborhood Self-Help Development Project Grant Program, 104
U.S. Department of Housing and Urban Development, Secretary's Regional Representative, 171-178
U.S. Department of Housing and Urban Development, Section 8 Program, 116
U.S. Department of Housing and Urban Development, Urban Development Action Grant Program, 114
U.S. Department of Justice, 125-126
U.S. Department of Transportation, 128
U.S. Department of Transportation, Urban Mass Transit Administration, 158-159
U.S. General Services Administration, 173
U.S. Marine Corps, 40, 42, 45
U.S. Navy, 16
U.S. Postal Service, 74
U.S. State Department, 147
U.S. Supreme Court, 150
United Way, 65
Uno, Chick, 20
Uno, Shigeko, 20, 27, 77, 78, 163, 180
University of Puget Sound, 65
University of Washington, 17, 26, 38, 51, 60, 71, 104, 136
Univesity of Washington Daily, 11
University of Washington Educational Opportunity Program, 71
University of Washington School of Fisheries, 141
University of Washington School of Social Work, 96, 167
Uwajimaya, 77, 130, 153, 163, 187, 188

V

Veloria, Velma, 170
Vera Cruz, Phillip, 69, 70
Vides, Felipe, 168

Viernes, Gene, 12, 57, 86, 98, 103, 123, 142, 143, 144-145, 146, 147, 148, 149, 150, 151
Vince's Barbershop, 22
Vista Volunteer Program, 63
Volchok, Zollie, 88

W

Wada, Paul, 109
Wagner, Dan, 159
Wah Ching, 108
Wah Mee Club, 152-153
Wards Cove Packing Company, 142, 150-151
Washington Education Association, 185
Washington Hall, 32
Washington Hotel, 20
Washington Iron Works, 130
Washington State Asian American Advisory Council, 73
Washington State Attorney General's Office, 133, 156
Washington State Commission on Asian American Affairs, 73
Washington State Convention and Trade Center, 59, 176-177
Washington State Department of Engineering, 156
Washington State Department of Health, 91, 165
Washington State Department of Transportation, 99, 156
Washington State Department of Vocational Rehabilitation, 91
Washington State Highway Commission, 75
Washington State House of Representatives, 117, 132, 143, 170, 184
Washington State Legislature, 131, 135, 146, 170
Washington State Liquor Control Board, 164
Washington State Penitentiary, 150
Washington State University, 99
Watanabe, Wendy, 161-162
Welcome Hotel, 113
West, Mae, 123
Westin Hotel, 140
Whitaker, Junko, 169
Whitebear, Bernie, 35, 38, 48, 49-50, 51, 56-60, 64, 65-66, 118-119, 132, 139
White House Conference on Aging, 72-73, 165
White River Dairy, 20, 27
Williams, Charlie, 44
Williamson, Don, 66
Wilson, Roy, 61
Wing Luke Asian Museum, 58, 117-118, 126, 158, 166, 170
Withey, Michael, 146, 149
Wizard of Oz, 15, 24
Wong, Benson, 168
Wong, Dean, 100
Wong, Diane, 94, 121
Wong, Dorothy, 168
Wong, Harry, Jr., 59
Wong, Harry, Sr., 57
Wong, Laura, 59
Wong, Robert, 180
Wong, Tek, 179, 181
Wong, Theresa, 59
Woo, Ben, 74, 77, 82-83, 85, 111, 112, 113, 115, 163
Woo, Clinton, 181
Woo, Curtis, 181
Woo, Danny, 19, 86, 102, 179, 180

Woo, George, 73
Woo, Irene, 168
Woo, Michael, 141
Woo, Paul, 111, 112, 180
Woo, Ruth, 170
Woo, Shari, 72, 86, 127, 164
Woo, Teresa, 181
Woo, Wilma, 57, 58, 89, 102, 179, 180, 181
Workman, Tom, 44
World of Music, 29
World Trade Organization, 176-177

Y

Yaguchi, Pauline, 39
Yamagiwa, Bob, 94
Yamaguchi, Rose, 22
Yanick, Judge Barbara, 120-121, 122
Yanko, Pat, 16
Yee, Donna, 73, 77, 78, 96, 165
Yee, Wayne, 180
Yesler Terrace Housing Project, 28, 33, 34, 35, 74
Yip, Eddie, 180
Yoshimura, Bruce, 180
Yoshimura, Irwin, 180
Yoshioka, Art, 128
Yoshitomi, Joan, 117
Young Asians for Action, 72
Young, Carlos, 77
Young, Elaine, 180
Young, James, 112
Yuasa, Gerry, 97, 109-110
Yumal, Joe, 33